STRUCTURALISM AND THE LOGIC OF DISSENT

Structuralism and the Logic of Dissent

Barthes, Derrida, Foucault, Lacan

Eve Tavor Bannet
Associate Professor of English
University of South Carolina

M
MACMILLAN
PRESS

First published 1989

Published by
THE MACMILLAN PRESS LTD
Houndmills, Basingstoke, Hampshire RG21 2XS
and London
Companies and representatives
throughout the world

Typeset by Wessex Typesetters
(Division of The Eastern Press Ltd)
Frome, Somerset

Printed in Hong Kong

British Library Cataloguing in Publication Data
Bannet, Eve Tavor
Structuralism and the logic of dissent:
Barthes, Derrida, Foucault, Lacan.
1. Structuralism
I. Title
149'.96   B841.4
ISBN 0–333–44343–8 (hardcover)
ISBN 0–333–46948–8 (paperback)

To Jacob Bannet, who made this book possible

Contents

Acknowledgements

I am profoundly indebted to the old *Lycée Français de Londres* under the late M. Gaudin, both for its draconian discipline and for enabling each of its pupils to become different.

I would like to thank Jerome Mandel and Meir Sternberg at Tel-Aviv University, for arranging for me to have the leave I needed, and Dorothea Krook-Gilead and the late Wylie Sypher for reading and commenting on portions of this manuscript. Special thanks are also due to Frances Arnold at Macmillan for her wonderful tact, understanding and timely encouragement, and to Julie Coyne, Jane Gostling and the staff of the Brompton Library in London, who went well beyond the call of duty in locating and procuring books for me.

I would like to thank the editors of *Orbis Litterarum* for permission to rework my article, 'Critical Play: a Reading of Roland Barthes'.

This book could not have been written without the constant help and support of my husband, Jacob Bannet, who lived with it from its inception with better than good grace, or without my two lively small sons, Jonathan and Alan, who helped by puncturing abstraction, making me laugh and by allowing me to sleep – at least most nights.

EVE TAVOR BANNET

Abbreviations

LACAN

Ec. I	*Écrits*, Vol. I
Ec. II	*Écrits*, Vol. II
Sem. I	*Le Séminaire: Livre I, Les écrits techniques de Freud*
Sem. II	*Le Séminaire: Livre II, Le moi dans la théorie de Freud et dans la technique de la psychanalyse*
Sem. III	*Le Séminaire: Livre III, Les psychoses*
Sem. XI	*Le Séminaire: Livre XI, Les quatres concepts fondamentaux de la psychanalyse*
Sem. XX	*Le Séminaire: Livre XX, Encore*
Tel.	*Télévision*

BARTHES

BR	*A Barthes Reader* (ed. Susan Sontag)
CV	*Critique et Vérité*
DZ	*Le Degré Zéro de l'Écriture*
EC I	*Éssais Critiques*
EC IV	*Éssais Critiques IV: Le bruissement de la langue*
ES	*L'Empire des Signes*
Frag.	*Fragments d'un discours amoureux*
GV	*Le Grain de la Voix: Entretiens 1962–80*
ITM	*Image–Text–Music*, essays selected and translated by Stephen Heath
M	*Mythologies*
Mich	*Michelet*
MT	*Myth Today* (in *A Barthes Reader* – BR)
NEC	*Nouveaux Essais Critiques*
PT	*Le Plaisir du Texte*
R	*Sur Racine*
RB	*Roland Barthes par Roland Barthes*
SFL	*Sade, Fourier, Loyola*
Soll.	*Sollers Écrivain*

FOUCAULT

AS	*L'Archéologie du Savoir*
HF	*Histoire de la Folie*
HS	*Histoire de la Sexualité*
LCP	*Language, Counter-Memory, Practice* (ed. Donald F. Bouchard)
MCH	*Les Mots et les Choses*
NC	*Naissance de la Clinique*
OD	*L'Ordre du Discours*
PK	*Power/Knowledge* (ed. Colin Gordon)
PTS	*Power, Truth, Strategy* (eds Morris and Patton)
SP	*Surveiller et Punir*

DERRIDA

CP	*La Carte Postale*
Diss.	*La Dissémination*
ED	*L'Écriture et la Différence*
G	*De la Grammatologie*
M	*Marges de la philosophie*
Ot.	*Otobiographies*
Pos.	*Positions*
Ton	*D'un Ton apocalyptique adopté naguère en philosophie*
VP	*La Voix et le Phenomène*

Introduction:
The Voice of Someone

'It's about the voice of no one – but it is, that's just it: it is about, it is always about the voice of someone.'

Roland Barthes

It would be impossible to write this or any other book if God and the self were really dead; if the author were really absent from his work; if language were nothing but an alien circuit which each of us is condemned to repeat; if society were really irredeemable and man irreparably alienated from his world. In the absence of any human form of mind, in the absence of any possibility of truth, meaning or change, in the absence of all capacity to say what has not been said before and to add to the stock of our culture, there would be nothing worth saying, no one to say it, and no one to say it to. There would not even be any point in declaring that God and the self are dead, that language and culture are tiresomely repeated by every speaking and acting subject, and that man is alienated from himself, from his culture and from his social world.

This is why, although these are central tenets of Lacan, Barthes, Foucault and Derrida as well as of many other modern writers, they are tenets which are stated – and then honoured more in the breach than in the observance. Lacan, Barthes, Foucault and Derrida, to name only those with whom we are primarily concerned here, are not in fact absent from their *oeuvres*. They use absence, death and carefully orchestrated silences as indicators of their form-giving presence and as affirmations of their desire for being, individuality and truth. Their often enigmatic texts tease the reader to seek the self which has been concealed the better to be revealed, and which manifests itself in the uniqueness and originality of their style as much as of their thought. Their works are not repetitions of each others' works or of any works that went before. They are new creations, which conform to no pre-existing genre,

1

which observe few cultural or linguistic conventions, and which transform what they repeat. The writers in question have all spent their lives teaching and working in prestigious French institutes of higher learning, like the *École Normale Supérieure*, the *École Pratique des Hautes Études*, the CNRS or the *Collège de France*, which underpin and help to reproduce the very culture and society which they condemn. And they have sought beyond the automatism of culture and the darkness of negation to find the thin small wedge from which it is still honest and honourable to speak.

It is this rupture at the heart of modern writing which makes this book possible. It re-legitimates explication and commentary. And it raises the central questions of these studies: how can dissenting intellectuals like Lacan, Barthes, Foucault and Derrida think and write creatively within a culture, for a culture, and ultimately to perpetuate a culture which they view as all-dominant, all-encompassing and utterly inauthentic, once they no longer believe that successful revolutionary change is on the agenda of world history? How do they come to terms with alienation in their writings, and how do they represent it? As we will see, each writer gives a very different answer to these questions. But the continuing struggle to find these answers is fundamental to their writing, as well as to their uses and discussions of other peoples' writings. It underlies their individual styles, governs the different structures of their thought, and dominates their architectonic thematic concerns.

Alienation in their work is no longer the relatively monolithic thing it was in Marx – man's failure to realise his species being and his inability to recognise himself in the product of his labour. Nor is it the amorphous thing it has become in the social sciences – a feeling of not belonging. In the work of the writers in question, man's alienation from himself is reformulated as a profound split or division within the subject, as the death or loss of the self, or as the development in which man became an object to himself. Man's alienation from other men is reformulated as his difference, or as his separation from others by the barrier of a common language. Man's alienation from culture and society is reformulated as *atopie* – placelessness – or as an effect of exclusion and control. As we will see, these views of alienation as different forms of 'Otherness' bring in their train views of man, language, culture and society which differ markedly from those of Hegel, Marx and their followers. As we will see, too, these redefinitions of the problem and these ways of breaking it down into its elements are part of the process of tackling alienation and of finding new ways to speak it. If the blanket term, alienation, has come to seem rather old-fashioned to us today, it is in no small measure due to the efforts made by Lacan, Barthes, Foucault and Derrida to redefine it and to deal with it in smaller and more manageable sections.

These writers are generally known as 'structuralist' or 'post-structuralist' writers. But, as John Sturrock has pointed out, the label 'structuralist' is doubly problematical if it is regarded as a description of their common method. It is problematical, in the first instance, because, beyond a certain number of technical terms taken from structural linguistics and particularly from the work of the Swiss linguist Ferdinand de Saussure, Lacan, Barthes, Foucault and Derrida appear to have very little in common. And it is problematical, too, because, unlike Lévi-Strauss, none of them 'would be at all happy to be labelled "structuralist" which each would see as a gross violation of his freedom of thought'.[1]

The label 'structuralist' may prove more enlightening, however, if we cease to regard it as a description of method, and begin to think of it ideologically, as a description of all that Lacan, Barthes, Foucault and Derrida, each in their different ways, bitterly opposed. It must be remembered that Parisian intellectual life was, and remains, highly politicised. This means, among other things, that there has been little 'pure' or 'apolitical' and 'disinterested' theorising. Furthermore, most left-wing intellectuals have viewed with intense disfavour the emergence of the centralised, highly planned, authoritarian and bureaucratic State which accompanied Gaullist attempts to modernise and industrialise France after the Second World War. It was in this context of dissent that Lacan, Barthes, Foucault and Derrida were writing.

The ideological implications of structuralism in France are made clear, for instance, in Henri Lefebvre's influential book, *Position: Contre les Technocrates*. *Position: Contre les Technocrates* (1967) was in fact an attack on structuralism, which had recently become the fashion in Parisian intellectual circles. Most particularly, it was an attack on what Lefebvre described as structuralism's central ideological tenet: that 'language as a system defines society as a system and also the forms of thought', that 'it brings into accord, because it engenders, mental structures and social structures'.[2] Lefebvre argued that structuralism's emphasis on 'System', on the 'Law', and on the constraints which govern mental and social structures make it homologous with the ideology of the technocratic architects of Gaullist neo-capitalism. 'Bureaucracy', he pointed out, 'is essentially structuring and structured'.[3] It classifies, it orders, it programmes; it endeavours to control and determine every aspect of life, leaving no place for innovation, creativity and non-conformity. Its technocrats presuppose that society is a rational system and, through their planning, they endeavour to make it one. Structuralist systems with their rational coherence and transparent cohesion, with their claim to encompass all essential relations and their complete but unconscious determinism of social and mental life, are a technocratic ideal.

> If the notion of System has arisen and come to the fore in [structuralist] theory, therefore, it is because in practice, an attempt is being made to systematise everywhere; to determine social boundaries which are capable of expansion but invariable as boundaries; to stipulate order, norms and rules; to formulate efficient 'models'; to organise equilibriums and 'feed-backs'.[4]

If Foucault, for instance, protested that he was not a structuralist, it was not at all because he disagreed with this view of French society. On the contrary, like Lacan, Barthes and Derrida, he largely shared it. His point was that he was not a supporter of the technocrats, that he was not trying to extend the System or to increase its domination and its constraints. Like Lacan, Barthes and Derrida, he was trying to show it up for what it was, and in so doing, to question it and subvert it. Where Lévi-Strauss saw structuralism as a universal and unconscious law of human society and of the human mind, Barthes, Lacan, Foucault and Derrida saw it as an unwelcome development of modern society. The ludic quality of these men's texts, their lack of conformity either to the constraints of language or to the norms of academic writing, their creativity, their innovativeness and their diversity are all aspects of their rejection of the 'structuralism' of the bureaucratic and 'technocratic' mental and social System. The logic which informs their writings is the logic of dissent.

Moreover, as these studies will show, Lacan, Barthes, Foucault and Derrida were not only *anti*-structuralist writers; they were also *counter*-structuralists. They not only sought to unmask and to displace the determinism and the domination, the rational coherence and the control of structural systems and to subvert all attempts to impose the alienating stamp of invariable sameness.

They also sought to replace such systematic structures with structures of their own – structures which define new spaces of nonconformity and freedom. Different as they are from one another, Lacan, Barthes, Derrida and Foucault all developed structures of language and thought characterised by gaps, discontinuities and suspensions of dictated meanings in which difference, plurality, multiplicity and the coexistence of opposites are allowed free play. Implicitly or explicitly, they all tried to present these nondeterministic and non-determining structures as alternatives to the deterministic and determining structures inherent in the society, in the university, in the field of knowledge and in the language they had inherited. Here, too, the logic which informs their writings is the logic of dissent. It is one of the ironies of history that these alternative structures of dissent should have lent themselves so readily to imitation and repetition, and that widespread imitation and repetition should have turned what had once been manifestations of non-conformity and freedom into new forms of academic conformity and constraint.

It is not fortuitous that these *anti-* and *counter-*structuralist writers, who spent all, or most, of their working lives teaching and researching in institutes of higher learning, should have been so preoccupied with the self's problematical relationship to language and to the culture embodied in it. Nor is it fortuitous that their investigations should have become so firmly entrenched in the universities in recent years. Broadly speaking, intellectuals may be defined as workers with words and significations. Academics who profess to what the French like to call 'the human sciences' (essentially the humanities and the social sciences) are a particularly pure example of the 'intellectual'. Where doctors, scientists, engineers and technicians admix the verbal with the practical manipulation of bodies, substances and objects, literary critics, philologists, philosophers, linguists, structural anthropologists, political scientists, historians and psychoanalysts pursue words and are pursued by them. Words and significations form the object of their studies; words and significations are what they proffer in their books, in their articles and in the media; words and significations are what they exchange in the conference hall, in the classroom, in the proverbial smoke-filled room and in the no less proverbial Left-Bank café. The pacts which unite academics in 'schools', orthodoxies and counter-orthodoxies, the conventions which regulate the flow and movement of opinion, and the rules which govern admittance to their society, are constituted of words and significations. Language and culture, repetition and innovation, writing and speech and their reality or unreality – these are problems of intellectuals; they are problems for intellectuals, more than for any other class of people in society.

But before Lacan, Barthes, Foucault and Derrida, they could not be seen in this light, at least outside France. Intellectuals – both those who, if Marxist critics are to be believed, have for centuries been producers of consciousness for one social class or another, and those who for the past 150 years have tried to produce a class consciousness for the proletariat – have had remarkably little consciousness of themselves as a class. As we will see throughout these studies, Lacan, Barthes, Foucault and Derrida begin to reverse this irony of history by raising the questions and by exploring the roles played and playable by intellectuals in the arts, in the human sciences and in the modern world. This aspect of their work has aroused a great deal of interest recently, especially in America, where it has reawakened attempts to resolve the 'crisis in English Studies', and provoked thinkers as different in other ways as Gerald Graff and Richard Rorty to redefine the place and functions of professors of the humanities in culture and society.

Understandably, however, Lacan, Barthes, Foucault and Derrida's preoccupation with language, culture and the role of the intellectual were, in the first instance, a response to a specifically French situation. For one thing, French education has been centred on the mastery of language skills to an extent unequalled anywhere else. Without the ability to 'dissert' with ease, clarity and rhetorical grace, it is impossible to graduate from a French secondary school, much less to obtain admission to a *Grande École*, to rise in the university hierarchy or to call oneself a cultured Frenchman. Prospective doctors, scientists or business executives are no more exempt from this rhetorical requirement than are teachers, lawyers and politicians. For the French educational system has, until recently, been geared almost exclusively to producing a homogeneous liberal élite, which 'governs itself, enlightens itself, judges itself and justifies itself by speech' and whose hallmark is 'knowledge of the art of writing and speaking in a certain humanist style and tradition'.[5] Lacan, Barthes, Foucault and Derrida all rejected this humanist style and tradition, as they rejected the philosophy of man implicit in it. But in seeking a different, individual, non-conformist mode of writing and in elaborating the formal and rhetorical difficulties of their texts, they remained as preoccupied with problems of style and expression as their humanist predecessors.

But beyond this, and like many other dissenting French intellectuals after the Liberation, they realised that the humanist arts of writing and speaking and the 'republic of professors and advocates' associated with it, were becoming increasingly irrelevant to a society which was very rapidly becoming technocratic, technically oriented, and, in their view 'americanised'. Their endeavour to redefine the place of creative intellectual writing in this, to them, alien symbolic and structural order, and to give dissenting intellectuals a new, non-humanist and non-traditional function within the society and culture they condemned is one of the factors which led them to view writing and speech in a much broader and more complex intellectual and cultural framework than traditional humanist critics have been wont to do. It led them to break down the conventional compartmentalisation of disciplines. As Edward Said has rightly pointed out, they do not distinguish clearly between literature, literary criticism, philology, philosophy, linguistics, anthropology, psychoanalysis and political science, or even between theory and practice – 'their common method is incorporative'.[6]

Because they are usually so innovative and challenging in the different disciplines they work with, and because they often invite their readers to be innovative in their turn, commentators have felt 'at liberty to pillage [their] repertoire' and to 'select' from it whatever they think useful in their particular field of interest.[7] But, as we are perhaps beginning to realise, selection and pillaging have their dangers.[8] As Lacan, Barthes, Foucault and Derrida were well aware, ideas, methods, structures and styles of writing are never 'neutral'; they always have social and political consequences. Pillaging does not neutralise these social and political consequences; it merely ignores them. And by ignoring them, it allows them to operate 'unconsciously' – unchosen, unquestioned and unchecked. If intellectual and academic responsibility consists, in the first instance, in responsibility for the ideas and the methods one is propagating, then the first step towards responsibility is to seek to understand the place of ideas and methods and styles of writing in a writer's 'system' and in their social and political contexts.

The approach in this book, then, consists in the first instance of treating the work of each writer incorporatively as a self-referential philosophical and narrative world, as a coherent piece of creative intellectual 'Writing', in some sense as a fiction. This is not as fanciful as it may seem, nor is it in any way inconsistent with the assumptions of the writers in question.

All of them deny that words in any way reflect reality. They argue that reality is either beyond our ken or beyond the possibilities of speech, insisting that the symbolic order creates its own realities according to its own laws. And they all have a horror of repetition. Accordingly, their aim is not to elucidate – and thus to repeat – the literary, philosophical, psychological and historical texts they discuss, much less to get at what positivists would consider 'the real facts' about them. Viewed in their own terms, the continuing debate about their accuracy as psychoanalysts or historians or linguists is essentially beside the point. For they use literary, philosophical, historical and psychological texts as Thomas Mann used the Bible in *Joseph and his Brothers* or as Shakespeare used Holinshed in his plays – as myths, as stories or legends to be invested with new life, new logic and new significations. And they use the different languages of the human sciences – structural anthropology, cybernetics, Freudian psychology, linguistics, Marxism, existentialism, phenomenology, semiology, traditional logic, traditional rhetoric and *explication de texte* – as a medium, a vehicle, for their critique of modern man's condition and as elements for a new creation of their own.

Like avant-garde art forms, the often experimental forms of these writers' texts are designed to show, rather than to state or demonstrate. They are designed to figure forth significations which have hitherto been unuttered and unutterable. Their texts are as individual, as original and as various as these significations, and therefore they are difficult. To penetrate the form is usually to grasp the significations and the significations are usually the key to the form. This closed – some would say vicious – circle means that Lacan, Barthes, Foucault and Derrida are writing texts that focus the reader's attention on themselves. They force the reader to consider them as objects in their own right. They are designed to prevent the reader from looking *through* them at some external referent; they are designed to make the reader look *at* them and to work at them, actively involving him in their construction or recreation. As Barthes points out, the difficulty and indeterminacy of such texts prevents the reader from consuming them at a gulp and throwing them away. The reader cannot simply glance through a Lacanian, Barthian, Foucaldian or Derridean text, extract a discursive message and shelve the book. He must come back to the text again and again; he must brood on it; he must relate to it as a puzzle or a game, in which he participates by deciphering the allusions, by reconstructing the relations between different parts, by seeking the significations which govern the form. Sartre's epigram that 'reading is directed creation' and Barthes' distinction between reading a text and 'scripting' it are of the essence here.

Because their texts are so self-consciously difficult, because they draw attention to themselves as created objects in their own right, and because they demand the active participation of their readers, Lacan, Barthes, Foucault and Derrida's writings have provoked a phenomenon heretofore associated almost exclusively with literary texts. They have provoked conventional criticism. A whole new industry, of which this book is an epiphenomenon, has grown up around their texts, to elucidate them, to comment on them, and to place them in some identifiable ideational context. This is not inappropriate if we think of the writers in question as embodiments of Wilde's programme for the critic in 'The Critic as Artist'. For, as will be recalled, Wilde pointed out that: 'Criticism of the highest kind treats the work of art as the starting point for a new creation . . . [it] is in its way more creative than creation, as it has least reference to any standard external to itself, and is its own reason for existing'.[9] If we qualify this by saying that our creative critics would probably say that criticism of the highest kind treats *any* text or discourse as the starting point for a new creation, then we have a pretty fair description of their work and grounds for approaching it incorporatively as a self-referential 'Writing'.

At the same time, like the greatest writers of fiction, and indeed like the humanist critics they reject, these *anti-* and *counter-*structuralist artist-critics have a tendency to lapse into universals – to portray their insights into their own situation as truths about the Human Condition, about Literature, about Modern Neo-Capitalist Society or about Western Philosophy – which can be misleading. Small as the world is becoming, it is not yet identical in all its parts, and as Matthew Arnold, among others, understood, the man requires the moment. These artist-critics lived and worked in a Paris buzzing with concern about the Plan or about the fate of the 1968 student uprising. They lived and worked in a Paris where left-wing intellectuals were vocally opposed both to the autocracy of Gaullism and to the dictatorship of the French Communist Party, to which dissenting intellectuals might otherwise have allied themselves. They lived and worked in a society which had been predominantly agricultural until the Liberation and which was trying to do in twenty years what America did in two centuries and what England has not yet altogether made up her mind to do. They lived and worked in a traditional humanist university, feudal in organisation, prescriptive in approach and bursting at the seams with students it was no longer equipped to train. This moment, this society and this university to which Lacan, Barthes, Foucault and Derrida were speaking are not identical to any other. They are not universals, but particulars.

This is not to say that there are not important lessons to be learned from Lacan, Barthes, Foucault and Derrida by intellectuals with a different experience. The rapidity of France's modernisation and the acuteness of the crisis in her universities may well have made French intellectuals see more clearly and resolve more expeditiously problems with which intellectuals in other countries have learned to live. But it seems to me that the applicability of the solutions to other countries and other situations can best be judged when the nature of the problems they were designed to resolve has been explored, and when Lacan, Barthes, Foucault and Derrida have each been awarded the privilege they sought for others, but often failed to grant them: the privilege of being different from each other and from everyone else.

In the chapters which follow, therefore, Lacan, Barthes, Foucault and Derrida are each discussed as far as possible in their own terms and in their own specific contexts. No reference is made to what each had to say about the other. Such references can be misleading. For instance, Barthes' generous acknowledgments of his debts to Derrida and Foucault tend to conceal what they had in fact learned from him, since he was often practising what they preached in texts written long before they came on the scene. Derrida's very necessary attempts to differentiate his spaces of non-being from Lacan's, and his use of division and *renversement* from Foucault's, tend to conceal the fundamental structural similarities in the work of all these men.

The concluding chapter is devoted to discussing the nature of these structural similarities and the complex response they constituted to the intellectual, institutional, political, social and textual contexts in which Lacan, Barthes, Foucault and Derrida were writing. These 'recontextualisations' will, I hope, help intellectuals writing, working and teaching outside France to identify areas of applicability and non-applicability to their own situation and to perceive more clearly the social and political implications of some French structures and ideas.

This book is not a paean of praise written by a faithful follower – if 'imitation is the sincerest form of flattery', then these studies, which make no attempt to imitate either the style or the methods of the writers they discuss, cannot be described as flattering. But neither is this book a critique designed to show where Lacan, Barthes, Foucault and Derrida were wrong or to defend an established position against their encroachments. The reality of reality has been doubted and disproved at more or less regular intervals since Sextus Empiricus, but like Uncle Toby, people have always found they could still get up and walk across a room. Indeed, after being exposed to fictions of doubt and to the illusions of argument, people have generally found that they longed for the solid evidence of that room. Moreover, Lacan, Barthes, Foucault and Derrida are far from being as nihilistic or as value-free as they are sometimes portrayed as being.

Barthes died in 1980; Lacan died in 1981; and Foucault died in 1984. Their vogue passed in Paris with the realisation that to provide oneself with a *maître-à-penser* is also to provide oneself with a master who enslaves one's thought. Their domination is passing elsewhere too. But their structures and many of their assumptions remain – in the work of English scholars like Anthony Giddens and Tony Bennett and in American 'New Historicism', for instance. Repeated and varied and put to more traditional uses, their logic of dissent is beginning to be absorbed into the academic establishment. These studies mark the interval between domination and absorption, the interspace when it seemed possible for a moment to approach Lacan, Barthes, Foucault and Derrida with the pleasure of a lover of fictions, with the curiosity of a lover of ideas, and with a historian's sense that language, fictions and ideas were all once grounded in the social, institutional and political dynamics of a specific time and place.

1

Lacan and the Alienation of Language

*'Who goes there? Who goes there? Is it you Nadja? Is it true that
the beyond, all the beyond is in this life? I do not understand you.
Who goes there? Is it I alone? Is it my self?'*

André Breton

THE VEL OF ALIENATION

'When you don't understand what you are being told, don't
immediately assume that you are to blame; say to yourselves – the
fact that I don't understand must itself have a meaning' (Sem. I,
253). Coming from a teacher who chose to mask his teaching in
obscurity and who sardonically assured bewildered readers of his
Écrits that he preferred access to his ideas to be 'difficult', this
observation of Lacan's to his seminar students carries considerable
personal weight. It reminds even practised ears that the art of
listening involves understanding not only what is being said,
but also the meaning of the barriers erected to prevent ready
understanding of what is being said. Like the poetical and rhetorical
resources of language which Lacan used so extensively, Lacan's
obscurity and stylistic difficulty are themselves significant statement. They are neither fortuitous nor disconnected from the
essence of his ideas because, for Lacan, language *is* thought, and
speech, the man.

Various and often contradictory explanations of the laconic
mystery have been advanced by Lacan's students. Some are
socio-historical: Lacan's obscurity is thought by one student and
analysand to have been an expression of complicity with those who
had excluded him in 1953 from the International Psychoanalytic
Association and from free interchange of ideas with the wider
psychoanalytic community – it made it impossible for Lacan's work

to be picked up and judged by anyone outside the group of believers who worked with him. Some explanations are political: Lacan thought his doctrine subversive and revolutionary and was convinced that if 'they' knew what he was saying, they would never let him say it. Some explanations are biographical: in his youth, Lacan was immeasurably attracted by the superbly poetic yet uncommunicative style of his paranoiac patients in their delirium, and 'he later made of the uncommunicative strangeness of this delirious style a calculated force'. Other explanations are psychoanalytical: 'In many ways,' we are told, 'Lacan's discourse is like the flow of language of a person in analysis, dense with associations and unexpected transitions. . . He wants his communications to speak directly to the unconscious and believes that word-play, where causal links dissolve and associations abound, is the language which it understands'.[1] In his preface to *Télévision*, Lacan himself insisted that he was not 'speaking so that idiots can understand me', but that he was 'speaking to those who know what it's about, to non-idiots and presumed analysts' (Tel., 10).

Lacan's remarks apart, these explanations remain incomplete and unsatisfying because they overlook the central paradox in Lacan's writing. They assume either that Lacan's style is fundamentally communicative or that it is fundamentally uncommunicative. In fact it is both. As Catherine Clément has put it: Lacan 'plays a subtle and dangerous game of communication and non-communication, of light and obscurity'.[2] This paradox of communication and non-communication is already implicit in the act of writing or speaking so as to make access to one's ideas 'difficult'. For Lacan, the act of writing or speaking is by its very nature an act of communication. It is also more than this: it is a reference to an other, a pact, an exchange of gifts, and the condition for human intersubjectivity. To use one's speech to estrange the other, to subvert the pact, to withhold the gift, and to bar human intersubjectivity, is to inscribe a paradox. Yet this is what Lacan does, and he does it to embody in his discourse the central structure of his thought. For Lacan's theories of signifier and reality, of language and individual speech, of ego and unconscious, of self and other, are all rooted in a tragic paradox: that each is irrevocably bound to the other, yet at the same time hopelessly alienated from it.

Despite Lacan's frequently Hegelian terminology, alienation here and in Lacan's work as a whole is not to be understood in the Hegelian-Marxist context of a subject objectifying himself through his activity on the external world and recognising – or failing to recognise – himself in the products of that activity. Lacan's use of Hegelian terminology and references for distinctly non-Hegelian concepts is wilfully misleading; it is a *leurre*, a deception, and part of the process of alienating readers from the text.[3]

Firstly, as Lacan never tires of pointing out, Lacanian psychoanalysis is not a humanism. There is in Lacan no autonomous, self-conscious subject in whom, as in a container, knowledge, experience and emotion inhere, whose relationship to the social environment can be measured in terms of creativity and self-recognition. Lacan's model for man is not – as in Hegel or Marx – the artisan who puts something of himself into every object he makes and who can therefore see what he has made as his own, or the factory worker who has been deprived of his natural, specifically human, right to artisanal satisfaction. Lacan's model for man is the computer. Man is a machine whose predetermined, linguistically programmed circuits are governed by binary structures: closed–open, absent–present, 01.[4] And like its inanimate counterpart, the human computer is largely programmed by others – by those who occupy the place of father, mother or brother, and by those other laws of culture and society which are embodied in language. Not entirely surprisingly, therefore, the question of the subject is conceived by Lacan as the question of where – if anywhere – the subject may be found and who – if anyone – it may prove to be. In the words of Breton's novel, it is a question of 'Who goes there? Is it you, Nadja? . . . Is it I alone? Is it my self?'

A second reason why Lacan should not be viewed in a Hegelian context has to do with what Lacan means by the term 'dialectic'. There is in Lacan no Hegelian tri-partite movement from subject to object and back to subject again, and therefore no possibility of closing the circle. What Lacan calls a dialectic is a binary movement without dialectical *Aufhebung*. The two terms of the binary opposition – let us call it self and other here – are ineluctably separated by a gap or *béance*; and unity, which in Hegel reconciled opposites, is demoted in Lacan either to a fiction or to a profound and primitive human desire which is doomed to remain forever unsatisfied. Alienation thus ceases to be what it is in Hegel and Marx – a moment of the dialectic which can and should be transcended by man's recognition of himself in the other. In Lacan, recognition of the self in the other becomes one pole of alienation. And in keeping with the computer model, alienation becomes a binary movement, an alternation of opposites. Lacan describes it as a *vel*, an 'or'. It is an alternative in which choosing one term of the opposition results either in the 'fading', the *aphanisis*, of the other term, or in the destruction of both. And in this form, alienation pervades Lacan's entire system.

According to Lacan, alienation is introduced into human experience with the child's first imaginary identification with another. This occurs some time during the child's first year of life when he (or she) is held in front of the mirror and jubilantly recognises himself in the mirror's reflected image. For the child does not see himself as the uncoordinated, powerless and fragmentary subject he is at this rudimentary stage in his development; he sees himself in the image of himself which confronts him in the mirror. A gap or cleavage is thus established between the subject and the image which he assumes as his own. Not only is the image a mere image or *imago* which is outside him and external to him, but it is other than he is. Its mastery of physical functions is remote from his own as yet almost complete physical dependence, and its fixed and statuesque unity bears no correspondence to his own anarchical and dynamic spontaneity. This fundamental opposition between subject and image means that when the child identifies with the *Gestalt* in the mirror, when he sees himself in the image of the other, he is also seeing himself *as* an other; he is conceiving of himself as other than he is. There is a fading or *aphanisis* or the subject, in favour of the imaginary image. It is in the imaginary image that the child sees his identity and his unity, around the image that he orders his experience and his environment, and to the image that he attaches his desire.

The opposition between subject and image in this initial 'mirror stage' of development is, in Lacan, the basis and pattern for the subsequent opposition of ego and unconscious. The principal difference between these two oppositions is that in the latter, the *vel* of alienation has been internalised. The ego is the introjected other, the unconscious, the subject in his *aphanisis*. Lacan describes the ego as 'a certain image we have of ourselves' (Sem. II, 273). Like the image in which the child first sees himself, the ego is a mirage, a fiction, an ideal of unity and mastery with which we mistakenly identify ourselves and to which we attach our perceptions, our desire, our experience and what we take to be our knowledge (Sem. I, 203; Sem. II, 61). But in fact, since it is made up of the sum of introjected images of others with whom the subject has identified in the course of his personal history (Sem. II, 187, 197), the ego is not identical with the subject. It is a mask of conformity, a collection of bric-à-brac gathered in society's shop of accessories, a system of preconceptions and prejudices, a socialised envelope or detachable skin (Sem. XI, 98; Sem. II, 56, 187, 197). The ego is other than the subject, and only tangentially coincides with the subject's real development. As Lacan puts it, borrowing a phrase from Rimbaud: 'I is another' (Sem. II, 16). When the subject sees himself in the ego, when he sees himself *as* an ego, he is seeing himself as other than he is, and what he is as a subject fades into the unconscious. This is why Lacan insists that there is a profound cleavage at the heart of man, that the ego is fundamentally alienated from the subject and that the subject is 'excentric to' or 'decentered from' the system of the ego.

According to Lacan, the subject's imaginary identification with the other without and the other within is responsible for the fundamental aggressiveness and destructiveness of human nature. The subject is constantly introjecting images of other people to form his idealised self-image and then re-projecting this self-image onto other people. On occasion, when another person appears to conform fully to the subject's idealised self-image, he becomes an object of narcissistic investiture, and the subject 'falls in love'. As Lacan puts it: 'In love, it is one's own ego that one loves, one's own ego realised on an imaginary level' (Sem. I, 163). But for the most part, the subject's relationship to other people is based on rivalry, on competition, on the *vel* of alienation: 'It's him *or* me'. Because it is through identification with another, who appears to enjoy a more complete satisfaction, to be more whole, more perfect or more masterful, that the subject grasps himself as an ego, the other is also someone who can deprive the subject of what he sees as his own. The other can rob the subject not only of an object he desires, but of his very self-image. For when a subject sees himself in an other person, his ego disappears; and to see himself in his ego again, he requires the disappearance of the other person. Identifying with the other, his desire projected onto the other, the child is jealous of the baby at his mother's breast; he desires the disappearance, the destruction of his rival: 'It's him or me'. Watching another, more accomplished child at play, the little girl says happily: 'Me break Francis's head'. 'This', says Lacan, 'only manifests the most fundamental structure of human beings on the imaginary plane – the destruction of whoever is the locus of alienation. . . The aggressive tension of this 'me or other' is absolutely integrated into every aspect of the functioning of man's imagination' (Sem. I, 194; Sem. III, 110). The *vel* of alienation, therefore, appears within the individual, in the mutually exclusive relationship of subject and ego. And, according to Lacan, it also appears in interpersonal relationships, at whatever age, whenever human beings relate to each other on this imaginary level, as hatred, violence, and a radical intolerance for the existence of others. It pervades modern society, where, Lacan argues, it manifests itself in man's exploitation of man, in the social struggle for power and prestige, and in what Lacan calls 'our culture of hate'.

If men do, nevertheless, manage to live with one another in society, and if subject and ego do, nevertheless, manage to coexist, it is because, in human development, imagination is overlaid by language. Lacan sometimes dates the child's entry into language from his first cries to his mother, and sometimes from the resolution of the Oedipal phase. But, in either case, the point is that the acquisition of language represents the introduction of law and harmonisation into the jungle of human rivalries. As Lacan puts it somewhat aphoristically: 'the law of mankind is the law of language' (Ec. I, 150).

There are three reasons in Lacan for this identification of law and language. The first is that words give permanence and regularity to otherwise transient human perceptions. For Lacan, as for Locke, objects are always perceived fleetingly by the imagination; on the imaginary level, it is always a matter of what is present before the eye at any given moment; and as the eye shifts its focus, so the object appears or disappears. This is why on the imaginary level, it is always a question of 'I *or* you' – if it is you who are present to the eye, then I am not; and if it is I, then you are not. But language enables objects to be present even in their absence. The word fixes the existence of the object even when it is not immediately present to the eye. 'The word', says Lacan, 'is a presence made of absence which allows absence to be named' (Ec. I, 155). Thus the ability to say 'I' gives the subject a fixity, a permanence, an existence, which removes the threat of immediate annihilation. And since language is a system of paired oppositions in which the 'I' is always learned in reference to the 'you', the coexistence of I and you is embodied in language and therefore in the law of mankind.[5]

The second reason for Lacan's identification of law and language is related to this. It is that language represents a pact among people. A sound or 'signifier' can only name an object if people agree that it does. From this point of view, language is a completely arbitrary phenomenon, and different peoples can (and do) agree to use different sounds to signify objects.

Naming constitutes a pact by which two subjects agree at the same time on the recognition of the same object. If human subjects did not first name the major species (as in Genesis), if subjects did not agree on this recognition, there would be no world, even perceptually, which could be sustained for more than an instant (Sem. II, 202).

Language's function of fixing objects depends on a pact of recognition among people.

Finally, law and language are identified by Lacan because for him there can be no law which is not embodied in language. There is no such thing for him as a natural, intuitive or unverbalised law. Lacan's favourite example of the inextricability of law and language is the law governing human alliances, because he argues that this is the fundamental law which substitutes the reign of culture and society for indiscriminate natural coupling. Animals couple with their mothers or sons as soon as the relationship has been obscured by time and absence, because they have no way of fixing their identities or of marking the relationship. The orders of preference and the taboos which define who is permitted to whom in human society depend on the possibility of naming family relationships across the generations and of giving each individual a clearly denoted place within them. It is language which fixes identities and relationships, which marks taboos and embodies the pact. And as such, language is more than a set of words; it is a symbolic order.

Yet, although the symbolic order makes human coexistence possible by enabling subjects to transcend their destructive imaginary alienations, it also involves them in two further alienations.

The first is an alienation from reality itself. For Lacan, language is a self-referential system which coincides only tangentially with the experienced reality of things. Here again, while Lacan uses Saussurean terminology to make his point, he is far from being an orthodox Saussurean. For Lacan, sounds or 'signifiers' do not stand for things even at a second remove. Signifiers stand for meanings or significations which grow out of their associations with and oppositions to other signifiers in the language. The word 'day' for instance, derives its signification not from any natural experience of day, but from its opposition in the symbolic system to 'night'. Where experience yields only a series of modulations, an alternation of light and obscurity with the gradual transitions between them, the word day is clearly demarcated from night. It means not only day, but also all that is not night, all that can be in the absence of night. And because it derives its signification in this way, it can acquire connotations, poetic, philosophical or metaphysical, which are even more remote from any basis in immediate experience. Thus language involves what Lacan calls 'an original murder of the thing' (Sem. III, 196). The symbolic order substitutes itself and its patterns of signification for things, so that things themselves, experience itself fades from view. It consists of 'oppositions which do not emerge from the real world, but nevertheless give it its construction, its axes, it structure, which organise it, and in effect make a reality for man in which he can find his way about' (Sem. III, 226). Far from reflecting reality, language creates it: 'It is the world of words which creates the world of things, which are first confused in the *hic et nunc* of everything in its becoming' (Ec. I, 155). For Lacan, language not only creates what the German idealists called 'a second nature', a human and humanised world in which men move and work; it also hangs a systematic network of significations over nature and reality, which substitutes itself for nature and reality, so that these fade from view and become indistinguishable because inexpressible.

The acquisition of language by the child also involves a second alienation from the self, because, for Lacan, language is an impersonal order external to the subject which determines both the nature and scope of his understanding and the form of his identity. The pact of language makes human exchanges possible, but it also predetermines the nature of these exchanges. The mere act of giving a child a name ineluctably determines that child's position within the symbolic order, and thus within the order of culture and society. He is someone's son, brother, nephew, cousin, uncle. The symbolic relationship of father and son, says Lacan, determines what happens far more than the fact of procreation. The subject's realisation of his sexuality is similarly determined by the symbolic order. As Lacan says: 'The subject finds his place in a pre-formed symbolic mechanism which lays down the law for sexuality. And this law no longer permits the subject to realise his sexuality except on the symbolic plane. This is the meaning of the Oedipus' (Sem. III, 191). The Oedipal phase marks the child's acceptance of the fact that he can only be a sexual being in the terms laid down by the symbolic order.[6] And as with this, so with everything else in his life. It is the symbolic order which makes us teacher and pupil, salesman and buyer, judge and accused, sinner and saint, ruler and citizen. What we are, both in terms of our personal identity and in terms of our relationship to each other, is pre-determined by the possibilities contained in the symbolic order. All other possibilities, all possibilities not given in this order, fade into non-existence.

By the same token, while language permits the subject to state, and thus to recognise, his desires and imaginary experiences, it also means that these can only be stated and recognised in terms of the words and concepts already in language. All that is inexpressible in the public and pre-existing order of language, all that has not already been 'created' by words, is repressed – banished to oblivion. And what can be stated can be stated only as distorted by a symbolic network which has its own structure and significations and which exists outside the subject, prior to the subject, and completely independently, not only of the subject's existence and experience, but also of the 'real' world of objects. Language thus determines the terms in which things, experience, and even the self, can be understood. It determines the very shape and content of thought: 'To think is to substitute the word 'elephant' for elephants, and a circle for the sun' (Sem. I, 250).

For Lacan, the consequences of this virtually complete take-over of perception, desire, imagination, thought, experience and reality by the symbolic order are two-fold. First, it imposes conformity and abolishes individuality to the point where 'the collective and the individual are the same thing' (Sem. II, 43). Secondly, it leads to a situation in which 'we are spoken more than we speak', in which what we do and say is entirely governed by the mechanisms of language, so that we become little robots echoing language:

Human beings are not masters of language. They have been flung into it, entangled in it, and are caught in its meshes. . . We should wonder at the paradox. Man is not master in his own house here. There is something in which he integrates himself which already reigns by its combinations. . . In the last analysis, the symbolic function controls us more than any direct apprehension whatsoever. This is why we always try and explain human beings in terms of a mechanism (Sem. II, 353, 43).

To Lacan, men are pawns of the symbolic order, slaves of the binary oppositions and significations already inherent in the structure of language, agents of the word rather than its masters. Men do not express themselves through language: language expresses itself through men.[7]

More significantly still, this alienation of the subject in language is not limited to consciousness and the ego. In Lacan, as in Lévi-Strauss, the symbolic order penetrates the unconscious, which Lacan describes as 'the speech which speaks within me, beyond the me' (Sem. II, 203). As the conscious subject is little more than a mechanism which repeats the signifiers and significations already in language, so the unconscious is a mechanism which repeats what has been repressed. As the conscious subject is the pawn of the symbolic order, a slave to the senses already embodied in language, so the unconscious is a slave of its non-sense, of symbols functioning purely as symbols according to their own peculiar laws. The unconscious is a 'dreaming machine' in which 'displacements, puns, word-play and games operate all by themselves' (Sem. II, 97). As the conscious subject is little more than a link in the continuity of the symbolic order, which existed before him and will exist after him, so the unconscious subject repeats the errors and aberrations of his fathers and transmits them to his sons. Here again, 'the collective and the individual are the same thing,' and the unconscious is 'the discourse of the other', no less than is consciousness. Consciousness and unconsciousness are two linguistic circuits running simultaneously within the individual, both of which are determined from without.

The relationship of the conscious and unconscious linguistic circuits to each other within the individual repeats the relationship of subject and ego on the imaginary level: it is again a matter of alternation, of alienation, of one *or* the other. Consciousness and unconsciousness cannot speak simultaneously: when the ego is speaking sense, the unconscious fades into oblivion; and the non-sense of the unconscious can only be heard when sense is not. The result is a relationship of rivalry and mutual destruction. The conscious ego tries to banish all that does not fit into its circuit into the depths; the unconscious circuit seeks to re-emerge, to displace what has displaced it, and to substitute its message for that of consciousness. The ego endeavours to bar, to strike out, to expunge the message circulating in the unconscious, to prevent it from being heard; the unconscious tries to subvert the conscious order by manifesting itself in disturbing or destructive symptoms and by annihilating sense.

For Lacan, alienation not only pervades every aspect of human life and every dimension of man's being; it is also completely inescapable. As Lacan puts it, another way of articulating the 'either/or' of alienation is 'not one without the other' (Sem. XI, 197). Opposed terms are not only mutually exclusive alternatives; they are also linked pairs. The ego may be 'an alienated form of being', but without it the subject would have no form, no focus for his perceptions, no guide to his experience. The subject's desire may be alienated in the other, but it is also realised in the other, by the other and through the other. Language may alienate the subject from the reality of things, but it also gives man his own world, a human, cultural and social world which is proper to him. Language may alienate the subject from his most profound and most personal experience, but, without it, there could be no intersubjectivity, no human communication or exchange, no co-existence in society. For Lacan it is 'either subject *or* ego, either subject *or* language, either self *or* other, either consciousness *or* unconsciousness', but it is also 'no subject without an ego, no subject without language, no self without others, no conscious without unconscious'.[8]

At the same time, it must be asked: if the subject is alienated both consciously and unconsciously in the significations and images of others; if he is programmed to the depths of his being by a symbolic order which is external to him and which pursues its course despite him; and if what he is is nevertheless inextricably bound up with these alien others, what remains of the subject and of his fabled freedom and autonomy? What is there left for the subject to be? Can, he indeed, *be* at all? Lacan answers this question with ruthless logical consistency: 'The subject is no one' (Sem. II, 72). The subject is the unborn, the unrealised, all that has not come into being. He is that which was fragmentary, incoherent and torn, which saw itself in the other and never became. The subject is the opposite of the other. If the other is +, the subject is −. If the other is presence, being and life, the subject is absence, lack of being and death. If the other is a unified image of the self, the subject is ineffable. If the other is what manifests itself in speech, the subject is what never comes to utterance. 'The subject is nothing' (Sem. XI), pure negativity, and this, we shall see, is its strength. As Lacan puts it, somewhat cryptically: 'A true signifier is, as such, a signifier which signifies nothing. Experience proves it. The more it signifies nothing, the more indestructible it is' (Sem. III, 210).

THE BEYOND IN THIS LIFE

Lacan characterised man as a standardised, mass-produced repetition of extant models, and the modern world as a world in which individuality, autonomy and freedom have disappeared. He argued that the subject as a unique, independent, sovereign ego was an invention of the seventeenth century which is no longer applicable because the subject has become little more than the slave of an all-pervasive social mechanism which rules him primarily through its manipulation of the word. Lacan rejected all philosophies – romantic, idealist, existentialist, or Marxist – which sought to preserve for man some vestige of his 'humanity' or which held out to him some vision of a golden age in the future or in the past. He insisted that there is no difference between exploiters and exploited in society, since they are both equally subject to the economy as a whole, and that there is no present possibility of a revolution which would not simply replace one tyrannical symbolic order by another, equally arbitrary. Despite the continuous 'delirious discourse' about individual autonomy and freedom in the modern world, therefore, he felt that men did, that men must, resign themselves to the status quo (Sem. III, 150–2).

Lacan saw, discussed and believed all this, but he could not accept it. Conformity of any kind was anathema to him. This is clear both from his life and from his style. Refusal to conform to the views, terms or pressures of others not only led to his leaving the French Psychoanalytical Association; it led him to dissolve, one after another, each of the psychoanalytic groups he founded, as soon as he felt that they were beginning to question or to limit his own unique and sovereign freedom; and it led him to behave like an *enfant terrible*, flouting convention and good manners, and shocking people as much as he could. In his life, as in his style, Lacan strove to be master and creator of the word, rather than its imitator and slave. A son of the high Parisian bourgeoisie, Lacan still desired what the bourgeois tradition had taught him to desire; to be a free, creative and autonomous individual capable of genuine and meaningful encounters with others.

In systemic terms, there was only one place to put this desire: the place where the alien other did not reign supreme, the place of the subject. Having boxed himself into a dialectic without transcendence and without reconciliation, there could be no transcendence or reconciliation for Lacan which did not inhabit the opposition. But since the subject was nothing, this involved Lacan in a *creatio ex nihilo*: he had both to create something in the place of nothing, and to make nothing something. And to do this in a manner consistent with his system of linked oppositions, he had to make nothing an inverted mirror reflection of something. This is why in Lacan, truth, reality, desire, language, life, presence, being and the Other are all present in inverted form in the subjective realm of negativity.[9]

Thus it is through a process of inversion that the subject's lack of being becomes the precondition for genuine being:

> If a [human] being were only what he is, there would not even be a place from which to talk about what he is. A [human] being comes to exist by virtue of his lack [of being]. It is by virtue of this lack in the experience of desire that the [human] being attains a sense of himself in relation to being. It is by pursuing this beyond which is nothing, that he becomes conscious of a self which is not a mere reflection in the world of things (Sem. II, 262).

A structure can only be perceived against its limits. It is only by standing at some distance from a configuration that one can see what it is. The subject as pure negativity, as absence and lack of being, is that point from which symbol, society and socialisation can be seen for what they are: alien forms of being which prevent the subject from becoming anything at all. The discovery in the experience of desire that the subject 'desires nothing that can be named' (Sem II, 261), that his desire can be satisfied by no object, goal or experience in the social and cultural order, is the impulse which makes him conceive of himself as something other than what the social and cultural order makes him. This is why Lacan compares the subject to a zero in the denominator of a fraction[10] and why he defines the subject's freedom as freedom to destroy all that is: the subject is free to be 'the signifier which kills all meanings' (Sem. XI, 227). The subject is the 'lethal factor' in the *vel* of alienation which destroys all extant oppositions. He is free to subvert and annihilate all that is in order to open a path to an impossible possibility of being.

At the same time, if it is 'through lack of being that being exists' (Sem. II, 261), and if, as Lacan says, it is only by virtue of the existence of the subject as pure negativity that men are able to speak 'as men' rather than merely as members of a herd, the question arises as to how the subject can manifest its being? How does it come to speech, and in what can its speech consist, if all language, and all symbol are the property of the alien order? Lacan's answers to these questions are graphically portrayed in his interpretation of Freud's dream of Irma. Here, first, is the text of the dream:

Dream of July 23rd–24th, 1895
A large hall – numerous guests whom we were receiving. Among them was Irma. I at once took her on one side, as though to answer her letter and to reproach her for not having accepted my 'solution' yet. I said to her: 'If you still get pains, it is really only your own fault.' She replied: 'If you only knew what pains I've got now in my throat and abdomen – it's choking me' – I was alarmed and looked at her. She looked pale and puffy. I thought to myself that after all I must be missing some organic trouble. I took her to the window and looked down her throat, and she showed signs of recalcitrance, like women with artificial dentures. I thought to myself that there was really no need for her to do that. – She then opened her mouth properly and on the right I found a big white patch; at another place, I saw extensive whitish grey scabs upon some remarkable curly structures which were evidently modelled on the turbinal bones of the nose. – I at once called in Dr. M. and he repeated the examination and confirmed it. . . Dr. M. looked quite different from usual he was very pale, he walked with a limp, and his

chin was clean shaven. . . My friend Otto was now standing
beside her as well, and my friend Leopold was percussing her
through her bodice and saying: 'She has a dull area low down
on the left'. He also indicated that a portion of skin on the left
shoulder was infiltrated. (I noticed this, just as he did, despite
her dress). . . M. said: 'There's no doubt it's an infection, but
no matter; dysentery will supervene, and the toxin will be
eliminated.'. . . We were directly aware, too, of the origin of the
infection. Not long before, when she was feeling unwell, my
friend Otto had given her an injection of a preparation of propyl,
propyls . . . proprionic acid . . . trimethylamin (and I saw before
me the formula for this printed in heavy type). . . Injections of
that sort ought not to be made so thoughtlessly. . . And probably
the syringe had not been clean.[11]

Lacan divides this dream into two parts, the first of which
concludes with the image of Irma's gaping throat.

In Lacan's interpretation, the first part of the dream shows the
ego close to its waking state, and the ego's imaginary associations.
Freud discusses Irma's symptoms with professional interest,
expresses his conscious displeasure at what he takes to be her
unjustifiable resistances to his treatment, and on the imaginary
level, he condenses in the figure of Irma features belonging both
to his wife and to another woman he would like to treat. The
consequence of Freud's need to know the human mind appears in
the culmination of this part of the dream as a horrifying revelation of
the dangerous, anguishing and subversive nature of his discovery.
According to Lacan, the horrible image of Irma's gaping gullet is a
revelation of ultimate Reality, of that reality which is unnamable
and unmentionable, before which all words cease and all categories
fail. For to Lacan, Irma's gaping gullet is a representation of the
negative face of being: it is 'the flesh one never sees, the bottom
of things, the reverse side of the face, the secreted *par excellence*
. . . the depths of the mystery, suffering flesh, formless flesh,
which, as such, produces anguish' (Sem. II, 186). Irma's gaping
gullet is also for Lacan a representation of the limit, of the boundary,
the beginning and end of things: it is 'the abyss of the feminine
organ from which all life emerges, as well as the chasm of the
mouth in which everything is engulfed and the image of death
where all things end' (Sem. II, 196). Irma's gaping gullet is thus
for Lacan, the point where the dream penetrates the unknown to
provide an ultimate revelation of the 'You are this, that which is

furthest from you, that which is most unformed' (Sem. II, 186). Here, says Lacan, Freud should have woken up. But instead he moves on to something for which the intimation of ultimate reality in Irma's gaping throat is the precondition: namely the subject's separation from the ego, and his recognition of the falsity of all that belongs to the ego's world. Lacan argues that the three doctors in the second part of the dream represent some of the identifications which went into the construction of Freud's ego, and therefore that their presence in the dream indicates the decomposition of Freud's ego into its elements. In consulting the three doctors, in deferring to them, in allowing them to diagnose Irma, Freud withdraws behind them, and from here, as a subject, he begins to make his presence felt in a new way. At this point, says Lacan, 'once he has vanished, been reabsorbed, abolished himself behind them . . . another voice begins to speak . . . the voice of the subject outside the subject who structures the dream' (Sem. II, 196–7). The subject outside the subject speaks by acting as the puppet-master of Freud's ego identifications: he manipulates the doctors' dialogue and shows up its absurdity. The subject speaks by making the doctors appear as clowns; he speaks in the holes and *non-sequiturs* of their discourses, by making their dialogue non-sensical – for instance, the discontinuity between the infiltration in Irma's shoulder and Dr. M.'s suggestion that it will be eliminated by dysentery makes a mockery of the suggestion.[12] At this point, then, the subject, who is behind the signifiers of speech, speaks by subverting the ego's meanings and by annihilating the sense of the public order of language.

The culminating point in this second part of the dream arrives when the subject who is no one speaks in his own voice to utter the word: 'trimethylamin'. Lacan says: 'At the point where the Hydra has lost its heads, a voice, which is no longer anything but the voice of no one makes the formula for trimethylamin emerge as the last word on the matter, the word for everything. And this word means nothing, if not that it is a word' (Sem. II, 202). Where Freud in his notes on Irma's dream elaborates his associations with the word trimethylamin as he elaborates his associations with every other phrase in the text of the dream, Lacan insists that the significance of the word derives not from its associations, but from the fact that it is a word which has been uttered by the subject. Lacan denies that the word answers anything in the dream or resolves any of the subject's existential questions. To him the significance of the word trimethylamin lies in its hermetic, enigmatic character which draws attention to it purely as a word, as a word spoken by the subject. And as a word spoken by the subject, as a genuine act of speech, the word trimethylamin has two significant functions.

The first is to mark the place – or rather the lack of place – occupied by the subject and thus to bring his absence, his lack of authentic existence, to recognition. The word here acts 'not like the cry which is profiled against a backdrop of silence, but like the cry which makes silence come into view as silence' (Sem. XI, 28). In the realm of negativity which is the subject, the word can never fill the silence. It can never give the subject a being he lacks or answer his existential questions about who he is, whence he came and why he must disappear, because, by definition in Lacan's philosophy of language, the word murders the thing. 'The signifier already considers the subject as dead' (Sem. III, 247). But although the word can never fill the silence, it can indicate existence. Again by definition, words represent the presence of things which are absent. Words can represent non-being, absence and lack. And they must do so because 'before speech, nothing is nor is not' (Sem. I, 254). Without speaking the word which fixes the nature of his condition, the subject can have neither being nor lack of being. The word is necessary to enable the subject to state and recognise that he has lost himself, and that he desires what he has lost. This is why the appearance of the word in the second part of Irma's dream seems to Lacan a step beyond the vision of ultimate reality in Irma's gaping gullet. As he puts it to somewhat enigmatically: 'the dimension of speech hollows truth out of the real . . . [it] introduces the hole of being into the texture of the real' (Sem. I, 254). In other words, speech makes it possible for the subject to recognise his truth: the truth of his lack of being and the truth of his desire for *tuché*, for the genuine encounter with himself which can never take place because he is not.

The second significant function of the word as word is to signal the subject's desire for a genuine encounter with an other. When people recount their dreams, as Freud recounted his dream of Irma, they are recounting their dream to someone; they are speaking to someone through their dream and trying to get 'a direct declaration from the subject' across to their interlocutor. The actual meaning of the word or words used here is irrelevant. Lacan insists that when Ulysses' companions are turned into pigs, their grunts are genuine acts of speech, genuine messages addressed to others, because they are appeals for recognition or belief. 'An act of speech is essentially the means of being recognised. It is there before anything which may lie behind it. And this is what makes it ambivalent and absolutely unfathomable' (Sem. I, 264). The subject's communication through a dream can be very complex. It can contain more than the teller means to say and more than he realises he is saying. For instance, Freud's account of his dream of Irma includes intimations about his guilt for transgressing the conventional boundaries of human knowledge, about his desire for self-effacement as a corrective to his overweening scientific ambition, and his desire to exonerate himself for the failure of his treatment of Irma. But Lacan makes it clear that, as far as he is concerned, the value of Freud's dream lies beyond this, in the 'search for the word, the direct confrontation with the dream's secret reality, the search for signification itself' (Sem. II, 191). What counts is the act of speech as a demand by the subject, who is no one, for recognition by another subject.

In highly schematic terms, the course of this dream as described by Lacan is also the course of a Lacanian analysis. At the beginning of his analysis, the analysand is where Freud was at the beginning of his dream of Irma. He identifies himself with his ego, he relates to others as people who can either threaten or captivate him, and his *parole vide* – his empty utterances – 'wander in the machinations of the linguistic system, in the labyrinth of the systems of reference given by the cultural situation '(Sem. I, 61). The analyst responds by taking his stand in Irma's gullet: he 'plays the dead' and 'introduces the sign of exclusion, the either/or of presence or absence' (Ec. I, 237). In other words, the analyst's silence, the sudden breaking off of the analytic session, and the very uncertainty and unexpectedness of these responses, are intended to confront the analysand's ego with absence, with non-being, with the limit, to shake his certainties and to 'loosen the moorings of his speech' (Sem. I, 205), so that he can begin the process of examining his ego from 'outside it'.

The second phase of a Lacanian analysis corresponds to the decomposition of Freud's ego in Irma's dream. The analysand performs the work of reconstructing the history of his ego for an other, and in the process he rediscovers the 'fundamental alienation which made him construct it as an other' (Ec. I, 125). In the process of reconstructing his history for the analyst, the analysand 'becomes aware of the captivating images on which the constitution of his ego is based' (Sem. I, 205). The analyst's function here is to act as the midwife of the analysand's subjectivity. It is to listen for the gaps, the omissions, the slips and the discontinuities in the analysand's account of his history, to locate the truths behind the analysand's errors, lies and evasions, and to help the analysand to discover the way his hidden subjectivity has structured his history and spoken through it, unknown to his ego. At the limits of 'depersonalisation', when the ego has been dissolved, and at the limits of the analysand's discourse when it has become apparent that the same loss or lack has structured his entire history, the point of reality and truth is reached. And at this point, as in Freud's dream, a new type of speech comes to be heard, a speech which seeks recognition and which establishes itself between two subjects. Lacan calls it alternately the Other (capital O) or *parole pleine* – full speech, or utterances full of the subject – to distinguish it from *parole vide* – speech empty of the subject because alienated in the cultural reference system.

At this point, the analysis is over. Lacan interprets Freud's dictum *'Wo es war, soll Ich werden'* to mean 'I must arrive there where it – the subject of the unconscious, the last signifier, the Other – was'. The analysis is over, therefore, when the analysand has found the Other who spoke through him, the other self he sought unknowingly in his false identifications with others, and when he has discovered that this Other is no one, that the Other is what has not been able to become. To this extent, and to this extent only, the analysand is 'disalienated' and changed by his analysis.

By the term of the analysis too, the analysand has achieved a genuine encounter; he has broken through what Lacan calls 'the wall of language' and succeeded in getting the Other self within him heard and recognised by another subject – that of the analyst – who can follow him and respond to him at this level of Otherness; and he has thus achieved genuine 'intersubjectivity'. But in Lacan this experience has few implications for interpersonal relations outside the analytic situation, for Lacan believes that such disalien-ating encounters are possible only between an analyst and analy-sand.

REPETITION AND INNOVATION

Lacan's work is enormously repetitive. Lacan makes the same

points and presents the same fundamental structures again and again in different ways, in different contexts and in terms of different cultural reference systems. This repetitiveness is a significant part of his statement since, as we saw, Lacan regards all conscious discourse as a repetition of the signifiers and significations already in language and all unconscious discourse as the repetition of an insistent message which endeavours to make itself heard between the lines and in the gaps of speech. But Lacan's repetitiveness is also as ambiguous as everything else in his system, because Lacan turns repetition into innovation – by making a game of it. As he explains:

> Repetition requires novelty. It turns to the ludic which makes novelty its dimension. . . Everything in repetition which is varied and modulated is only the alienation of its meaning. The adult, or the more advanced child, demands novelty from his activity, from his play. But this slide [towards novelty] veils the real secret of the ludic, namely the more radical diversity constituted by repetition itself (Sem. XI, 59–60).

The pleasure of the Lacanian text begins when the difficulties and obscurities have been overcome, when the basic points have been grasped and when the inherent repetitiveness has been seen. For the pleasure of the Lacanian text lies in the wit, the unexpectedness and the intellectual dexterity with which the most diverse cultural and historical reference systems are used as counters in the same game and as vehicles for the same insistent message. Lacan alternates between the vocabulary of Freudian psychoanalysis, Saussurean linguistics, Lévi-Straussian anthropology, Platonic, Hegelian, Sartrian, Heideggerian and Merleau-Pontean philosophy, Greek, Roman or nineteenth-century realist literature, cybernetics, myth, rhetoric, mathematics, and graphs, images and algebraic symbols of his own invention. In Lacanian terms, these different vocabularies or reference systems can be described as metaphors or metonymies – as substitutions of one word or reference system for another, and as substitutions of parts for the whole. Or they can be described as varied or modulated repetitions which alienate the same meaning by putting it in other terms.[13]

Lacan can repeat his message in terms of virtually any reference system because he is speaking not as an analyst, a scientist, a philosopher or a literary critic, but as a subject who has no reference system and no words but those of others and who must make himself heard in, through and despite an alien medium. Which reference system is used – Freudian, cybernetic, philosophical, algebraic or literary – is therefore almost a matter of indifference in comparison to the question of how the subject can transmit his message through a symbolic order which is programmed to say something else. But fortunately – since all communication requires *some* measure of familiarity, of repetition – there are models in language and culture for this too: the Freudian model of how the subject speaks through dream materials, and the longer-standing model of esoteric writing. Lacan refers us to both:

> Freud shows us how speech, the transmission of desire, can make itself recognised through virtually anything, as long as this virtually-anything is organised as a symbolic system . . . [In *The Interpretation of Dreams*] he speaks of *Tagesreste*, materials left over from the day, which are, he says, disinvested from the point of view of desire. In dreams, they are errant forms which are of minor importance to the subject and which have been emptied of their meaning. They are therefore signifying material. Signifying material, be it phonematic, hieroglyphic etc. is made up of forms deprived of their proper meaning and taken up into a new organisation through which a different meaning expresses itself (Sem. I, 269–70).

> Maimonedes' *Guide to the Perplexed* is an esoteric work. [Maimonedes] deliberately organises his discourse in such a way that what he wants to say, which is unsayable – and he is the one speaking – can nevertheless be revealed. It is by means of a certain disorder, of certain ruptures and certain intentional discords that he says what cannot or must not be said. Well, the lapsuses, the holes, the contentions, the repetitions of the subject also express – but innocently and spontaneously this time – the way in which his discourse is organised (Sem. I, 269).

What the subject does innocently and spontaneously, Lacan does with conscious and calculating intent. Like the subject in the second half of Freud's dream of Irma, Lacan speaks through the most diverse signifying materials by the way in which he structures and organises these materials, and by emptying them of their accepted meanings so that they can become vehicles for the subject's message.

The most obvious way in which Lacan empties extant reference systems of their meaning and turns them into vehicles for his own subjective message is by using key words to mean something other than what they would normally mean within the reference system in question. As we have seen, Lacan uses key Hegelian terms like dialectic and alienation in senses diametrically opposed to their received meaning within the Hegelian system, and he does the same with other philosophical terms like Reality, Being, Subject, Presence and Other. In his *Écrits*, Lacan describes this as the 'sliding' of the signified under the signifier and points out that it permits the signifying chain to be used to say something quite different from what it says (Ec. I, 260). Elsewhere, he argues that it is characteristic of the evolution of language for human significations to modify the content of signifiers, so that words acquire new usages (Sem. III, 135). But either way, it is a practice which places Lacan's writing on the boundary of communication and non-communication. For, on the one hand, in so far as signification derives from the relation among signifiers in language, so that the meaning of words becomes apparent from their usage in different contexts, it is possible for the reader to work out the new senses Lacan is giving familiar words. But on the other hand, as Lacan was gleefully aware, using key words in unfamiliar senses can easily prevent the reader from following his argument:

> There is no way to follow what I am saying without using my signifiers, but using my signifiers is attended by a sense of alienation which incites people to seek what Freud calls 'the small difference'. Unfortunately this small difference makes them lose the thread of the implications I am indicating to them (Sem. XI, 198).

Another way in which Lacan empties extant reference systems of their meaning and turns them into vehicles for his own subjective message is by restructuring received ideas. For novel as Lacan's ideas invariably seem, they are not in themselves radically new. For instance, the idea that language is capable of creating an order of reality which differs fundamentally from the natural order goes back to Plato and has accompanied us in one form or another down the centuries. The notion that words represent ideas in the mind

rather than real things goes back to the sceptics and becomes
important from Locke on. From the middle of the seventeenth
century, the realisation has been growing that society is not an
ineluctably God-given hierarchy, but an artificial human order
which differs profoundly both from society to society and from the
natural order. Under the dual influence of nineteenth-century
sociology and Marxism, men have long been exploring the ways
in which society socialises individuals to its norms and
assumptions. The negative effect of the machine and of modern
technology on human freedom and self-expression was a central
theme of the Chartists and of writers and philosophers throughout
the nineteenth century. The opposition between Being and Nothing
has been central to modern philosophy from Hegel through to
Heidegger and Sartre. In our own century, cybernetics and the
development of the computer have focused the study of language
on binary oppositions and mathematical combinations. And the
attempt to explain all reality in terms of one dominant principle is
familiar throughout the history of human thought – whether in
the pre-Socratic form of a single natural element or in the later
forms of theology, economics or the symbolic order.

Lacan restructures such received ideas by his use of gaps
or omissions. As he warns us: 'the notation of an absence is
extraordinarily important for the localisation of a structure' (Sem.
III, 142). As we have seen, what is absent in Lacan is the traditional
notion of the subject – man as creator, man as master of himself
and his world, man as a free agent. And this absence penetrates
and profoundly transforms every idea that Lacan takes over. For
instance, for Lacan, as for so many before him, language, culture
and society represent an artificial human order which makes man
whatever he is. But, for Lacan, language, culture and society
are not human creations, embodiments of the human spirit,
monuments to man's struggle to make himself and his world. In
the absence of man as creator, language, culture and society
become 'the voice of no one', an impersonal circuit into which
each of us is integrated whether we will or no, which remains
irrevocably alien to the subject. Or again, for Lacan, like many
others before him, man is socialised into language, culture and
society. But in the absence of any concept of man as a free,
individual or controlling force, the traditional opposition between
man and society collapses, and language, culture and society
become identical with man.

In this way, through absence or omission, Lacan makes every received idea a vehicle for the same subjective message: 'I, the subject, am not'. This practice, too, places Lacan on the boundary of communication and non-communication. It sends readers and students off in complicated circles if they assume that they are being trained in anything other than the art of listening to Lacan. But then Lacan never made a secret of the fact that he regarded his seminars as analytical situations in which he was speaking as an analysand to a roomful of analysts. Even in the preface to *Télévision*, he reminds us that he is speaking 'to those who know what it's about, to non-idiots and presumed analysts.' And when all is said and done, it must be said that learning to listen to Lacan is pretty good training for listening to anyone.[14]

Lacan uses literary texts in the same way that he uses received ideas. He speaks through them rather than about them. His purpose is not to show how they are made, but to make them what he wants to show. At the same time, Lacan's use of literary texts indicates that, in his view, literature has a function and a centrality in culture and in human life which vastly exceeds the roles of instruction and entertainment traditionally attributed to it. For Lacan treats literature as an instance of the symbolic structures which determine the patterns of conscious and unconscious thought. In Lacan, literature is an integral part of the symbolic order and shares its laws. As man becomes human by repeating the structures and significations already in language, so man becomes human by repeating the concepts, the roles, the myths already in literature. And subsequently, literature, like language, provides man with the means to speak of the patterns they have repeated. The Oedipus story is an obvious case in point. The Oedipus story is something which each of us unconsciously relives. It is something which each of us must repeat to become what we must be within the confines of our specific social and cultural order. And since Freud, it is also something which gives us the symbols, the words and relations, to convey what we have lived. In restructuring received texts to convey a subjective message, in emptying literary texts of all meanings but his own, then, Lacan is doing more than simply using extant literature as a vehicle for speech. He is creating symbols, structures and significations which can be repeated by others, either as models for patterns of thought or as a language for experience. This may help to explain why, since Lacan, the myth of the absent subject who is spoken more than he speaks has taken such root in the language and in the culture.[15]

From this point of view, the part of the Oedipus story which interests Lacan is not the part represented in *Oedipus Rex* which usually concerns Freudians, but the very end of Oedipus' life at Colonus, when Oedipus's destiny has been fulfilled and he is at the point of death. Standing before the sacred grove of the Euminedes – which serves the same function in *Oedipus at Colonus* as Irma's gaping gullet in Freud's dream of Irma - Oedipus can see what his life has been and what life, all life, must inevitably be. According to Lacan, at the boundary of life and death, Oedipus sums up his insight in a single phrase: 'Is it at the moment when I am nothing that I become a man?' For at the point of non-being, when his destiny has been lived out and all that he was has been, Oedipus can see that his life has been nothing but the realisation of the words pronounced by the oracle before he was born. He can see that his destiny has been determined throughout by others acting on these words – his parents who exposed him at birth, the people of Thebes who gave him Jocasta to wife, the old man who crossed his path – and that 'he had nothing to do with it'. Even at Colonus, when the ambassadors, sages and politicians of Thebes come to beg him to return to the confines of the city, he perceives that they do not do so from any feeling of charity or humanity, but as agents of the word, the word spoken by the oracle who warned them that Thebes would lose its greatness if Oedipus did not return.

For Lacan, Oedipus is the very type of the man who has been placed in a symbolic chain which begins before he is born, continues after his death and determines his life and being whether he will or no. Once he has lived out what has been dictated, he is nothing. Once Oedipus has acted out his destiny, he is 'junked, obsolete, a mere residue on the face of the earth' (Sem. II, 20). Oedipus' nothingness outside the terms of the symbolic order is the death, the absence, the non-being which, according to Lacan, not only precedes and succeeds life, but subsists with it. This non-existence of the subject always accompanies the living ego, giving life and the ego their form and their value, and this, to Lacan, is what *Oedipus at Colonus* ultimately demonstrates:

> *Oedipus at Colonus*, whose being is entirely in the utterance formulated by his destiny, presents the conjunction of life and

death. He lives a life which is dead, the life that is there directly under life. . . Life is a stubborn detour, in itself transitory, decaying, lacking all meaning. This life of which we are captive, a life which is essentially alienated, ex-sisting, life in the other, is as such conjoined to death. It always returns to death, and is drawn into larger and more circuitous detours only by what Freud calls elements of the external world (Sem. II, 271–2).

If Oedipus who, according to Lacan, understands the alienness of his destiny and his own innocence in all that has befallen him, nevertheless accepts his destiny, it is because he also recognises that life cannot be different. The only way to avoid fulfilling what is commanded by the word would be to be born other than we are – and this, says Lacan, is impossible (Sem. III, 277). This is why the choir says: 'Better never to have been born, or, if one has been born, to die as quickly as possible'. Dying here means not so much dying the physical death which puts an end to life, as abolishing one's life in the symbolic order, becoming nothing that can be named in the symbolic order, in order to become a man who speaks despite and through that order. The rather surprising question with which Lacan leaves us here is whether the speech which speaks through language and despite it is, in the last analysis, any more human, any more individual, than the other which it strives to displace:

Why in the manifestation of life which is called man does something occur which insists across that life, and which is called a meaning? We call it *human*, but is that so certain? Is it as human as all that, this meaning? (Sem II, 271).

Lacan answers this question in his treatment of Poe's short story, 'The Purloined Letter'.

Lacan uses 'The Purloined Letter' to show that this supposedly human subjective meaning is as repetitive, as mechanical, as transindividual, and as pre-determined as the alien significations it seeks to displace, because 'even that something which is called the subject' is organised and absolutely determined by the play of the symbolic order. To this end, Lacan empties the key words 'purloined' and 'letter' of their received meanings. In the Lacanian text, the letter is not merely a missive, a written communication; it is a metonymy for language itself. Like the word trimethylamin in

Freud's dream of Irma with which Lacan identifies it, the letter in Lacan's version of Poe's tale is a pure signifier, which speaks for the unconscious subject and marks its absence. As a pure signifier, it can also pass from subject to subject, making each what he is by virtue of the role it gives him.[16] This is why Lacan also performs a very erudite and probably inaccurate, etymological analysis of the word 'purloined' to show that we have to do not with a stolen letter, but with a letter which has been diverted from its course and held in abeyance in such a way as to prolong its circuit and to make its repetitive character more apparent. In Lacan, the purloined letter thus becomes a symbol of the linguistic circuit which operates in the unconscious. Thereafter, Lacan has only to show how, unbeknownst to them, the letter imposes repetitive predetermined roles on the participants in Poe's drama as it passes from hand to hand. And he does this with some elegance.

It might be as well here to recall Poe's plot: In a first episode, an incriminating letter is stolen from a high personage at court, the Queen. She is interrupted in her reading of the letter by the sudden entrance of her husband, the King, who is accompanied by a minister. Anxious to conceal the letter, she hastily places it in full view on a nearby coffee table, in the hope that it will escape notice by virtue of the innocuousness of its position. The letter does indeed escape the king's notice, but not that of the minister. Observing her ploy and fathoming her secret, the minister calmly replaces her letter with a similar looking letter of his own, and walks off with the original. The Queen, of course, dares say nothing lest the king learn of its existence. In a second episode, Detective Dupin does what the police have failed to do despite a minute search of the minister's house. He retrieves the letter. And this is how he does it: he visits the minister's house on some pretext and spots the letter in full view in a card rack over the fireplace. He then goes home, prepares a facsimile of the letter he has seen in the card rack, and arranges for a diversion to be created in the street outside the minister's house while he is again visiting the minister. While the minister is at the window trying to see what is going on in the street below, Dupin exchanges the letters, and walks off with the original without the minister's knowledge.

Lacan points out that these two episodes are repetitions of each other. In each case, there is one character who sees nothing of what is going on; another who sees that the first has seen nothing and who deceives himself into thinking that he has succeeded in hiding the letter; and a third who sees the ploy and realises that the letter is open to all takers. But, Lacan argues, the two events differ from one another in that these roles or positions *vis-à-vis* the letter are occupied by different individuals. In the first case, it is the king who sees nothing, the Queen who does the hiding, and the minister who sees what is hidden. In the second case, it is the police which see nothing, the minister who does the hiding and Dupin who sees what has been hidden. The displacement of the letter among the characters thus corresponds to a displacement of roles. The minister who was shrewd enough to see through the Queen's manoeuvres in the first episode is displaced to her position in the second episode. As a result, he finds himself behaving exactly like her. He demonstrates traits of femininity, passivity and luxury previously associated with the Queen. Like her, he resorts to a prominent hiding place to ensure that the letter escapes detection; like her he must thereafter wait and hope that no one will notice it; like her, he is helpless before the character who occupies the same position in the series previously occupied by him. For as the minister once saw the Queen's ploy, so Dupin, now in the position of seer, sees the minister's.

In Lacan's hands, then, the purloined letter becomes a graphic image of the way in which causality and destiny are governed not by anything in life or character, but by the dictation of the word: 'the displacement of the signifier', he says, 'determines subjects in their acts, in their destinies, in their refusals, in their blindnesses, in their success and in their fate, despite their innate gifts and social acquisitions, without regard for their character or their sex; whether we like it or not, all psychological givens must follow in the train of the signifier' (Ec. I, 40). Lacan insists that the characters in Poe's story must obey the unconscious signifier even though it presents a menace to the pacts, the engagements, the positions of the characters in the conscious social order, which is represented for Lacan in the story by the marriage of King and Queen. And this makes the letter 'a signifier which materialises the incidence of death' (Ec. I, 33) in a double sense: on the one hand, the letter represents treason – a threat to the life and stability of the conscious order; and on the other hand, it marks the absence of the subject as a free and original individual. For the letter which passes from hand to hand and catches everyone in its web is the symbol of the repetition compulsion which makes us all relive, even in the depths of our unconscious, what has already been written. 'To come into possession of the letter is to be possessed by it' (Ec. I, 41).

Lacan also gives Poe's short story another dimension which relates it to the analytic situation. From this point of view, the character who sees nothing of what is going on is to be identified with the ego; the character who sees that the first has seen nothing and who deceives himself into thinking that he has succeeded in hiding the letter is to be identified with the unconscious; and the character who sees the ploy and realises that the letter is there for the taking is to be identified with the analyst. Lacan uses this parallel to make some instructive points about the task of the analyst. The first lesson to be learned by analysts is that they should not behave like the policemen in the story, who assume that the letter must be hidden very deeply and very cleverly, and who pull up the floorboards and take apart the furniture in the minister's house to find it. After all, both the Queen and the minister think the letter is safe because it is under everyone's nose. The letter is never where one thinks it will be, and if the police cannot find it and Dupin can, it is because the police do not know what they are looking for and Dupin does. The second lesson to be learned is that, despite what he pretends in his reference to the children's game with odd and even numbers of marbles, Dupin does not find the letter by any process of identification or empathy with the minister (now in the place of the unconscious). Because he understands that the unconscious is structured like a language, that it always and inevitably repeats 'the discourse of the other', Dupin knows that finding the letter depends exclusively on understanding the rules of the symbolic game. The key to both conscious and unconscious life is the law of language; and 'if the different registers of being are anywhere, they are, in the last analysis, in words' (Sem. III, 224).

Lacan's emphasis on the dominance of the symbolic order and on the inevitability of repetition precludes him from really understanding creativity. Lacan recognises that language itself has a history, and that new concepts are introduced into language in the course of history. For instance, he discusses the words introduced into language by the *précieuses* (Sem. III, 133–4) and the way the surrealists changed the conventions of imagery; he describes poetry as 'the creation of a subject assuming a new order of symbolic relations to the world' (Sem. III, 91); he argues that like the mathematical sign $\sqrt{}$ which was invented at one point in history, or like the concept of the 'self' which did not exist until the sixteenth or seventeenth century, Freud's discovery is an 'historical event' (Sem. II, 23); and he presents his own psycho-analytical approach as some thing historically new: 'It is', he says, 'required by particular aims which are historically defined by the elaboration of the notion of the subject. It posits this notion in a new way, by taking the subject back to his signifying dependence' (Sem. XI, 73).

But although Lacan recognises that history is a process in which new ideas, and new symbols come into being, he cannot explain this phenomenon. Do the changes in man's view of the self over the centuries represent 'a concrete turn-about in man's relation to himself, or simply a recognition of something that had not been seen till then?' (Sem. II, 23). Lacan does not know. The closest he comes to an explanation of historical change is a glancing reference to the Hegelian-Marxist idea that the seeds of every new order grow up within the framework of the old:

> One cannot anticipate categories which will come later and which are not yet created; that is completely impossible – human beings are always plunged in the same cultural network as their contemporaries and cannot have different notions from theirs. To be a precursor is to see what our contemporaries are in the process of constituting – in thought, in consciousness, in action, in technique, in political forms – and seeing it as it will be seen a century later. That, yes, that may well be (Sem. II, 45).

But this is an evasion of the problem. For if no one can anticipate what has not yet been created, who does the creating? Our contemporaries? But that is only to say that creation always remains the act of others and that, like the symbolic order itself, it always belongs to the other. This does not explain creativity, but presents it as something alien to the individual, who can only hope to see what others are somehow, mysteriously, in the process of creating, as it will be seen by still others in the future. In the absence of any free and authentic subject and in a situation where we are all penetrated to the depths of our unconscious by the laws of the symbolic order, even innovation must be firmly anchored in the extant, contemporary cultural network.

And this is true of Lacan's practice. For Lacan the entire symbolic order – everything in language, culture and society – is alien to the subject. The symbolic order governs all the registers of man's being and condemns authentic subjectivity – the untrammelled, dominant, highly individualistic subjectivity idealised in the nineteenth and early twentieth centuries – to fading, to *aphanisis* and to non-being. Lacan presents himself as an authentically individual subject by speaking in the name of this subjectivity – which existed, if at all, only in Western culture, and only for a period of a hundred years – through the interstices of the alien symbolic order and by means of endless repetition. This is the enigma at the heart of his system and the secret of his difficult style. As he says: 'It is often what appears harmonious and comprehensible which conceals some opacity. And conversely, it is in the antinomy, in the gap, in difficulty that we find a chance of being transparent. This is the point of view on which our method is based, and I hope our progress too' (Sem. I, 126).

THE INTELLECTUAL AND THE OTHER

Despite the absolute domination of the symbolic order and the conscious difficulty of his style, Lacan succeeded in speaking as a subject and in making himself heard. There is, however, a great deal of truth in Anthony Wilden's observation that Lacan's psychology was 'a psychology for intellectuals, not for people'.[17] For despite attempts to popularise Lacan in the French press and media, Lacan spoke throughout his life primarily to intellectuals. He spoke to psychoanalysts. He spoke to artists like Dali and the surrealists. He spoke to philosophers, lay-analysts, anthropologists, literary critics and linguists in his various psychoanalytical groups, in his Seminars at the *École des hautes Études* and later at Vincennes. And he spoke to all shades of the French Left which was, like Lacan himself, largely middle-class, intellectual, anti-American, anti-bureaucratic and anti-establishment.

At the time, these groups of French intellectuals heard him rather differently from the way in which he has since been heard in England and America. What often appears in England and America as an abstract and theoretical formulation of the insidious and largely hidden role of language and culture in modern societies was grasped in France in much more concrete and immediate terms: as a description of the actual constraints operated by the established order both within the educational system and without it, upon the individuals processed by it. It should be remembered that the French system has, for most of this century been more centralised and authoritarian than either the American or the British, and that France clung to its rigid, hierarchical traditions long after the British had begun to dismantle theirs. Still largely rural and agricultural after the Second World War, France was transformed into one of the most industrial and technologically-advanced countries in Europe within about twenty years by means of rigorous centralised control. Under Gaullism, France was given up to the planners and administrators in Paris. They not only planned the economy; they controlled the programmes put out on the ORTF – both the news programmes prepared by journalists and light entertainment programmes; and they ran the entire French educational system, including the Universities, on rigidly standardised lines, leaving local administrative and teaching staff little or no say either in the curriculae or in the decisions made about them. At the same time, teaching in the schools and Universities was highly structured and authoritarian – 'ritualistic and fideist' is what one Frenchman has called it[18] – as well as distinctly traditional in content. There was very little emphasis on science, and great emphasis on the rhetorical mastery of the French language and of French philosophical and cultural traditions. Students were treated paternalistically by University adminis-trations which, *in loco parentis*, imposed innumerable petty rules on them; and both the Universities and the professions were organised feudally around the fiefdoms of the *grands patrons* – mandarins whose favour and approval had to be sought by all those who hoped to advance in the hierarchy, and whose opinions had to be deferred to. There was little leeway in this system either for participation or for eccentricity. For French intelectuals there was, therefore, nothing abstract or theoretical about the rule of the other.

In this situation, Lacan did not offer a panacea for society, an educational programme of reform, or even a model for relations among people in their ordinary lives or in their professional *milieux*. He did not endeavour to determine a future course of action or to prescribe a mode of being. He espoused no party ideology and made no decisions for the subject of any kind. Lacan's teaching and psychoanalysis only aimed to show the subject in what position he was placed. Lacan aimed to make his students and analysands aware that they were controlled to the depths of their being by the other — by an alien symbolic, cultural and social order which failed to satisfy their deepest needs and desires and which condemned real subjectivity to oblivion. And for those who failed to grasp the point from his teaching and from their training analyses, Lacan instituted the *passe* – a qualifying examination which mocked the system it was qualifying them for.[19] To make students realise their total dependence on others and their utter helplessness in the face of it, Lacan made the student submitting to the *passe* 'take the position of the dead' while others discussed him and determined his fate. And to make students understand that they could nevertheless only make themselves heard in language and through the other, he decreed that each student must first speak to one of his peers, who would in turn be responsible for pleading his case to others.

Equally important, Lacan taught French intellectuals that they need not be of the party of the other. He gave analysts a role, and writers and teachers the model of a role, which did not simply involve helping people to conform and adapt to the demands and constraints of the established order in France.[20]

This is how, apolitical as he appeared to be, Lacan nevertheless managed to intervene in the intellectual and political conflicts of his time. Lacan hinted at the manner of his intervention when he pointed out in 1964: 'the "cause" of [Lacanian] psychoanalysis is the cause of the unconscious; this cause must be conceived as a fundamentally lost cause. That is the only chance there is of winning it' (Sem. XI, 117). The post-war years in France were years when both the political left and the political right were profoundly divided among themselves; when the Soviet Union's example inspired increasing numbers of French intellectuals with severe doubts about the efficacy of organised Marxist revolutions; and when France's long-standing cultural traditions were being effectively changed, not by a much needed increase of liberty, equality and fraternity, but by American technology and Gaullist centralised planning. There was thus no immediate prospect of destroying the extant social and cultural order except, as Lacan put it, 'in effigy' – through language and speech, as Lacan does in his system and in his analyses. In these circumstances, the humanist cause of a spontaneously creative individual who was master in his own house might well have seemed a lost cause. And as Lacan saw it, the only remaining hope lay in reminding people that they were being turned into automata and in keeping alive the realisation that there was no longer any place in language and culture for individuality, intersubjectivity and the humanist conception of man. For if people realised what was missing, if they became aware of their own profound desire for an existence they lacked, there might yet be a chance of regaining what they had lost.

The efficacy of Lacan's intervention in politics became apparent in the historic uprising of 1968. As several commentators have pointed out, the May 1968 revolution in France was a revolution of the intellectual class.[21] It was led by University students, by *lycée* pupils and by their teachers. It was joined by artists, journalists, technicians, engineers and professional workers. It grew up without any reference to the organised political parties of the French Left, and, in its initial and formative phases, without any relation to the working class as such. The May revolution was an almost spontaneous attempt to bring down the 'masks', conventions and constraints of French society and to regain subjective autonomy, freedom and self-expression. As Shelley Turkle says, people spoke of May as '*la prise de la parole*' – the seizure of individual speech.[22] During its brief moment of glory, the May revolution put control back into the hands of the individual subject by means of thousands of action committees where people were free to speak out, to participate in decisions and to carry them out for themselves.

Lacan was one of the cult figures of this revolution; he was also one of those to whom disappointed intellectuals turned when it failed. Lacan himself stood apart from the attempt to create a world consonant with the subject and watched impassively as subjective energies were dissipated and overruled by the authorities. But he continued to be respected because he had posed the problem in terms which had been borne out by the events of May: he had long argued that the desire of the subject must either flounder in a formlessness which would preclude it from attaining any enduring, collective mode of being, or turn into its opposite – a new tyrannical and alien symbolic order which merely replaced the one it had displaced. It was with this impasse as defined by Lacan and with the events of May, that other thinkers, like Foucault, were going to have to contend.

Lacan's effect on French literary criticism and critical theory has been no less marked. Before Lacan, French literary criticism wavered between the well-trodden paths of *explication de texte* (close textual analysis) backed by superficial biographical histories, and the more avant-garde Marxist *sociologie*. This has been changed, in part because of Lacan. For Lacan's model of the location of the subject in Freud's dream of Irma and in Lacanian psychoanalysis has been almost literally transposed into an influential theory of literature, by Roland Barthes and Pierre Macherey among others. In his *S/Z* and his 'Textual Analysis of a Tale of Poe',[23] Barthes uses the Lacanian structure for purposes of his own – as we will see in the next chapter. But Macherey's book, *The Theory of Literary Production*,[24] is almost entirely expository.

Macherey conceives of the literary text as Lacan conceives of the analysand's: as a discourse 'coiled about an absent centre which it can neither conceal nor reveal'.[25] Like the analysand's discourse, the literary narrative is a 'diversion'; it circles around an enigmatic truth which it cannot say, and exists only as the postponement of an ultimate revelation. Like the language in which the analysand's discourse is presented, the literary text is caught up in the labyrinth of symbolic reference systems: it repeats established literary models and narrative methods familiar from other texts and speaks with a plurality of diverse and often conflicting voices borrowed from extant ideologies and from the forms of everyday speech. It does not reflect or represent reality, but banishes the objects it names and constitutes itself as a purely self-referential system in which 'language speaks of itself, its forms and its objects'.[26] Like Freud's ego in Irma's dream, or the analysand's in the first phase of Lacanian psychoanalysis, the literary text derives its structure, its outline and its limits from the absence symbolised in Irma's gaping gullet. As Macherey explains: 'silence shapes all speech . . . it is the silence which tells us – not just anything, since it exists to say nothing – which informs us of the precise conditions for the appearance of an utterance and thus its limits, giving it real significance without, for all that, speaking in its place'.[27] And like the vision of Irma's gaping gullet in Freud's dream, this silence annihilates all the significations of the text. Macherey compares the text to a 'double picture' in which a landscape conceals a policeman's hat: as soon as we perceive the hidden shape, the landscape disappears. Macherey argues that since no text is fully conscious of this, its other face, and since it 'gives no hint of the absence of what it does not and cannot say',[28] it is for the critic to seek the text's 'unconscious' and to discover 'in what relation to that which is other than itself the text is produced'.[29] The critic's task is to display the conflicts among the text's diverse voices and to extricate the structure of the work from his standpoint in the silence. For Macherey, then, 'the critic is an analyst: he performs a structural analysis like Lacan, Lévi-Strauss and Martinet in their fields'.[30]

In fact, this is not quite the case. For in Macherey's version of the Lacanian structure no *textual* voice speaks in the silence seeking recognition and no indication is given in the *text* of what the text cannot say. At no level is Macherey's writer a 'subject' in the Lacanian sense of a creator expressing his anguishing inability either to create or to be – he is merely a producer of books, a cypher in the chain of book production and distribution. The result is that what Macherey calls the text's 'unconscious' has no language but what the critic endows it with. Where the Lacanian analyst listens for the voice of the subject pronouncing the ultimate word, Macherey's critical analyst replaces the subject. It is his task to say what the work does not say, to say 'something else after another fashion', to give the text its meaning. This distortion of Lacan, which stems from a conflation of the roles of analyst and analysand in Lacan's work, leads Macherey into a contradiction. It leads him to deny that the writer is a creator in any humanistic sense, while insisting that 'thought' – presumably the critic's thought – has 'the capacity to generate novelty, to actively transform its initial data'.[31] And this in turn leads to further distortions. For, whereas in Lacan the subject of the unconscious is playful, ambiguous, subversive and above all 'negative', the subject who replaces him in Macherey's transposition of Lacan is a serious, unambiguous, expository 'positive critic'. Instead of either destroying all the significations of the text or playing with them for his own subjective purposes, Macherey's 'positive critic' shows how the text is 'made' and says what it 'does not and cannot say'. But since in Lacan's model there can be no positive utterance which is not by definition already alienated in the symbolic order, the critic's positivity inevitably leads him to explain the text in terms of the reference systems of 'others' – even if they are up-to-date others like Lacan or Lévi-Strauss – and this repetition excludes him both from 'novelty' and from the possibility of articulating any genuine subjectivity. Macherey's positive critical analyst, therefore, ends up doing precisely what Lacan warned his analysts against doing: he allies himself with the ego and with the extant symbolic order, and imposes his own (intellectual) ego ideals on the text before him.

Barthes makes none of these mistakes. Like the Lacanian analyst whose role is to mark by his silence and by his breaks in the analysand's discourse the inauthenticity of the ego's utterances, Barthes is content to take his stand in the silence. In *S/Z* and in his 'Textual Analysis of a Tale of Poe', Barthes organises the silences – the gaps, the spaces – around the plurality of cultural voices in each text and in the critical discourses about them in such a way as to bring out their babbling, repetitive and hopelessly conventional character. Like the Lacanian analyst whose role is to recognise the voice of the subject when it finally speaks rather than to speak for him, Barthes is content for his critical text to be a 'mirror' of the literary text he is discussing. Since his mirroring of the literary text is done after his *own* fashion, Barthes' critical texts are neither empty repetitions nor mere transpositions of the text into another terminology; they represent acknowledgments that the text's 'unconscious message' has been heard and fully compehended and demonstrations that a genuine encounter between the critic and the text has occurred. In his choice and treatment of M. Valdemar's words from beyond the grave – 'I am dead' – and in the sign S/Z, which represents the inverted mirror relationship between the symbolic world of the ego and the castration or nothingness of the subject, Barthes shows that he has heard and recognised the voice of the Lacanian subject who is nothing and can never come to be. And in his playful manipulation of extant critical models – including Lacan's – for purposes of his own, Barthes shows his understanding of the ludic character not only of the unconscious, but also of the entire Lacanian enterprise.

Lacan, then, gave French intellectual theory and practice a new starting point and a new impetus, to an extent which cannot be fully explored here. Far from confirming that man's mind is nothing but what the extant symbolic order has made it and that the linguistic and cultural circuit goes its own autonomous and impersonal way regardless of the subject, Lacan's work and Lacan's impact on the often innovative work of others demonstrate that it is still possible for subjects to transform what they have received. They prove that, however intractable social and political forces may prove to be when it comes to actual revolutions, tyrannies in the world of words and significations, in which people also live, can be overthrown by those who are most at home in it. This contradiction in Lacan has been no less fruitful than anything else in his system. For from it Foucault learned that the rules of the symbolic order which govern the way intellectuals think and speak must be explored from the point of view of their periodic transformations.

2

Barthes and the Pleasures of Alienation

'Atopia. Fiché: *I am pinned on a fiche, assigned to a place (intellectual), to residence within a caste (if not a class). Against which only one internal doctrine: that of* atopia *(a habitation adrift).'*

RB by RB

Barthes turned life into language and his alienation in Writing, Play and Pleasure. Barthes' writings are repetitive: they unfold from the same key words and fundamental patterning structures. Like Yeats, Barthes has his own ex-centric vocabulary of interlocking terms and his own ex-centric mythology. But Barthes' writings are also always different, always new: they change with the changes in Barthes' intellectual environment and with the growing boldness of his mental, emotional and sexual striptease.[1] Because Barthes translated the languages and conventions of his culture, his readings, his thinking, his 'art of life', his habits, his loves, his 'perversions', his tenderness and even his own texts into Writing (*Écriture*), there remains, in his own words, 'no person behind' the plural surfaces of his texts. Indeed, one could conceive of writing about Barthes exclusively by putting together a patchwork of citations from Barthes. For instance:

It is my profound conviction (and it is linked to all my work during the past twenty years) that everything is language, that nothing escapes language, and that the whole of society is penetrated by language (GV, 145). Each of us speaks only one sentence which can be interrupted only by death (GV, 101). I write . . . by a mixture of obsessions, of continuities, of tactical detours (GV, 259). The history of what I have written is the history of a game, it is a successive game in which I have essayed texts (GV, 137). I am someone who always tries to give voice

49

to a certain marginality (GV, 264). Language is this paradox: the institutionalisation of subjectivity (EC I, 154).

But despite Barthes' attempts to turn everything into language and to make his Writing 'a mask that points a finger at itself' (EC I, 107), the finger remains elliptical and Barthes' Writing obscure. What needs to be retraced is how, in his play-texts, Barthes translated the complex realities of his historical, political and intellectual situation into a network of competing languages and wrote himself within them as an other – a playful, nihilistic and atopical – voice; and how, increasingly, he sought to rewrite this atopical voice as a positive moral, political, aesthetic and individuating value.

THE DUPLICITIES OF CRITICAL PLAY

Barthes' critical play is both a subversion of conventional critical and cultural practices and a re-creation which enables the critic to overcome his alienation from himself, from others and from his cultural world. Its effectiveness on both counts depends entirely on the recognition that he *is* playing. If this is not recognised, Barthes' play-texts have the opposite effect. Far from subverting anything, they give rise to new orthodoxies with their professionals, professors and priests. Far from overcoming alienation, they encourage the growth of 'scientific' critical metalanguages which exclude and alienate all but the most hardened initiates. In the 1970s, fearing that his play-texts were being misunderstood in this way, Barthes wrote *Le Plaisir du Texte* (the only one of his books not to be commissioned), which might be described as an aesthetic of the play-text. He also wrote a number of articles and gave a number of interviews in which he tried to describe the 'transgressions', 'trickery', 'duplicity' and 'ludic practices' by which the play-text achieved its suspension of meaning. But again, he was not understood, and commentators of his work continue to take him 'seriously' in the conventional way.

Barthes' critical play began long before the 1970s. It was initially conceived as a means of escaping an impasse outlined in Barthes' earliest Marxist works, *Le Degré Zéro de l'Écriture* (1953) and *Mythologies* (1957). Marxism, which provided the tools for 'unmasking' or 'demythologising' bourgeois ideology, robbed Barthes of his faith in the 'innocence' or disinterestedness of traditional ideas, values and methods. Once supposedly universal and self-evident truthes could be shown to embody narrow political class interests, once all cultural forms were perceived to contain suspect interpellent ideological messages, it was no longer possible, in good conscience, to espouse them. Yet, partly because Marxism failed to create a social revolution in France, and partly because new proletarian cultures do not spring full-blow from the head of latter-day Zeuses, it became apparent to Barthes that Marxism had failed to provide a positive alternative to bourgeois ideology, and that it was, as a consequence, impossible to escape the domination of bourgeois cultural forms. This was the painful lesson of *Mythologies*.

In *Mythologies*, Barthes attempted to show that even things as familiar, as apparently 'natural' and 'self-evident' as a child's toy, a film star's face or a wrestling match conceal bourgeois myths which are consumed with the cultural product unbeknownst to the consumer. Barthes set out to unmask and describe these surreptitious myths. The problem which became apparent to him was not only his characteristically intellectual way of demystifying the bourgeois world – 'even objects will become speech if they mean something' (MT, 95) – but, more disturbingly, what he made them mean. Given tongue, a boxing match became 'a Jansenist sport'; a wrestling match 'a great Spectacle of Suffering, Defeat and Justice', either in the Tragic or in the Comic mode, depending on whether the wrestler protagonist imposed himself as a 'primitive Pietà' or as a Molière character; and Garbo's face partook of 'the rule of Courtly love' where the flesh gives rise to 'mystical feelings of Perdition'. In demystifying or unmasking cultural objects, Barthes had simply replaced one set of bourgeois myths by another, more up-market set of bourgeois myths.

In *Myth Today* (1957), Barthes admitted that he was trapped: 'it is a measure of our present alienation,' he said, 'that we constantly drift between the object and its demystification, powerless to render its wholeness. If we penetrate the object (unmask it) we liberate it, but we destroy it; and if we acknowledge its full weight, we respect it, but we restore it to a state where it is still mystified' (MT, 149). And he drew his conclusions: 'In a bourgeois society, there is neither proletarian culture, nor proletarian morality, nor proletarian art; ideologically, all that is not bourgeois is obliged to borrow from the bourgeoisie' (MT, 127). This was a lesson Barthes never forgot. Throughout his subsequent writings, he insisted that it was impossible to speak from 'outside' bourgeois society and bourgeois culture, and that one could not write counter-culturally without basing oneself on stereotypes and working with 'fragments of the the language which already exists' (GV, 145).

As Barthes makes clear in his articles and interviews as well as in his texts, Marxism had also failed him in other ways. In Russia and China, the revolutions had proved 'disappointing'. The State had not perished, there were the Gulags, and far from freeing man from oppression, Stalinist discourse 'policed' everyone, put everyone on trial. In France, Marxist discourse had become institutionalised: it had come to impose a vocabulary and set of values which seemed to Barthes as repetitive, as stereotyped, as boring, as dogmatic and as dictatorial as bourgeois discourse. There was no more possibility of freedom within the universe of left-wing language than there was in the Communist State. Barthes' condemnation of intellectual left-wing writing in *Le Degré Zéro* reveals what was to become a fundamental and enduring characteristic of his thought:

> writing here becomes like a signature one places at the bottom of a collective proclamation . . . Instead of an ideally free language which would not report on me, which would leave everyone in ignorance of my past and my choice, the writing to which I here entrust myself is already all institution; it exposes my past and my choice, it gives me a history, it parades my situation, it engages me without my having to say so (DZ, 23).

The disappointing reality of the communist revolutions taught Barthes that revolution could only now be conceived as an imaginary utopia outside reality and outside the determinations of any familiar social 'place'; while the reality of left-wing intellectual writing taught him that liberty must be sought outside the dictats and collective proclamations of institutionalised languages. It taught him to eschew 'gregarious' positions, to change his vocabulary and his style of writing as soon as these were taken up and repeated by others, and to seek, at least for a while, a form of writing that would allow him anonymity.

Critical play, as a form of brinkmanship between extant institutionalised ideologies and silence, between meaning and its absence, was an expression and resolution of this double bind situation. It was a supposedly 'neutral third term' which enabled Barthes to write without 'borrowing' either from the bourgeoisie or from its left-wing opposition, and without leaving anyone any idea or form with which to subvert his subversion of both warring camps. However, since as far as Barthes was concerned, there were in modern French society no words, languages or meanings *other* than those which had to be subverted, since it was impossible to get *outside* the languages which already existed, the game could only be played within them. Barthes therefore played with and in extant languages, indicating his game in his play-texts by 'cutting the discourse, making holes in it without rendering it senseless', thus by 'supervised ruptures, fake conformities and indirect destructions' (PT, 18). This is what makes his games so easy to overlook, and what makes it so tempting to assume that Barthes is 'really' trying to say something about language, criticism or culture when he is in fact trying to 'suspend all meaning'.

Myth Today was Barthes' first play-text. On the face of it, *Myth Today* presents a 'scientific' semiological model for the way myth introduces itself into human communications. Since 'mythical speech is made of material which has *already* been worked on so as to make it suitable for communication' (MT, 95), myth appears as a second level of communication which uses extant words, sentences or images to convey a supplementary and alternative message. Barthes provides a suitable scientific diagram to illustrate the way this supplementary and alternative mythical message introduces itself into the order of language. He dignifies each aspect of this interlocking semiological structure with a suitable scientific terminology (on the level of language, the *signifier* and *signified* produce a *meaning* which in turn becomes the *form* of a mythical *concept*, which together constitute the mythical *signification*). And Barthes provides the necessary examples. For instance:

On the cover [of *Paris-Match*], a young negro in French uniform is saluting with his eyes uplifted, probably fixed on a fold of the tricolor. All this is the *meaning* of the picture. But, whether naively or not, I see very well what it signifies to me: that France is a great Empire, that all her sons, without any colour discrimination, faithfully serve under her flag, and that there is no better answer to the detractors of an alleged colonialism than the zeal shown by this negro in serving his so-called oppressors (MT, 101–2).

Barthes points out that when the meaning of the original picture ('a black soldier is giving the French salute') becomes the form of the mythical concept ('the success of French colonialism'), the meaning of the original picture is not suppressed. It is merely held at a distance, temporarily emptied out, but in such a way that it can be retrieved at will. And he creates a typology of different possible readings of myth based on this 'duplicity' of meaning and concept. The first type of reading focuses on the picture-image as the unambiguous form of the mythical concept, so as to see the negro as a 'symbol for French imperiality'. This type of focusing is also that of 'the producer of myths . . . who starts with a concept and seeks a form for it' (MT, 115). The second type of reading distinguishes between the meaning and the form, and, under-standing the distortion of the original image by the myth, it receives the myth as an 'imposture'. In this type of reading, which is the reading of the mythologist, the saluting negro becomes 'the alibi of French imperiality'. The third type of reading, that of 'the reader of myths', focuses on the ambiguity of meaning and form and 'lives the myth as a story at once true and unreal' (MT, 115).

Plausible as all this may seem, Barthes has, as he admits in a footnote, resorted to 'trickery'. The trickery becomes evident when we follow Barthes' advice to retrieve the meaning of the original picture ('a black soldier is giving the French salute') and compare it with what Barthes says about it in the passage quoted above. For in that passage, Barthes describes the soldier not as 'a black soldier giving the French salute', but as 'a young negro in French uniform saluting with his eyes uplifted, *probably fixed on a fold of the tricolor*' (my italics). Without the introduction of this completely imaginary French flag, a black soldier giving a salute could lend itself to many other interpretations; with the imaginary French flag, the picture becomes the unambiguous form of the concept of French 'imperiality' and Barthes becomes the very type of the first kind of reader – the producer of myths. As he says: 'whether naïvely or not, I see very well *what it* [the picture] *signifies to me*' (my italics). What follows in the passage quoted above is written in the voice of the mythologist who understands the myth as a distortion of the image and who recognises that the negro saluting the flag is an alibi for French 'imperiality' against its detractors. In a nice touch, this mythologist also distances himself from the detractors of French 'imperiality' by suggesting that the language of their detraction is as mythical as the patriotic alibi ('alleged colonialism', 'so-called oppressors').

The reader who reads Barthes' description of the cover of *Paris-Match* in this way is reading the myth he has produced ambiguously, and 'as a story at once true and unreal'. It is true to say that a picture of a black soldier loyally saluting the French flag on the cover of a French magazine could represent a justification for the French presence in Africa. It is true that a Frenchman might well receive this image with simple patriotic pride, or, if he were a left-wing opponent of French policy in Africa, as an imposture and an alibi. But true as this may be, this reading is unreal because it is not based on the picture as it really is. For this reason, it is also true that French 'imperiality' and French colonialism are distortions of the real picture. But French 'imperiality' and French colonialism are also unreal because they are manifestly politically loaded French cultural myths which have little to do with the real feelings or loyalties of black soldiers in their native land.

The same mixture of truth and unreality afflicts Barthes' entire 'scientific' semiological enterprise in *Myth Today*. Everything Barthes says about mythical speech in *Myth Today* is true in so far as it is borne out by his examples and by the ways he repeats and varies them. At the same time, everything he says is unreal. It is unreal in so far as his examples are 'faked'. And it is unreal in so far as Barthes' complex scientific account of myth as a semiological system is only what Barthes himself calls 'an artifice of analysis'. Barthes account of the 'duplicity' of myth is a true account of *Myth Today*, however. It is true in so far as Barthes' semiological edifice in *Myth Today* is a myth which Barthes simultaneously produces and unmasks as an imposture.

What is being subverted here? First, the scientific pretensions not only of semiology, but of all the new fields of research which concern themselves with the problem of meaning. Barthes associates psychoanalysis, structuralism, eidetic psychology and some types of Bachelard inspired literary criticism with semiology as 'sciences dealing with values' which 'are not content with meeting the facts [but] define and explore them as tokens for something else' (MT, 96). Barthes' analysis of myth in *Myth Today* is a demonstration that to use facts (like the cover picture on *Paris-Match*) as a token for something else is to use facts as a token for a subjective meaning, and to make them vehicles for the values and myths of the researcher who defines and explores them.

The second thing which is subverted in *Myth Today* is Barthes' own approach in *Mythologies*. In *Mythologies*, Barthes was in the position of the mythologist in *Myth Today* – he could understand distortions, decipher mythical significations and unmask the imposture of myth. But like the mythologist in *Myth Today*, he could only do so in terms of other myths (French imperiality/colonialism). As Barthes pointed out some years later: 'in placing oneself outside certain types of language . . . we must not forget that we always do so from another language, and never from a non-language. Thenceforth, we are engaged in an infinite critique of ourselves, a critique of our own language' (GV, 145). *Myth Today* was the first of these self-critiques.

The third, and perhaps the most remarkable thing which is subverted in *Myth Today* is *Myth Today* itself. What remains if both the language of the Right (French imperiality) and the language of the Left (French colonialism, French oppression) are mythical? If reader and researcher alike bring their own myths to any material they work on? If the scientific metalanguages of all the sciences concerned with meaning and the semiological analysis of myth itself are mythical? What remains but the unreality of myth and the truth that we and our realities are completely alienated in myths? Barthes 'vanquished myth from the inside' by 'mythifying it in its turn' and by producing 'an artificial myth' (MT, 123) which reveals the factitious character of 'knowledge' and the mythical nature of cultural ideologies and 'explodes' them without replacing them with anything else.

Two further examples of Barthian play-texts should suffice: the first is the well-known 'structuralist' essay on Jacob's struggle with the Angel (1971); the second, *S/Z* (1970).

Barthes subjects 'Jacob's Struggle with the Angel' (Gen. 32: 22–32) both to an 'extremely classical and almost canonical structural analysis' and to a textual analysis designed to show how the text is 'unmade', how it 'explodes, disseminates' into various significances. The classical structural work of people like Greimas and Propp had been designed to locate and describe a single structural model underlying all texts of a specific type (myth, folktales, etc.), and thus to reduce all texts to a single fundamental format. In his 'almost' canonical structural analysis, Barthes applies these models. He finds three structural sequences in the biblical text: the Crossing, The Struggle, the Namings – a series familiar in structural studies of mythical narratives as the Ordeal. Applying Greimas' actantial model to the characters in the biblical text, he finds the following:

Subject (of the quest/action)	–	Jacob
Object (of the quest/action)	–	Crossing the Ford
Sender (initiator of the action)	–	God
Receiver	–	Jacob
Opponent (who hinders the subject)	–	God
Helper (who helps the subject)	–	Jacob

Propp's functional model of narrative acts in folktale is then adduced to show that in the biblical narrative God is 'structurally stamped with the role of the Villain'. But this, of course, is a palpable absurdity. As Barthes points out in the article with dry humour: 'Propp would have been unable to imagine a more convincing application of his discovery'.

The textual analysis provides the methodological key for 'exploding' or 'unmaking' this structural reading for anyone who does find it convincing. Illustrated in Barthes' analysis of Gen. 32: 22 and 23, the textual method consists of showing how 'abrasions' or discontinuities in the text open it to multiple significances. A close reading of the biblical text and of Barthes' structuralist analysis of it shows that the structuralist reading described above has been arrived at by *glossing over* one such abrasion or discontinuity: that between Gen. 32: 29 and 30. The openness or (to borrow a term from S/Z) the enigmatic quality of the biblical text derives from the abrasion or discontinuity between Jacob's question of the Angel: 'Tell me, I pray thee, thy name' (v.29) and the Naming: 'And Jacob called the name of the place Penuel: for I have seen God face to face and my life has been preserved' (v.30). God becomes the Opponent or Villain and Jacob his own Helper only when this discontinuity is glossed as a continuity: when the name Penuel (the face of God) is taken to be an answer to Jacob's request that the Angel name himself, thus when Penuel is read as the name of the Angel and when the number of actors is correspondingly reduced from three to two.[2]

What is subverted in this essay? First, structuralism itself.[3] As Barthes points out: 'Structural analysis in the strict sense of the term would conclude emphatically that 'the struggle with the angel' is a true fairy-tale, since according to Propp all fairy-tales belong to the same structure, the one he described', i.e. the one which stamped God as the Villain or Opponent. Textual analysis, Barthes explains, tries to see each text in its 'difference'. The absurdity of structuralism is clearly that it does not. As Barthes says elsewhere: the attempt to 'see all the narratives of the world in a single structure . . . is a draining and ultimately undesirable undertaking because the text loses its difference' (S/Z 9). And as far as he is concerned, the text's difference is constituted not by its individuality in any conventional sense, but by the unique way in which it borrows and uses 'the infinity of texts, languages and systems' (S/Z 9). This form of difference becomes an important characteristic of his later 'novelistic' writings.

The second subversion is ideological. The traditional view of God is subverted by the mere possibility that the text which is supposed to provide authoritative knowledge of Him might mean something else. The abrasion between the traditional view of God and Barthes' structuralist presentation of Him produces a blurring of categories: God as Helper or Opponent? God as force of Good or as Villain? Ironically enough, this subversion works by exploiting a virtue on which most bourgeois intellectuals would pride themselves: their readiness to entertain all possibilities.

The third subversion is a subversion of all significance. Barthes concludes the essay by explaining that 'the problem, the problem at least posed for me, is exactly how to manage not to reduce the text to a signified, whatever it may be (historical, economic, folkloristic, kerygmatic) but to hold its significance fully open'. The structuralist folkloristic signifiance adduced by Barthes is clearly not what the biblical text signifies; the traditional religious signifiance has been subverted; and no other possibility is presented. As in *Myth Today*, Barthes' essay has shown up the unreal and mythical character of some of the elements in bourgeois culture without providing an alternative. The essay leaves the reader nothing to appropriate – except perhaps the complex paraphernalia of structuralism emptied of all meaning and all applicability.

In *S/Z*, Barthes inverts a well-known nursery story, the Emperor's New Clothes. In the nursery story, everyone was told that the Emperor was wearing new clothes when he was in fact naked. In *S/Z*, Barthes does the opposite. He tells everyone that the Emperor is naked: instead of clothing Balzac's short story *Sarrasine* in a single totalising meta-meaning as criticism of all kinds is wont to do, Barthes is going to open the text to multiple possibilities of meaning. First, he is going to chop up Balzac's narrative into what he calls *lexes*, arbitrary units of reading which consist of anything from a phrase to a paragraph and constitute a 'decomposition' of the work of reading. Then he is going to demonstrate the text's plurality by showing that these *lexes* are coded in terms of five codes, 'each of which is one of the forces which can monopolise the text' if taken on its own (S/Z 28). These codes are: the hermeneutic code which describes the way the narrative posits a secret or enigma and then delays its revelation or resolution till the end of the story; the proairetic code, which represents the sequence of actions in the narrative; the semic code which relates to what is signified; the symbolic code, which relates to what is symbolised; and the cultural code which relates to a variety of references to contemporary science, history or popular wisdom. By juxtaposing these different codes in his commentary on the lexes without attempting to show how they cohere with each other, Barthes presents each code as merely 'one of the voices weaved into the text' and he presents the text as a 'network' of multiple voices. Finally, instead of using the conventional 'dissertational' style of criticism with its authoritative tone and its synthesizing, 'subjugating' interpretation, Barthes is going to fragment and pluralise his observations by dispersing them in the form of digressions among the lexes and coded commentaries.

Despite all these pluralising and liberating gestures, however, 200 pages of lexes chopped irregularly and 'arbitrarily' out of *Sarrasine*, of coded commentaries and dispersed digressions shows not only that Barthes' text has been clothed in a single totalising meta-meaning from Barthes' first commentary but also that what Barthes has been doing is weaving a cast-iron dress for it.

The meta-meaning of *Sarrasine*, the meaning which Barthes shows that every line and every single coded level of the text cooperate to affirm, confirm and reaffirm, is that given in Barthes' rather enigmatic title: *S/Z*. Z is the 'initial of castration'. According to the rules of French phonology, SarraSine should be pronounced SarraZine; but this Z is transposed from Sarrasine's name to that of Zambinella, the eunuch with whom Sarrasine falls in love mistaking him for a woman. Barthes explains: 'S and Z are graphic inversions of each other; it is the same letter seen from the other side of the mirror; Sarrasine contemplates in Zambinella his own castration' (S/Z, 113). Sarrasine falls in love with Zambinella, the brilliant castrated boy singer and fails to realise what he has done because he is himself a brilliant sculptor who has been castrated in his youth by the overly maternal care of his parent and mentor. In Zambinella, Sarrasine recognises himself. In a very brilliant, perfectly classical analysis, Barthes shows that every single line and every code of Balzac's narrative either serves to conceal or to reveal this fact and that Balzac's alternately hints at this meaning and uses 'decoys' to delay comprehension. Indeed, it is only because every code and every line lead to the same point in this way that Barthes can claim that the text (both his and Balzac's) can be 'entered anywhere'.

Barthes' analysis of *Sarrasine* in fact obeys a critical programme given not in *S/Z* but in *Critique et Vérité* (1966):

> Criticism unfolds meaning by making a second language, that is to say a coherence of signs, float above the first language of the work. It is, in short, a sort of anamorphosis in which it is understood on the one hand that the work never lends itself to pure reflection . . . and on the other, that anamorphosis itself is a supervised transformation which is subject to optical constraints: it must transform *everything* it reflects; it must transform only according to certain laws; it must transform always to the same effect. These are the three constraints of criticism (CV, 64).

In *S/Z*, the meaning of the Balzacian text is unfolded by a second language of lexes and codes, by a coherence of critical signs suspended above the Balzacian text. The language of codes ensures that everything in the text is transformed according to the same laws and to the same effect. The lexes ensure that this transformation covers everything ('a system of meaning is not complete unless *all* utterances have an intelligible place'). And the discrepancy between what we are told the lexes and codes are going to do (open the text, constitute a plural) and what they in fact do (close the text, lock it into an inescapable singular) is an anamorphic reflection of the structuration of the Balzacian text. The classical text is 'a game with two partners: the decoy and the truth' and so is Barthes' text.

In Barthes' text, the denotative level of the critical language serves as the decoy, its connotative level represents the truth. 'Structurally', it is the existence of these two levels which 'permits the text to function as a game', a game of communication and counter-communication because it permits the text to signify one thing at one level and to contradict this signification on another level. As Barthes explains, connotation produces a counter-communication by the formation of 'meanings scattered like gold-dust on the apparent surface of the text' into 'nebuli of signifieds' (S/Z, 14–16). Thus the denotative level of Barthes' critical language with its name codes, numbered lexes and disruptive digressions communicates the presence of a plurality of different meanings and interpretations. But the aggregated meanings scattered throughout these codes, lexes and digressions establish 'a correlation immanent in the text' which locks it into an inescapably singular totalising meta-meaning, that given in the title: S/Z. Like *Sarrasine* itself, S/Z has to be re-read retrospectively for the 'ludic interest' of seeing how Barthes has 'multiplied signifiers'. Retrospective re-reading does not yield some ultimate signified that was not perceived the first time; it shows how many different ways have been found to say the same thing.

Like *Myth Today*, S/Z operates on three levels – that of the producer of myth, that of the mythologist and that of the reader of myths. The lexes represent the level at which language is produced as myth (by Balzac); the coded commentaries represent the level of the mythologist where the reader or critic's subjectivity appears as 'the wake left by all the codes that make him' so that subjectivity manifests itself as 'the very generality of stereotypes' (S/Z 17); and the digressions represent the level of the reader of myths, where the game of communication and counter-communication indicates its own truth and unreality. Dispersed and discontinuous as they seem, Barthes' digressions constitute something approaching a coherent and connected meditation, and he indicates this fact by organising them in the form of a 'Reasoned Table' in Annex 3 of the book. The digressions provide the rules for writing and reading the game in S/Z. They are literally 'an index; they point but do not say . . . they are what is on the tip of the tongue, and will later let fall the truth' (S/Z, 69).

What is being subverted here? First, what Barthes calls in one of his digressions 'language as nature', the assumption that at least at the level of denotation language can be relied upon to be simple, literal, 'true'. As Barthes showed in *Mythologies* and goes on to argue in S/Z, this apparent reliability of language at the level of denotation has the function of 'innocenting culture' and 'domesticating artifice' because it blinds us to the interpellent ideological messages hiding, like the traditional devil, in its seemingly natural and innocent face. If we expect ambiguity, indirection, interpellent messages and the play of language at all (as we do in literary but not in scientific, critical or philosophical texts), we do not expect them at the level of denotation; we expect them at the level of connotation, at the level of what is 'after' or 'above' denotation. Barthes subverts language as nature in S/Z by subverting and inverting this hierarchy which he claims is characteristic of all Western discourse. In S/Z, the level of connotation is simple and 'true'; the level of connotation is not.

Another thing which is subverted in *S/Z* is the very possibility of criticism. As we have seen, this subversion includes, almost parenthetically, a subversion of the 'imperialist' claim of any critical school to exclusive validity. Psychoanalytical, historical and thematic criticism, structuralism, semiology and traditional *explication de texte* (echoed in Barthes' step by step lexical approach) appear in *S/Z* as a 'babble' of voices all of which are woven into the text. If Barthes had stopped here, it would be a moot point whether, as has been argued, he was denying the superiority of any critical approach or, as has also been argued, whether he was preaching the peaceful coexistence of all critical schools in a cooperative study of literary texts. He does not stop here, however, but once again takes criticism to the brink of silence.

'The critique of references (cultural codes)', he explains, 'can only ever be established by a ruse, at the very limit of Full Literature, where it is possible (but at the price of what acrobatics and what uncertainty) to accomplish a critique of the stereotype (to vomit it) without having recourse to a new stereotype: that of irony' (S/Z 113). The ruse in *S/Z* is given in the title. To paraphrase a quotation given earlier, Barthes' text and Balzac's text are graphic inversions or mirror images of each other. It is not by chance that Barthes uses the same pictorial metaphor of 'framing' to represent both the way classical realism sets about describing reality and the way criticism sets about describing a literary text. Both superimpose a 'frame' on the objects they purport to describe and then depict what is within that frame by means of a set of stereotyped cultural codes. If Balzac's text is a 'pastiche' of cultural codes, so is the Barthian text which re-codifies and re-names them. If 'realism consists not in copying the real, but only in copying a (painted) copy of the real', what can be said of criticism, except that it contemplates in realism its own castration? Balzac's text moves inexorably to the ultimate revelation of Zambinella's castration, a castration which represents for Barthes 'the emptiness which has replaced his centre', and it moves to Sarrasine's ultimate realisation that both he and his statue of Zambinella are afflicted by the same hollowness, the same lack as Zambinella him/herself. In the same way, Barthes' text moves to the revelation that it, too, is an edifice with a hollow centre, a playful verbal artifice which remains within cultural codes and cultural myths and within the limitations of anamorphic transformation and is castrated by its inability to penetrate the real.

The stroke (/) in S/Z represents 'the wall of hallucination, the trenchant bar of the antithesis, the abstraction of the limit'. In other words, it represents the paradigmatic opposition which, according to modern linguistics grounds all meaning: male/female, life/death, denotation/connotation. Each is what it is only by virtue of its opposition to the other. When the line opposing the literary text to the critical text is removed by criticism's anamorphic reflection of the literary text, the S of BartheS' criticism and the Z of the BalZacian text join hands to form a closed circle of cultural codes, an echo chamber of repeated structures and reformulated stereotypes, an endless and inescapable tautology. Both concealing and revealing 'the wound of the lack', they teeter together on the brink of the real which cannot be spoken by culture and remains shrouded in silence. And in the process they merge, obliterating the distinction between creative 'literary' writing and instrumental critical writing, to become a form of writing which is neither one nor the other. 'It is lethal', Barthes points out, 'to remove the separating line, the paradigmatic bar which permits meaning to function (the wall of antithesis), life to be reproduced (the opposition of the sexes), goods to be protected (the rule of contracts)' (S/Z, 221). To 'transgress' such classifications is lethal because it is, like the castrati, to sentence oneself to occupy the 'untenable place of the ne-uter', the place of the 'neither/nor'. A form of writing which can be classified neither as criticism nor as fiction, which is neither entirely serious and instrumental nor entirely humorous or fictional, such as a form of writing has no predefined place either in the economy of academic disciplines or in the marketing of books. It is placeless, a-topical. But at the same time, criticism's lethal, self-destructive transgression of classifications, the 'abolition of the Wall and confusion with the Object' produces, at least in Barthes, an exquisite orgasmic pleasure which he dubs *jouissance* (S/Z, 124). S/Z is, if nothing else, a critical text which takes immense and endlessly refined pleasure in confusing itself with its literary object in such a way as to accomplish its own self-destruction.

Jouissance becomes a key concept in Barthes aesthetic of the play-text, *Le Plaisir du Texte* (1973). *Jouissance* is untranslatable in modern English, but has an equivalent in the Renaissance word 'to die', which meant orgasm, death, and the moment of self-obliteration (of death) at the height of sexual pleasure. Barthes describes the play-text, the *texte de jouissance*, as a text which takes erotic pleasure in accomplishing the death of its subject – in both senses of this word, as topic and as person. The *texte de jouissance* kills its topic by being a text where 'language is in pieces, and culture is in pieces' and where nothing can be reconstructed or recovered (PT, 82–3); by playing off cultural plagiarism or conformity to the 'canonical languages' of society against a vacuum in such a way as to 'hint at the death of language'; by liquidating metalanguages, by destroying 'to the point of contradiction' its own discursive category or genre, by creating 'pompous and ridiculous neologisms' and by allowing logical contradictions and antipathetic codes to coexist. *The texte de jouissance* also obliterates the subject as a determined and determinate identity. By erasing the writer as a magisterial voice arguing for some cause or some theory, the *texte de jouissance* produces a 'fading' of the subject; by destroying all possible meanings, it creates a 'hole' which 'swallows the subject of the game – the subject of the text' (PT, 23); and by 'rocking the reader's historical, cultural and psychological foundations and the consistency of his tastes, values and memories', it places him too 'in a state of loss' (PT, 25–6). The *texte de jouissance* is 'scandalously a-topical' because it cuts itself completely adrift from the standard topoi of culture, society, language and personal identity.

But the play-text, the *texte de jouissance*, is not merely a refuge from bad conscience, a way for someone standing outside warring camps to utter his subversive silence. It also waves the banner of good conscience; it represents a polemical affirmation in the ideological war, a *praxis*, and a way for the intellectual to overcome his estrangement and exclusion. In *Le Plaisir du Texte*, Barthes characterises the play-text as anarchical and nihilistic, but he also insists that it is, at the same time, 'always the trace of an affirmation' (PT, 35–6).

The key to some of these affirmative aspects of the play-text is to be found in an early article on toys in *Mythologies* in which

Barthes complains that most French toys are pint-size imitations of the adult world which teach the child to own, to use and to consume bourgeois culture but not to create with it. Given dynamic, do-it-yourself forms like building blocks on the other hand:

> the child does not create any meaningful objects, it matters little to him whether they have an adult name; the actions he performs are not those of a user, but those of a demiurge. He creates forms which walk, which roll, he creates life, not property; objects now act by themselves, they are no longer an inert and complicated material in the palm of the hand (M, 115).

Often set in blocks on the page, Barthes' play-texts are dynamic do-it-yourself forms both for their writers and for their readers. Barthes does not imitate the authoritative canonical codes which own and dominate bourgeois society. He dissects these codes into 'mobile, substitutive parts' and creates new networks with them. Instead of using them to explicate reality, Barthes assembles and reassembles them into text-objects which act 'by themselves', without the intervention of any magisterial voice, through hints, recurrences and associations. Writing is a *praxis* for the writer, then, because he is fabricating his text out of existing cultural entities, not imitating reality at second remove. This *praxis* also authentifies his relation to language. Like the woodcutter naming the tree he is felling, the writer names codes and stereotypes only to cut them down. Like the woodcutter before his tree, the writer treats pre-existing institutional languages as objects to be transformed by his labour. His language is authentic and 'unmythical' because it is 'fully and functionally absorbed in making' (MT, 135). It is 'operational' (MT, 134) or, as Barthes will later say, productive and performative.

The reader's reading is a *praxis* for the same reason. The reader of a Barthian play-text cannot read it passively in imitation of other readings, consuming the text at a gulp and throwing it away. If he does so, he will remain at the level of reading of the producer of myths, for he will turn Barthes' texts into purveyors of new theoretical or semiological orthodoxies. The reader of a Barthian play-text has to take time; he has to go back and reconstruct the text; he has to participate in the game by 'scripting' it for himself, and he 'scripts' it by fabricating a reading out of the entities given to him in the text. He must see the text not as a commentary on another text, but as something in its own write, 'a text, a fiction, a fissured envelope' (PT, 31). This is why Barthes insists that his texts should be treated as autonomous objects and it is why he asks that no referent in reality be sought for them. In children's games, too, no one assumes that the game is real; everyone is too intent on the actual playing of the game and on the enjoyment of his own skill in manipulating its 'mobile parts'.

Through this re-creative *praxis*, writers and readers transcend their alienation from each other and from cultural objects.[4] They transcend their alienation from each other in so far as the text is both an invitation and an agreement to play. The writer's exclusion is overcome by getting others to share it with him; the reader's estrangement is overcome by his participation in scripting a shared text. In this process, writers and readers also transcend their alienation from cultural objects because all fabrication is also an appropriation. Barthes' innovation here is to show that man's alienation from already extant 'dead' cultural forms can be overcome by the intellectual re-appropriation in ludic fabrication. In ludic fabrication, dead cultural objects are de-reified; in scripting, they are able to 'pass from a closed, silent existence to an oral state open to appropriation by society' (MT, 111). In this way, literary works from the past which are no longer 'readable' or even much read, can be given a new, albeit different, lease of life. As a result, far from subverting bourgeois culture and criticism, it can be argued that re-creative play helps to keep them alive.

Through this re-creative *praxis*, man also transcends his alienation from himself because, for Barthes, intellectual activity is the fundamentally human activity: 'the addition of intellect to the object has anthropological value in that it is man himself, his freedom and the very resistance that nature offers to his mind'. When Barthes seeks 'the natural in culture', he finds it 'not so much in stable finite, "true" meanings, as in the shudder of the enormous machine which is humanity tirelessly undertaking to create meanings without which it would no longer be human (EC I, 280)'. What is anthropologically valuable and essentially human here (the mechanistic image notwithstanding) is the process of adding intellect and of creating meanings: 'the fabrication of meaning is more important than the meanings themselves (EC I, 281)'. It is by fabricating meanings that man asserts his fundamental nature. The fact that Barthes tries to clothe this view of man in the erotic language of love's body does not change its fundamentally intellectual and abstract character – it simply links intellectual fabrication to the pleasure-principle of childhood. Only children and (it would seem) intellectuals can claim to derive pleasure and sensuous satisfaction from the playful creation of objects which do not have to mean anything either stable or nameable in the adult world.

Finally, re-creative *praxis* permits Barthes to transcend his alienation from himself by enabling him to objectify himself in his work on extant language and to recognise himself in the texts he produces.[5] For the play-text does not only obliterate Barthes as a determinate subject; it also asserts his individuality. As Barthes puts it, the subject of the play-text is 'a cloven subject who, through the text, enjoys the consistency of his ego at the same time as he enjoys its downfall'. (PT, 36) The play-text asserts the ego of the subject, his formal 'difference' from everyone else, by virtue of the fact that, unlike everyone else, the writer of the play-text absents himself by dissociating himself from all the codes, causes, positions and forms which usually define people in our society. It also gives this difference a substantive content, for Barthes often projects his own 'perverse' biographical and homosexual experience into his play-texts (in *S/Z* for example). This sort of rather daring exhibitionism is responsible for the 'thrill of fear' which Barthes insists is inseparable from the *text de jouissance*: will they see or will they not? And if they do, am I not, like the libertine in *Le Plaisir du Texte* 'cutting the rope on which he hangs at the moment of his greatest *jouissance*?' (PT, 15).

Barthes saw himself and wrote himself as a contradictory sociohistorical subject, and although he took no direct part in the events of 1968 or in the party-political debates of the 1960s and 1970s, he nevertheless defined a political position for himself and found his own way of trying to change the world. As we will see, this becomes more manifest in Barthes' later 'novelistic' writings, but it is already present in the play-texts and in Barthes earliest writings, as a portrayal of the non-place he felt he occupied and in the use he made of the idea of a post-revolutionary utopia.

In *Le Plaisir du Texte*, Barthes writes himself as an unplaced and contradictory subject when he explains:

I play the contradictory game of (cultural) pleasure and (noncultural) thrills at the very limit of a fine combination of biographical, historical, sociological and neurotic elements (education,

class, society, infantile configurations etc.) and I write myself as
a subject who is badly placed, who has come too soon or
too late (this represents no regret or mischance, only a non-
placement); an anachronistic subject, adrift (PT, 99).

Barthes writes himself here as he wrote the mythologist in *Myth
Today* and avant-garde intellectuals in the *Critical Essays* of the late
1950s and early 1960s. There Barthes had presented the intellectual
as a man who was cut off both from the yesterday he rejected and
from 'tomorrow's positivity', the post-revolutionary utopia which
he described as a Promised Land which was not even visible on
the horizon. Estranged both from the society in which he lived and
from the 'history in the name of which he professed to act', the
intellectual was for the old, part of the new, and for the new,
a left-over from the old. His 'status always remained one of
exclusion'.

Barthes' placement of himself in a non-place, a ne-uter, between
old and new represents his acceptance of an unresolved problem
which dates back to *Le Degré Zéro*. In *Le Degré Zéro*, Barthes had
tried – and failed – to find a 'neutral' form of writing which would
make it possible to write in bourgeois society. The flaw in his
argument there had been that the instrumentality, transparent
clarity and universality he attributed to zero degree writing (exem-
plified in France by Camus) also made it the direct heir to classical
French rhetoric as Barthes described it in the same volume. And
as far as Barthes was concerned, classical French rhetoric was far
from 'neutral': its emphasis on clarity, instrumentality and purity
of language perpetuated the bourgeois 'essentialist myth of man'; its
universality linked it to political authoritarianism and to intellectual
dogmatism. Barthes was acute enough to realize that Zero Degree
writing had not in fact accomplished a real break with its bourgeois
past, and he explains that away at the end of *Le Degré Zéro*, in
marxist fashion, by observing that 'the fundamental ambiguity is
that the revolution had no choice but to draw out of what it wishes
to destroy the image of what it wishes to possess'. The real question
however was whether instrumentality, clarity and postulated
universality made Zero Degree writing a 'utopian' but revolutionary
form – or whether it simply constituted it as a vehicle for a new
bourgeois myth of man. Barthes' abandonment of transparent
clarity and universality for the 'supervised ruptures, fake conformities and indirect destructions' of critical play represents his answer

to this question. It represents his realization after *Mythologies* that no extant form of writing could become the 'neutral' form he was seeking.

When play replaced Zero Degree writing as the atopical 'third term' the 'island of neutrality' amidst warring camps, it took over the 'fundamental ambiguity' of a revolution which was caught between a past it wished to destroy and a utopian future it could not bring into being, and it superimposed the two. The play-text partook of the bourgeois past not only in so far as it made it possible to reappropriate this past, to take renewed pleasure in bourgeois culture and bourgeois texts and to give them a new purpose and interest; it also partook of the past in so far as Barthes himself loved the bourgeois 'art of life', bourgeois texts and bourgeois culture, and in so far as he saw the bourgeois past as an intrinsic part of 'the consistency of his ego'. But at the same time, the play-text embodied Barthes' conception of the post-revolutionary utopia. In the late 1960s and early 1970s, he conceived this still, as he had conceived it in *Le Degré Zéro*, as a world where both language and the subject were 'ideally free', a world where nothing was given or dictated, without stereotypes, conformities or myths, where the battle of ideologies had been silenced, where the subject could be fearlessly and democratically 'different' and where it was possible to eschew violence and conflict and be at peace. And this is what he embodied in the form of his play-texts.[6] By raising the paradigmatic bar which founds antithetical meanings and by signifying nothing ideologically monotheistic, the play-text 'expressed the utopia of a world which is at once strictly semantic and strictly atheistic' (GV, 82), 'the utopia of a lifting of signs, of an exemption of meaning, of an individuation of language, of a transparency of social relations' (GV 185).

Barthes was content to be an 'anachronistic subject' – to 'participate at the same time and contradictorily, in the profound hedonism of all culture (which penetrates him peaceably under the cover of an 'art of living' of which ancient books are part) and in the destruction of this culture' (PT, 26). He was content to be contradictory and anachronistic in this way because he understood that this contradiction defined his real socio-historical situation. It reproduced the real situation of dissenting intellectuals in a bourgeois society which showed no prospect of changing, for whom 'the disalienation of culture could only take utopian form' (GV 143). It reproduced the contradictory reality of a society in which the revolutionary ideal and revolutionary action had to 'cohabit, almost institutionally, with the norms of bourgeois and petit bourgeois morality' (EC I, 88) and make themselves felt within it. It also represented the divided consciousness of an intellectual who desired to participate in the society from which he excluded himself; who believed that his culture must die but, like Orpheus, could not 'turn his back on the thing he loved'; and who found himself adrift politically and historically because he was repelled by the institutional reality of the Left and had no other place in society to wait until, by some magical historical 'spiral', the bourgeois world he both loved and hated was recreated at some higher level in the disalienated world of the post-revolutionary utopia.

There is no 'third term' to resolve the contradiction among the different aspects of the play-text. Critical play is wilfully ambiguous. It is the writing of a conscious antithesis: the antithesis of exclusion and participation, of subversion and recreation, of absence and presence. It speaks with the voice of a 'living contradiction', seeking to transgress both the rules of logic and the nature of personal identity in our society. And it enables Barthes to write himself as:

> the fiction of an individual . . . who would abolish in himself all barriers, classes and exclusions, not by synchretism, but by simply getting rid of that old spectre: the *logical contradiction*; who would mix all languages, however incompatible; and who would silently put up with all accusations of illogicality and infidelity (PT, 9).

'THE INTELLECTUAL WRITER THAT I AM'

Even when he was not playing, Barthes did not read literary texts like an academic critic. He did not try to define a writer's 'philosophy' or his place in history, to summarise writers' work or to explicate their meaning. He did not write what he called 'instrumental' or 'institutional' criticism. For Barthes, 'the critic is a writer' (EC I, 9). Barthes read and wrote about literature like the great writer-critics from Sidney to T. S. Eliot, who read their predecessors and contemporaries for what they could themselves learn and use, and who invariably saw themselves and their own image of writing in the works of every writer they discuss.[7] In his non-playful critical writings, Barthes wrote a a would-be writer 'looking over the shoulder' of other writers as they wrote (Soll., 79): what interested him was the logic and intelligibility of writers' structures, the meaning or images embodied in the articulation and organisation of their writing. At the same time, much like Chateaubriand in his *Vie de Rancé*, Barthes invariably introduced his own concerns, his own conception of writing and his own contemporary experience into his accounts of others, either interweaving his voice with theirs (as in the essays on Sollers, Bataille or Voltaire) or, when he wholly or partially remade writers of the past in his own image (Racine, Sade, Loyola and Fourier for example), producing something akin to a 'composite voice' (NEC, 111). As Barthes pointed out in his preface to *Essais Critiques*, the critic can never say 'I' or speak of himself in the third person as a novelist can; he can only speak of himself indirectly through his discourse about another and hope that this indirect discourse will be recognised as 'the very sign of his existence' (EC I, 18).

When Barthes came to write his more obviously 'novelistic' works – *L'Empire des Signes* (1970), *Roland Barthes par Roland Barthes* (1980) and *Fragments d'un discours amoureux* (1977) – he applied what he had gleaned from other writers or what he had worked out for himself in the process of writing about them, and he allowed his own voice to come out of the critical closet. From his point of view, it is appropriate to say of Barthes' critical writing what Barthes says of Proust's oeuvre, namely that it 'describes an immense, an incessant apprenticeship' (NEC, 125) and represents 'the history of a writing' (NEC, 121).

At the same time, too much should not be made of the distinction between Barthes' 'novelistic' work and his critical essays, or of that between his playful and non-playful critical writings. All were in their own way experiments in writing. All were 'essay-istic'. All were, to one degree or another, fictions. And all were part of the same obsessive quest for a utopia of writing which would both subvert all extant hierarchies of subject-matter, language and genre and hold out the utopian image of a text which is disalienated, performative and 'ideally free'. The differences are matters of degree rather than of kind: in the novelistic works, where Barthes was able to dispense with the constraints of seeming to discourse about somebody else, he was freer to seek formal equivalents for his utopian image of disalienated writing, reading and social intercourse. Barthes' 'novelistic' books are not novels: they lack character, plot, sustained narrative, adventures and closure. But they have certain elements of the novel: they embody something imaginary (GV, 211), and they are 'writings about life' (GV, 124) which impersonalise and fictionalise moments of Barthes' own experience and aspects of his intellectual, emotional and hedonistic 'art of living'. In this respect, all Barthes' novelistic writings are versions of Roland Barthes by Roland Barthes.

Having said that, the fact that Barthes did come to novelistic writing through critical writing has a certain practical significance. It means that the critical essays can help to make Barthes' often obscure and always complex novelistic books more intelligible – they provide the building blocks, so to speak, out of which the novelistic texts were constructed. The critical essays also demonstrate Barthes' need to work out intellectually, indeed almost philosophically, how he was going to write novelistically. Barthes was, as he himself put it, an 'intellectual writer'. He distrusted spontaneity, which he claimed is always banal, stereotyped and fundamentally inexpressive. But he considered quotation without quotation marks both legitimate and unavoidable in a world where it is impossible to speak without using 'fragments of the language which already exists'. In such a world, he insisted, 'there are no creators, only combiners' (EC I, 14). Quotation of other peoples' literary forms and literary techniques, of other peoples' phrases, even of Barthes' own previous writings, were the raw materials he 'wove' together in his novelistic texts in such a way as to produce what he insisted was a 'new' language.[8] Not without a certain amount of self-mockery, in *Roland Barthes par Roland Barthes* he even went so far as to appropriate Michelet's awful migraine headaches.

Barthes' fundamental unit of novelistic writing was the named fragment. Like all French schoolchildren, Barthes had been taught to take notes on the books he was reading as he was reading them by the '*fiche*' or index method – that is to say, he had been taught to note down everything about a given character or theme on a separate piece of paper and to put the name of the character or theme clearly at the top of each piece of paper. Barthes continued to work in this way, and as he matured, he found that he was not only copying down onto the *fiches* relevant quotations from the book he was reading, but writing whole sentences and paragraphs of his own about the subject matter of each *fiche* as the ideas came to him (GV, 173). This was the basis of the named fragment. It corresponded to the 'first gesture of construction' (GV, 174), the first discontinuous organisation of materials and ideas. The second 'gesture of construction' that French schoolchildren are taught is to turn the materials in their *fiches* into a coherent essay or *dissertation* by making a plan and constructing a continuous argument with suitable transitions and an appropriate 'development of ideas'. This was something Barthes always had trouble in doing. In his first publication, 'On Gide and his Journal' (1942), Barthes admitted that he had failed to find any connection among his notes, and announced that he was going to 'offer them as such – as notes – and not try to disguise their lack of continuity' (BR, 3). Although Barthes learned to hide this deficiency better in his later critical writings, he always, as he says, tended to 'a short mode of writing, which procedes by fragments, by small tableaux, by paragraphs with titles or by articles' (GV, 198). Moreover, most of his critical essays explore the possibilities of discontinuous writing, and the way writers from La Rochefoucauld to Sollers and Bataille constructed and ordered their short 'articulated' units. When Barthes decided to write novelistically, he had only to 'reactivate [this] long-standing taste for the fragment' (GV, 198), to systematise it, and to give it a theoretical justification. Not the least enjoyable aspect of this justification was Barthes' insistence that named fragments were a way for the text to 'offer it own work to be read' (Soll., 24) and, at the same time, a 'deconstruction of the dissertation' and of the 'myth of the plan' (GV, 173).

When listening to what Barthes has to say about reading, about writing and about fragments, it is important to visualise him sitting at his desk reading a book and writing down, by hand, with the same sort of fountain pen that he had been expected to use at school, the names at the top of his *fiches*, passages from the book, and ideas which 'curiously came to him already in the rhythm of sentences' (GV, 173). It is important, too, to think of him looking at his completed fiches spread on the table before him like 'a rain, seeds, a dissemination, a web, a tissue, a text, a writing', before he polished each *fiche* into one of his named fragments and arranged them alphabetically to form a book; for these very characteristic Barthian practices explain a great deal that would otherwise seem eccentric or perverse. They explain, for instance, why Barthes insists that reading is always a process of naming and that 'to hold a system of names is to hold the essential significance of a book, its profound syntax' (NEC, 128) – to start his *fiches*,

Barthes had in fact to name what he felt to be the essential significances of the book he was reading and thus to translate the book into a system of names. They explain why Barthes insists that reading and writing are aspects of the same activity, and why, for him, 'writing is the hand' (GV, 182), or 'the tension of the body trying to produce language' (Soll., 65) – this is not a metaphysical insight, but a literal description of what Barthes was doing at his desk. And above all, they explain the relationship between a Barthian fragment and its title.

Perhaps not surprisingly for someone who spent every morning on his *fiches*, Barthes was fascinated by the way names or nouns 'essentialised' a multiplicity of different meanings and by the way, as he proceeded with his reading, he found himself progressively discovering, 'deciphering' or 'unfolding' the different significances of each name or noun which he had selected from the book. Names or nouns were ambiguous 'topoi' or places to be explored not for their referents in reality, but for the many, often contradictory, ideas they signified.

Since the ideas signified by each name or noun all appeared under it on the same page of the *fiche*, these ideas could also be visualised as having spatial relationships to each other. Indeed, Barthes saw and presented these ideas in configurations, or in the form of what he called 'figures'. Barthes' figures are often rhetorical, since he was well versed in classical rhetoric and since he conceived of rhetorical figures spatially as different ways of cutting things up and reorganising them; but his figures were not exclusively rhetorical. The figures he uses most frequently within the fragments are the antithesis and the circle, where ideas are juxtaposed in such a way as to go all around the subject without encapsulating its 'centre'.

The structure of Barthes' named fragments, then, is that of the *fiche*: it consists of a name whose various meanings are 'unfolded' in the text of the fragment, where they are arranged in the form of one or more 'figures' and often combined with quotations, some of which have quotation marks and some of which do not. Usually terse, dense and elliptical, each polished fragment has to be read as one would read a prose poem. For instance:

Atopia
Fiché: I am pinned to a *fiche*, assigned to a place (intellectual), to residence within a caste (if not a class). Against which only

one internal doctrine, that of *atopia* (a habitation adrift). Atopia is superior to utopia (utopia is reactive, tactical, literary, it proceeds from meaning and fools with meaning) (RB, 53).

In this fragment, there are two antitheses. The first turns on two meanings of the word *fiché* – *fiché* in the sense of being indexed or filed or tabulated in a certain way, and *fiché* in the sense of *ficher le camp*, i.e., getting the hell out. This antithesis corresponds to the antithesis in the word atopia which gives this fragment its theme, since here the idea of *topos* (a fixed rhetorical place) is posited only to be denied (*a-topos*: non-place). The second antithesis is that between atopia and utopia, and it turns on an opposition between two kinds of place. Atopia is a non-place which is adrift from all extant social and rhetorical meanings, while utopia is a non-place (in the sense that it exists only as an ideal place) which can be defined in literary and tactical terms and in terms of what it is reacting against. At the same time, Barthes is using antithesis in this fragment to subvert the very notion of antithesis as a way of establishing meanings. For while the fragment establishes the meanings of atopia by a series of antitheses, it also tells us that atopia, which cannot be defined antithetically as a reaction against something, is superior to utopia which can. It presents atopia as a 'living contradiction': atopia is a non-place which is adrift from all social and rhetorical places and which cannot be defined in reactive, literary or tactical terms, but it is also a habitation, an internal doctrine (thus something which has a place) and a reaction 'against' being indexed socially or rhetorically. Moreover, the fragment presents this contradictory idea of atopia in a form whose literary and tactical nature cannot be denied. Like utopia, then, atopia is reactive, literary and tactical, and like utopia, it 'fools with meaning.' Atopia is utopian. The difference between them – if indeed difference there be – is that atopia is presented as a contradiction, whereas utopia is more traditionally conceived as a resolution of all contradictions. As in a poem, therefore, the meaning or meanings of Barthes' named fragments and the complexities of their form must be discovered or reconstructed by a reader who is prepared to read carefully, to read several times, and to work with words, associations and figures.

The named fragment provided Barthes with a unit of writing in which he could be simultaneously present and absent. Barthes is present in each fragment in two ways. He is present in so far as each fragment represents the way Barthes has fragmented and ordered the world of things and meanings: 'to appropriate is to fragment the world, to divide it into finite objects which are subjected to man in proportion to their discontinuity; for one cannot separate without naming and classifying, and from this, property is born' (NEC, 93). The choice of names and classifications in the *fiches* and in the fragments which grow out of them is neither objective nor ineluctably necessary. Different people will divide up the same book or the same life in different ways, will pursue different themes, and try to master different aspects of the same material. The way a person constructs his *fiches*, the way he chooses and explores his topics, represents the way he, as a particular subjectivity and a particular mind, masters and appropriates his material. If the way he does this is sufficiently original, sufficiently different from the average and the stereotyped, it constitutes what Barthes calls a 'writing': 'it is enough that there be an energy and singularity of thought sufficiently powerful to engender a new cut out (a new mapping) of the real (of literary discourse for instance): to classify vigorously and *of oneself* is always to write' (GV, 168). A writing in this sense always reveals the particular intellectual physiognomy of its author, the singularity of a man's mind. This is what Barthes means by 'the novelistic quality of the Intellect' (RB, 94).

Barthes is also present in each fragment in so far as each fragment represents a work of the imagination: 'to imagine', he says, 'is to unfold a sign' (NEC, 134). The ideas drawn out of each word and their configurations go beyond dictionary definitions, and they are intended to have no referent in reality. The fragments represent Barthes' imaginative elaboration and structuration of each name or noun; they represent what the name means to him or what he has made it mean. Accordingly, the fragments have to be read 'in a mythical perspective . . . as they are constructed by the writer' (NEC, 134), and for what they display of the writer who is, if he is Barthes, also seeking to be loved and desired in the fragmented and fetishised 'body' of his texts. He draws the reader's attention to this self-referential aspect of the fragments in the following sequence: 'Production of my fragments. Contemplation of my fragments (correction, polishing etc). Contemplation of my excretions (narcissism)' (RB, 99).

But if Barthes is present in each fragment as a specific Intellect and as a peculiarly verbal imagination, he is absent from them as a centred subject and as a traditional biographical character. There is no portrait of Barthes or of any other 'character' in any of the fragments, even in what is supposed to be his autobiography. Neither is there any narrative continuity among the fragments or any evidence of closure. 'The text starts off, but never arrives anywhere' (Sol.). Dispersed or disseminated in hundreds of non-sequential, alphabetically ordered fragments, Barthes' subjectivity cannot be pinned down narratively as the creator or product of a specific human destiny or as the emitter of an authoritative authorial message. It cannot be placed, but it can be found, as Barthes indicates in his metaphors for the way the writer disappears and appears in fragmentary texts:

> The writer is to be conceived as a man lost in a hall of mirrors: where his image is missing is the way out (Soll., 53).
> Text means Weave . . . lost in this weave – in this texture – the subject unmakes himself there; it is as if a spider dissolved herself in the secretions with which she constructed her web (PT, 101).
> I prefer the play of the kaleidoscope to the idea of a unitary subject: one gives it a shake and the pieces of glass put themselves into a different order (GV, 193).

In other words, Barthes' subjectivity, found and then lost at the level of the fragment, can be found again at the level of the text, not as the image of a man (a character, a centred subject), but as a pattern in the weave of the text. We are back at the idea that 'to hold a system of names is to hold a book's essential significances and its profound syntax' and to be able to distinguish the figure of the writer in the carpet – the two subjects are the same in Barthes' novelistic writings where the intellect and imagination of Barthes the subject are also the subject of the books. But before finding this ambiguous subject, we have to lose him again.

For, as Barthes points out with some glee, it is far from easy to use a *fiche* method to turn discontinuous fragments into a coherent system of names when each fragment yields an extremely heterogeneous collection of names and when no attempt has been made to clue the reader about their relative importance. 'Index these little pieces', says Barthes provocatively, 'let there be the words: fragment, circle, Gide, catch, asyndete, painting, dissertation, Zen, intermezzo; imagine a discourse which could link them' (RB, 97).

It is even more difficult to arrive at a system of names which encompasses the book's essential significances and profound syntax when the book in question is constructed 'kaleidoscopically' to yield a multiplicity of different possible patterns. Barthes' subjectivity and his 'essential meanings', dispersed and disseminated at the level of the fragment, are again dispersed and disseminated at the level of the text in the multiple possible systems of names that the reader can construct from the fragments.

The key to this multiplicity lies in Barthes' formal imagination and in the way it repeats itself. In the fragment, Barthes found a structure that was 'at once unique and varied' (NEC, 69). In so far as every fragment repeats the same structure (that of the *fiche*), unfolding from its name and disposing itself in the form of one or more figures, each named fragment can serve as the 'archetype' of all the others (NEC, 69). Its structure is unique. But this structure can be infinitely varied: because each fragment unfolds different meanings from a different name and uses different figures (including that of the fragment itself) in different combinations; because fragments can differ both in length and in scope; and because fragments can borrow any existing style or writing from the dictation to the dissertation, from the high to the low. On the level of the text as a whole, Barthes found another structure which was 'at once unique and varied' – that of the series. The model for this was given in *L'Empire des Signes* beside a picture of a vertical series of Japanese ideograms: 'Rain, Seed, Dissemination, Web, Weave, text, Writing'. The series founds meaning, not like the paradigm, by contrast, opposition and contradiction, but by a fine progression of affinities and differences between neighbouring terms. Many different series can be discovered in Barthes' novelistic fragments. For instance: Writing, Text, Play, Duplicity, Transgression, Subversion, Eros, *Jouissance*, Signifiance; or *Neutre*, Third Term, *Atopos*, Plural, Mixed, Transition; or negatively, Violence, Monocentrism, Repetition, Stereotype, Myth, Nature, Innocence, Spontaneity. Series such as these constitute Barthes' mental world. They consitute the very shape and figure of Barthes' mind and values and the subjects of his discourse. They are composed of words which Barthes has constructed and given meaning, words which can only be defined and explained as in a dictionary, in terms of each other, through the affinities and differences between them and by quotation from Barthes' work. The words in Barthes' series can therefore only be explained by re-writing Barthes under a different series of headings than the ones already attached to his fragments. This is why Barthes points out that 'the index of a text . . . is itself a text, a second text which is the relief map (what is left and the outline) of the first' (RB, 97).

To rewrite Barthes in this way, producing an annotated index of his index, a *fiche* of his *fiches*, in a sort of anamorphic reflection of his writing, would be amusing, but it would also be to miss the point of Barthes. For Barthes speaks less through what he signifies than through the ways in which he structures his writing. 'I am on the structure side, on the sentence side, where the text is a sentence' (RB, 96). Barthes' novelistic texts should not be read for their signification, for some ultimate or profound 'meaning'. As he says, 'in literature, everything is *given* to be understood and yet, as in our lives, there is *in the last analysis* nothing to be understood' (NEC, 113). In terms of what he signifies, Barthes offers only 'a simple plural of charms' (SFL, 13) – some very acute insights, some memorable images, some moving details, a certain inflexion of the voice, a tone of mind, a body of tastes and distastes. Barthes offers a fragmented subject to the pleasure of his readers, whom he conceives not in the mass or as an average 'ideal' reader, but as a series of differentiated individuals, with differentiated tastes, each of whom should be able to find something to please him in the variety and plurality of the text, and each of whom should be able to compose his reading at will, lingering here to ponder and taste, skipping there and coming away in possession of something he has loved. On this level, Barthes cannot be summarised or explained; the flavour of what he is and what he does cannot be conveyed; and there is no substitute for reading him, 'cruising' in quest of one's pleasure.

It is less through what he signifies, therefore, than through the ways in which he signifies that Barthes conveys what he calls 'the marvellously real', which is to him the very essence of novelistic writing. 'The marvellously real', he explains,' is precisely the signifier, or if one prefers, it is 'reality' marked, in comparison to scientific reality, by its train of phantasms' (SFL, 101). In other words, it is through the signifier, through the way Barthes uses fragments, series and pluralities to signify that Barthes conjures up the marvel-ous image of a utopian reality in which writer and reader alike are disalienated, performative and free.

. The fragment, itself made up of recognisable cultural repetitions and quotations, uses repetition and recognition both to subvert them and to suggest an alternative. It subverts the repetitive 'ancient text of culture, science and literature' by fragmenting it and by 'disseminating its traits according to unrecognisable formulae' (SFL, 15). In the process, it destroys the book as a reified object, as an object of recognition and consumption, in which the writer, distanced and alienated from his reader, encodes his authoritative messages. In so far as the fragment represents the writer's working notes and stops short of the 'second gesture of construction', the fragment reminds the reader that 'writing is an activity' (EC, 10) and that reading is the same. It offers itself as a form of 'play, activity, production, practice' (ITM, 162) leaving the reader to construct coherences and continuities for himself. By offering multiple possible forms of coherence and continuity, it allows each reader to exist in his difference. By lovingly polishing his working notes into dense, elliptical and poetical pieces of writing, the writer reminds the reader that 'writing is a task that carries its own happiness with it' (EC, 10) and that writers write not for the sake of publishing, but for the sake of writing itself (NEC, 136). At the same time, he offers each perfected, elliptical and poetic fragment to the pleasure of his reader, to be enjoyed for its own sake, to be read slowly for the pleasure it can yield. Above all, the fragment, the polished *fiche*, represents the point of juncture between reading and writing, the point where reading and writing are aspects of the same activity, and where in consequence, reader and writer are no longer 'other'. To read is always also to rewrite: the writer of the Barthian fragments is a reader who is rewriting the writing of others, and the reader of Barthian fragments is a reader who is rewriting Barthes.

None of this is unreal or 'ideal'. All of us know what Barthes is talking about. We all came to writing about books through our pleasure in reading books irresponsibly, for their own sake and our own. We have all enjoyed the intellectual activity of finding coherences and continuities in the books we have read, of establishing patterns and discovering meanings, of deciphering poems and penetrating indirection; and before writing as students or academics, many of us have written simply for the pleasure of writing and know what it is to enjoy writing for its own sake. All this is perfectly real. But Barthes also saw it as a phantasm in a society where books are consumed for escapism or information and in a university system where reading and writing have become artificial 'instrumental' activities, carried out in haste with a view to publishing or to obtaining a degree, and where it is infinitely wiser to write something that can be instantly recognised and understood. In the context of this world of reading and writing, the fragment was designed to conjure up the 'marvellously real' vision of reading and writing ex-centrically, creatively, at leisure and with pleasure, not for some ultimate purpose or truth, but from desire, from love of reading and writing and thinking.

If Barthes' fragments are intended to conjure up a vision of disalienated reading and writing, the plurality in his texts and the series into which they fall are intended to conjure up a vision of disalienated social relationships.[9] As he points out, 'alienation gives way as soon as the world becomes multiple' (R, 62). Plurality and the series are ways of making the world multiple. The plural text is a text in which a variety of different meanings, different forms of writing, and different formal and ideational quotations from literature and culture blend and clash, mix and counter, parody and echo each other in such a way as to preclude all forms of closure and to constitute a 'multi-dimensional space' (ITM, 146), which can be organised by the reader in a multitude of different ways. The plural text 'refuses to assign a "secret" an ultimate meaning to the text (and to the world as text)' (ITM, 147); it thus subverts all extant ideologies because 'to refuse to fix meaning is, in the end, to refuse God and his hypostases – reason, science, law' (ITM, 147). But it also holds up an image of a different world, and partakes of 'a social utopia' by constituting a space where no language or meaning or ideology is either dominant or subjected, where 'no language has a hold over any other' (ITM, 164) and where all languages are equally performative and free.

The series into which plural texts fall do not limit plurality – indeed, they are themselves plural – they merely provide plurality with a mode of being. They subvert the paradigm on which meaning is usually grounded in Western society, which disposes terms as rival contraries which cannot cohabit (A is not A) and must battle each other for supremacy (either/or); and by their *nuanced* progression of affinities and differences, they bridge oppositions and permit them to coexist. The series represents the vision of a world in which the weight of every term and the difference of every individual is respected; where every term and every individual can cohabit with every other because while each is different from every other, each is also linked to others by multiple affinities; and where terms and individuals are ordered and harmonised in such a way as to give each a number of possible places in different series. The series is not a humanist or a liberal concept: it is not centred on man viewed in one universal way, and it does not celebrate any man's uniqueness or individualism. The series represents the vision of a world without conformism and without marginality, without theologies and without separation, without domination and without subjection. It lacks any centre and is not itself a centre because many series are possible simultaneously. And its fine progression precludes any individuated unit from being either unique or identical with any other – each is simply different from all the others, and at the same time, like others and combinable with others in a multitude of different ways. The series is real in so far as *fiches* placed in a series in front of one relate to each other in precisely this way. But in the context of human relations, the series appears as a phantasm, as something marvellously real – or marvellous if it were real.

Fragment, plural and series are all structures which are at once 'unique and varied'. They are all 'decentered structures', entities which are 'organised among themselves and therefore have structural characteristics, but without making it possible to indicate a pivotal centre around which the structure is constructed' (GV, 99). They are all what Barthes calls *systématiques*. Where systems are fixed, centred, doctrinaire, authoritative, logical and developmental, *systématiques* are open, infinite, uncentred, disseminated, performative and capable of endless permutations. Where systems use language 'transparently' or instrumentally, and have as their goal some practical application in the reality outside language, *systématiques* remain within language and within writing and seem to be unconcerned with their social or practical applicability.

But they are, in fact, not as playful or as innocent as they appear. For in the context of the belief that 'words create reality' and that 'practice follows speech and is absolutely determined by it' (SFL, 40), and in the context of the belief that 'our life comes from books' (Soll., 20) – that our lives are in some sense a repetition and imitation of our reading – 'to change the book is to change life itself' (Soll., 39). This belief is not completely absurd in the aftermath of Darwin, Marx and Freud, to say nothing of Mao and Saussure. It is also far from absurd in Parisian intellectual circles, where books are taken seriously and where fashions in reading succeed each other sufficiently rapidly for their impact on people's thinking and living to become apparent. If Barthes characterised his writing as a revolutionary activity, it is because his writing was an attempt to change the book that people were imitating and in the process to change their relationship to the book. What he was trying above all else to change about the book – whether it was a left-wing bible like Marx, Lenin or Mao or simply the text of bourgeois and petit-bourgeois culture — was its dictatorial authority, its imposition of conformity and obedience, its assumption of truth. What he was trying above all else to change about peoples' relationship to the book was the idea that books can be taken over as programmes for living and that freedom of choice boils down to one's choice of book. Barthes' *systématiques* were an attempt to suggest that society and human life could be like his books: 'airy, light, spaced, open, uncentred, noble and free' (ITM, 168), and that with some energy and singularity of thought, everyone could '*of oneself*' engender a new writing, a new combination, an original mapping of reality, and individuate the book of his life.

Fragment, plural and series do not exhaust Barthes' *systématiques*. There are many other *systématiques* in his work. For instance: the alphabet, which is presented as the key to the structure of numerous Barthian texts; or the dictionary, where words are defined by other words *ad infinitum*, which is used to great effect in *Fragments*; or the pronouns 'I', 'he', 'you' and the initials RB in *Roland Barthes par Roland Barthes* which fragment the subject into decentred elements which can be contrasted, combined and varied in innumerable ways. There are even in *L'Empire des Signes* objective correlatives for the *systématique* (the Japanese meal, the Japanese house), for the series (Japanese faces, addresses in Tokyo), and for the fragment (the haiku, Japanese gift packaging). But to discuss all this would be to repeat oneself, for all are built on the same archetype. All Barthes' *systématiques* have the same decentred structure, the same capacity for infinite variety and combination, the same free and performative character. Barthes said that 'each of us speaks only one sentence which can be interrupted only by death' (GV, 101). And this was his sentence.

MYTHOLOGIES OF OTHERNESS

Despite his preference for empty, performative forms, Barthes coined innumerable paradigmatic oppositions. 'What for? Simply to *say something*: it is necessary to posit a paradigm to produce a meaning and set it adrift' (RB, 96). If Barthes felt justified in characterising himself as an ethical writer, it is because, in his paradigms, he set what he considered to be an evil against what he considered to be a good and managed to 'say something'. By positing such paradigmatic oppositions as Literature/Text, *Écrivant*/*Écrivain*, Professional/Amateur, Repetition/Play, System/*Systématique*, Doxa/Paradoxa, Full/Empty, where the first term represents a conventional cultural Sameness and the second term is purely Barthian, Barthes managed to *say* his Otherness, and at the same time to turn it into a series of positive affirmations.

The biographical and socio-historical core of these different oppositions of Sameness and Otherness is the paradigmatic opposition between centrism and marginality. For Barthes saw himself as a plurally marginal figure: a Protestant in a predominantly Catholic country; an atheist among religious and political believers; a homosexual in a predominantly heterosexual society, language and value system; an heir to the *grande bourgeoisie*, who was *déclassé* by his father's early death, his family's resulting poverty and his mother's need to resort to manual work to scrape a living, and who refused to join the ranks of any other class – despising the petit-bourgeoisie and insisting that the proletariat no longer existed; a boy whose tuberculosis put him 'outside the world' (GV, 245) in sanatoriums when his generation was going to war or to university and prevented him from taking the competitive examinations for the *École Normale*; and a teacher in what he described as 'marginal' institutions within the University (the *École Pratique* and the *Collège de France*) where he felt himself 'outside the bounds of power' (BR, 458). Barthes also felt himself to be marginal to society as an intellectual and as a writer. He felt that his position as an intellectual in society was governed by society's image of the intellectual as a person whose feet are not on the ground, a person who has lost touch with practical realities and sound common sense, who floats above reality in some stratosphere of his own, spouting hot air (M, 205). 'Intellectuals' he said, 'are the refuse of society. Refuse in the strict sense, i.e. that which is useless' (GV, 256). Barthes also felt that his position as a writer was determined by society's view of the writer as a person without any real social function, whose gratuitous products were bought and sold precisely for their uselessness, as luxuries or pastimes.

Barthes' innovation in the mournful history of alienations was to accept and affirm each of these marginalities and to transform them into positive creative and intellectual resources.

'The writer is largely without a function and this prompts him to develop a utopia of pure expenditure, of expenditure to no purpose' (GV, 222). If the writer is gratuitous to society, let him make the most of it; let gratuitousness be its own purpose. Instead of endeavouring to be applicable to the reality outside words, instead of producing systems and ultimate meanings, the writer might as well say nothing to the purpose and take 'perverse pleasure in words' (PT, 57) and in the play of ideas and signifiers for their own sake. He might as well expend his energies in creating texts purely for the sake of writing, and demand that the reader expend his energies on the text purely for the sake of reading.

'When positions seem to become reified, I always feel like going somewhere else. And it is in this that I can recognise myself to be an intellectual: the function of the intellectual being to go somewhere else when something "catches on"' (GV, 264). If the intellectual is viewed as being somewhere else in relation to the solid, non-intellectual citizens who produce society's wealth by physical labour, he might as well make the most of it. If the intellectual is the refuse of society, let him speak in the name of society's refuse, in the name of all that society has refused: let him speak of pleasure which is 'foreclosed' both by bourgeois and petit-bourgeois culture and by left-wing discourse; of the amorous subject, a subject more marginal even than the drug addict or the racial minority; let him speak of play, of emptiness, of the suspension of meanings, of the imagination, of all the subjects which have no place either in the cultural status quo or in the discourse of those who oppose it. And if the intellectual is someone who spouts hot air, who has nothing to say of any value, let him also speak in his own name and in the name of his own marginality: 'the intellectual does not have to speak in the name of the proletariat – he is not a proxy; he has to present the case for what he himself lacks, for the way his intellectual activities are diminished, for the alienations that present-day society imposes on him as an intellectual' (GV, 155).

Above all, if a man is a marginal subject in society – a religious and political unbeliever, a homosexual, *déclassé* from the bourgeoisie and from his peer group and 'outside the bounds of power' in the University – he can make the most of that too by speaking in the name of his own multiple marginalities, in the name of everything about himself which places him outside conventional social groupings.

Barthes turned his position outside religious, political and social camps into *atopos*, a non-place from which to show up the myths and stereotypes of all the warring camps in society and from which to produce myths of his own. He turned his place 'outside the bounds of power' in the University into a position from which to subvert the university's power over language, undermining the dissertation with its plan and logical development of ideas, the neat departmental division of subject-matters, the authority of teachers and of university instruction, and the traditional methods of approaching texts. More positively, he made this place outside the bounds of power in the university a 'happy Babel', a space where all languages could cohabit and intermingle.

Barthes turned homosexuality, perceived as the condition of being neither male nor female, into a third term, a ne-uter, which subverts all the reproductive paradigmatic forms of extant society.[10] And he made homosexuality's own practices – *la drague*, the cruising in quest of a series of acutely pleasurable but transitory sexual encounters, the close, accepting friendships with non-sexual partners and the perversion of exhibitionism with its thrill and fear of discovery – he made these his standard of pleasure, love and social disalienation and his counter-weight to extant social practices.

Barthes transformed being *déclassé* from the bourgeoisie, whose culture was in any case, he felt, being vulgarised and commercialised by the petit-bourgeoisie, into an 'art of living' which preserved the largely outdated values of the old bourgeoisie. Barthes celebrated in his life and in his writings the pleasures of the table, the pleasure of exquisite and rare objects, the pleasures of music, art and literature, and the even greater pleasures of making one's own music, trying one's own hand at painting, and doing one's own writing while being content to be an amateur at each. Barthes also enjoyed the more stolidly bourgeois pleasure of a day's work well done – he sat at his desk every morning struggling with the modern texts he confessed he did not enjoy – and like all successful bourgeois, he structured his day to exploit time to the utmost – he spent every morning at his desk, had a nap after lunch, put aside a time every afternoon for his music and his painting and for taking tea and, in bed at night, he read the classics for pleasure. Barthes even enjoyed the bourgeois' neat and functional ordering of space – he lovingly describes the tri-partite division of his study into spaces for writing, music and painting, the table for his typewriter beside the desk, the drawer for his diary and lecture notes, the boxes he made for his *fiches*, and the way he reproduced all these features of his Paris apartment in his country house. And he translated this pleasure in the neat and functional ordering of space into a human and textual imperative, arguing that it is impossible either to play or to be free without a coherent structure.

Barthes' 'drifting' paradigms, the paradigms of meaning he constructed within a single word, are as significant as his coinages. By positing such drifting paradigmatic oppositions as Politics/Politics, History/History and Subject/Subject, Barthes managed not only to *say* his political, social and historical Otherness, but also to transform it into a politically, socially and historically integrated position.

At the core of these drifting paradigms is the opposition between traditional Marxist notions of contradiction and Barthian ones. The political left argued traditionally that the contradictions which characterise capitalist society are evils which will lead dialectically to revolution and to the *Aufhebung* of all contradictions in the post-revolutionary era. But Barthes understood that in the absence of any extant post-revolutionary society which had succeeded in reconciling its contradictions – modern man and modern society are in reality left seething in their contradictions. Where the political left self-righteously distanced itself from the historical contradictions of capitalist society by speaking from the vantage point of the post-revolutionary era, therefore, Barthes spoke from the vantage point of the present and consciously assumed its contradictions: 'I claim to live to the full the contradictions of my time' (M, 8). Concerned as they are with formal problems of language, literature and writing, Barthes' works do not seem either particularly political or particularly historical. But as Barthes was at pains to point out many times, they were both – only their politics and their historicity must be understood in Barthian terms, not in conventional and stereotyped ones. Barthes' conscious historicity must not be sought where traditional socio-historical criticism would seek it – in the assumptions, forms or conditions be shared with his contemporaries, in what Barthes described as the 'institutional' and repetitive, as opposed to the creative and unique aspects of a man's work. Barthes' conscious historicity lies in his assumption of the contradictions of his time and in the creative use he makes of them as well as in the 'marvellously real' quality of his utopianism.

In conventional logic, contradictions exclude each other – it is either day or night, it cannot be both. In dialectical logic, each term of the contradiction is partly abolished and partly preserved in their higher dialectical synthesis. Barthes' contradictions stand in paradigmatic opposition to both these forms of contradiction. For in Barthes' contradictions 'one of the terms is not more "true" than the other' (EC IV, 311) and Barthes 'allows the superimposition of two absolute contraries to be read in the same body' (EC IV). In other words, there is neither the either/or of conventional logic nor the mitigation of contradictoriness of the higher dialectical synthesis. Both terms of the contradiction are allowed to stand in their absolute contradictoriness.[11] When Barthes writes himself as a contradictory subject, as a subject who is both present and absent, excluded and participating, subversive and recreative, bound to the past and rooted in the needs of the present, confined to 'fragments of the language that already exists' and yet capable of producing a 'new' language, or when he writes himself simultaneously as a writer and a critic, a fictionalist and an intellectual, he is using what he calls a 'concomitant syntax' (EC IV, 311). He is using a syntax which gives both terms of the contradiction equal weight and which unites them only in so far as they are both present in the same subject. The same is true of the Barthian Text, in so far as it represents a space where there is both work (production) and play, reading and writing, spectacle and performance, nihilism and affirmation, fiction and criticism, objectivity and subjectivity, reality and utopia, structural archetypal unity and complex pluralities.

This concomitant syntax produces – and is intended to produce – 'surprise: the wonder of a return, a juncture, a rediscovery' (EC IV, 311), because it is at once absolutely familiar and absolutely new. The contradictions themselves are absolutely conventional: work as opposed to play, spectacle as opposed to performance, reading as opposed to writing, exclusion as opposed to participation. What is new is their juncture, their conjunction, the fact that it is no longer necessary either to choose between them or to find a way to reconcile them by a third term like time. And what is new, as a result of this conjunction of contradictory terms is that we are led to re-examine the necessity which makes them contradictory. Must work really be opposed to play – could it not be possible to work and play simultaneously? Must we really either watch a performance or perform ourselves – is there not a way of doing both at once? Must we really separate writers from readers in our educational systems and reading practices – can we not find a point of juncture between them? Must we really be either critics or writers, objective or subjective, analytical or fictional – as critics are we not also writers and are our supposedly objective analyses of texts not at the same time in some way both subjective and fictional? Must we really see ourselves as either minds or bodies, thinkers or doers, workers of the intellect or sexual beings – are we not in reality both at once? The answers to these questions and to questions such as these produce the surprise of return and rediscovery as we find, as Barthes found, that at some level we already live some of these contradictions without any difficulty, and that, with some energy and thought, we could find ways of living others. Like Barthes, we could 'live to the full the contradictions of our time'.

From this point of view, Barthes' assumption of contradictions is not merely an acceptance of the fact that modern man and modern societies seethe with contradictions. It is also a subversion of contradiction itself, and the translation of the vision of a utopia where contradictions are no longer a problem into the realities of the present. Barthian contradiction is a structure in which past stereotypes and future utopias meet to destroy and recreate the present. It is as political and as revolutionary in its implications as Barthes' other innovative structures, the fragment and the series.

Barthes never bothered to work out the practical applications of these structures to society as a whole. But faithful to his view that the intellectual does not have to speak for any class but his own, he did give a great deal of thought to their applications in the academic world where the intellectual is a teacher and a writer.[12]

Barthes wanted to subvert the power and authority of the teacher and of his instruction. This power and authority, he felt, derived not so much from the fact that the professor was lecturing to his students, that he was transmitting previous knowledge, or even from the knowledge and culture he was transmitting, as from the nature of his speech itself. The professor's speech, Barthes argued, is always monosemic rather than polysemic; it is always 'on the side of the law' (ITM, 191), always legislative. Like all the institutional languages of society, it seeks to dominate, to subjugate, to order. The problem for Barthes was to find ways of 'presenting a discourse without imposing it' (BR, 476) and of recreating in the lecture hall and in the seminar room the same freedoms which he had introduced into his texts: freedom 'not only [as] the capacity to escape power, but also and especially [as] the capacity to subjugate no one' (BR, 461).

Barthes' solutions to these teaching problems repeat the solutions of his texts. His first goal in the lecture hall was to 'loosen' or to baffle the power of professorial discourse: 'I am increasingly convinced', he told his academic audience in his inaugural lecture at the *Collège de France*, 'that the fundamental operation of this loosening method is, if one writes, fragmentation and if one teaches, digression, or to put it in a preciously ambiguous word, excursion' (BR, 476). Instead of speaking clearly and unhesitatingly, developing one's ideas and conveying a coherent argument, Barthes thought that the lecturer should construct a series of discontinuous digressions around his subject, leaving his subject and coming back to it in different ways and from different points of view, bringing to it each time some small and apparently useless addition, and tracing around it 'a whole locus of play'. Rather than assume the role of the authoritative Father, Barthes argues, the lecturer should assume the role of the child playing beside his mother, leaving her and returning to her and in his play, allowing his phantasms free rein.

Moreover, as in his texts, Barthes' view of the subject to be presented by the professor's discourse is an ambiguous mixture of objectivity and subjectivity. On the one hand, he conceived of the subject of discourse to be the professor himself: 'in the *exposé*, more aptly named than we tend to think, it is not knowledge which is exposed, it is the subject (who exposes himself to all sorts of painful adventures)' (ITM, 194). Like Lacan, Barthes compared the professor speaking to his students to an analysand on a psychoanalyst's couch, speaking to his analyst as the 'exemplary Other', whose unnerving silence punctures his discourse and makes it question and subvert itself.

More objectively, Barthes saw the discipline of Literature as the exemplary subject of professorial discourse, in so far as it embodied, in an essential contradiction, the 'realistic' with the 'unrealistic'. Barthes makes an impressive case for the value of literature as a subject of study, even going so far as to say that if some new 'socialism or barbarism' were to abolish all the other disciplines, 'it is the discipline of literature which would have to be saved, for all knowledge, all the sciences are present in the literary monument' (BR, 463). The realistic value of literature, its value as an encyclopaedic subject, Barthes argues, lies in its indirection. Literature does not fix or fetishise any field of knowledge or present knowledge as either complete or final: it merely 'stages' the different forms of knowledge it contains (historical, geographical, social, technological, botanical, anthropological etc.) in such a way as to permit us to reflect on knowledge as such and to find, in the interstices of extant knowledge, new possible and as yet unsuspected spaces for language and thought. Literature also makes us reflect on language itself, because, unlike science, which is 'crude', instrumental and supposedly objective, literary language is always presented as the statement of an absent subject – it is always something once written by someone. This not only draws attention to language as 'an immense halo of implications, of effects, of echoes, of turns, returns and degrees', and as the representation of a subject who or which is both 'insistent and ineffable, unknown and yet recognised' (RB, 464). It also makes it possible to perceive the fundamental unrealism of knowledge, language and desire. For, Barthes argues, the real, which is pluri-dimensional, can never be represented in language which is a uni-dimensional order; the real can only ever be indicated or demonstrated. Literature's resulting failure to represent the real is its strength: it constitutes the history of literature (and of the forms of knowledge it contains) as the history of man's shifting and unsuccessful attempts to capture the real, and thus it takes language and knowledge to their limit. Moreover, literature's constant failure to represent the real enables it to perform an important unrealistic and 'utopian function' which Barthes insists can 'change the world', by creating a space in which man is free to speak 'according to the truth of his desire'. As Barthes explains:

> This freedom is a luxury which every society should afford its citizens: as many languages as there are desires – a utopian proposition in that no society is yet ready to admit the plurality of desires. That a language, whatever it be, not repress another; that the subject . . . may speak this or that according to his perversions, not according to the Law (BR, 467).

Barthes' alternative to the power of the lecturer and to the authority of his instruction was therefore fourfold: to subvert the lecturer's power by making him vulnerable, by making him 'expose' himself to the silent, pitiless gaze of his audience and present himself as a subject speaking according to the truth of his desires; to make professorial discourse playful, digressive and 'excursive' or decentered; to transmit previous knowledge indirectly through literature, where it is always plural and always staged and where it always subverts itself by manifesting its own unreality; and to hold up, both in his own discourse and in literature itself, the phantasm, the utopia of a space where no language and no person has the capacity to subjugate any other and where plurality and difference coexist in the possibility given to each to speak according to the truth of his desire.

Barthes' notion of the seminar was a more performative version of the same thing. But whereas in the lecture hall, the predominant figures are the fragment and the contradiction, in the seminar room, the dominant figure is the series. Barthes describes the purpose of the seminar as 'the production of differences', that is to say, its purpose is to arrive at a situation in which roles cease to be reproduced, other peoples' discourses cease to be repeated, and everyone, including the professor, 'originalises himself' (EC IV, 371). In Barthes' utopian seminar, the professor ceases to be either a magister or an examiner, to become either a demonstrator or a master of ceremonies. When he acts as a demonstrator, he behaves like a master doing his work while his apprentices watch: he writes in their presence. He does not explain what he is doing (reality cannot be spoken), but shows them what he does. And in the process, he once against makes himself vulnerable to them – Barthes compares it to sons watching their father in a state of erection.

When the professor acts as a master of ceremonies, he initiates a situation in which everyone in the seminar is engaged in writing a common text. 'In the seminar (this is its definition) all instruction is foreclosed; no knowledge is transmitted (but knowledge may be created), no discourse is held (but a text is sought)' (EC IV, 374). It is worth noting that at least one of Barthes' texts, *S/Z*, was written in one of Barthes' seminars. The professor's difference from his students in this situation consists only in his 'mothering' of them – in his affectionate support, encouragement and incitement of them to speak and write. Barthes compares it to a mother encouraging her child to walk. Like writing itself, the work of the seminar is completely gratuitous. It differs from classical institutional seminars where marketable knowledge is transmitted and students are trained to be specialists. Barthes compares such seminars to 'an alienated production line in which objects are transformed (the motor of a car) but subjects repeat themselves' (EC IV, 375). In the disalienated production line of his seminar, on the other hand, 'in the production line of *jouissance*, of knowledge, the object is a matter of indifference, but the subjects come through' (EC IV, 375).

The purpose of research, as far as Barthes was concerned, was not to produce work which could have an 'institutional future', work which teaches or repeats a dogma, a science or a method and which pretends to know. Barthes characterises research work which conforms to a reigning critical school ideology or method as 'mere opportunism' (ITM, 199) and insists that 'a piece of work which ceaselessly proclaims its determination for method is ultimately sterile . . . the researcher repeatedly asserts that his text will be methodological, but the text never comes' (ITM, 201). For Barthes, 'research is only ever a group of people who search (who search themselves?)' (EC IV, 378) and the purpose of research is to 'teach the scientist or scholar *that he speaks*' and that 'the epistemological condition of research is its nature as language' (ITM, 198). In other words, the purpose of research is to teach scholars and scientists to 'originalise themselves', to teach them to find something to say *of themselves*, and to make them see that they should assume the responsibilities of the writers *vis-à-vis* language, culture and society.

Barthes' (utopian?) academic writer is not a man who writes for publication or promotion or to satisfy institutional expectations, any more than he is a man who respects departmental divisions of subject-matter. He is a man who finds pleasure in reading and writing for their own sake, who enjoys sitting in his study before his desk every morning with a book in front of him and a pen in his hand, playing intellectual and intuitive hide-and-seek with a rewarding writer and constructing his own texts. Barthes' academic writer is a man who 'sacralises writing' and sees it as the purpose of his life, and he is a man who desires, through his writings to touch the lives of othjers and to be loved and remembered by them. Barthes' academic writer is a man who thinks 'of himself', a man of culture and counter-culture, a realist and a dreamer, an imaginative creator and innovator who speaks of the past to speak to the present and who speaks to the present to influence the future in the certain knowledge that his words can help to create realities. Barthes' academic writer is a fictionalised version of himself.

3

Foucault and the Archeology of Alienation

'Who speaks? It is always a multitude, even within the person who speaks and acts.'

Gilles Deleuze

Foucault begins from a radical unwillingness to accept the present order of things. Asked towards the end of his life what militant action might be expected of an intellectual, he replied:

> The project, the tactics and goals to be adopted are a matter for those who do the fighting. What the intellectual can do is provide instruments of analysis, and at present this is the historian's essential role. What is effectively needed is a ramified penetrative perception of the present, one that makes it possible to locate lines of weakness, strong points, positions where the instances of power have secured and implanted themselves in a system of organisation dating back over a hundred and fifty years. In other words, a topological and geological survey of the battlefield – that is the intellectual's role' (PK, 62).

Alienation occupies a focal position in Foucault's topological and geological survey of the present. It appears throughout Foucault's work as a series of 'dividing practices' in which 'the subject is either divided inside himself or divided from others'.[1] Foucault shows how these 'dividing practices' were built into the discursive and institutional order of society; how they permeated psychiatry, criminology and the human sciences; how they came to govern the supposedly objective epistemology of measurement, inquiry and examination; and how they came to serve the play of power relations in the confessional, in asylums, law courts, prisons, factories and schools. A product of knowledge and power, alienation in Foucault is a historical phenomenon which determines our

94

subjectivation, our view of ourselves and our relations with each other. It is therefore not limited to any one class of society. Administered by intellectuals – by doctors and psychiatrists, by judges and scholars, by philosophers and social workers – it affects all of society, both those whom it marks for exclusion and those whom it makes other to themselves. Foucault took seriously Lacan's insistence that all that we know, all that we do, and all that we are is predetermined by the possibilities inherent in the symbolic order. But unlike Lacan, he set out to describe and dislodge these determining possibilities, these implicit and unconscious 'prescriptions which govern exclusion and choice',[2] in order to permit us once again to move beyond them into a new chapter of human life. And, contrary to a widespread misconception, far from abolishing the subject, Foucault was actively engaged in the task of clearing the way for a new kind of subject, a subject who would no longer be subjected to the dividing practices inherent in the present mechanisms of power and in the forms of knowledge associated with them.

Many commentators on Foucault have hailed his 'instruments of analysis' as a way out of current impasses, whether these are defined as problems within Marxism, structuralism phenomenology, existentialism and critical theory, or as problems of political action inside or outside the Communist Party.[3] Few modern writers can have provoked so much constructive theoretical thinking or so much innovative historical research. Most of Foucault's commentators and followers, however, have attributed his brilliance to an approach supposedly outlined in *L'Archéologie du Savoir* which emphasises discontinuity, heterogeneity and dispersion and the multiplicity of untotalised and unsynchronised forces operative in social and discursive formations. This almost exclusive emphasis in many studies of Foucault on dispersion and discontinuity has led critics to deny that Foucault has anything that might be described as a system or methodology, and to seek to imitate him by refusing to deal with his writings in terms of their underlying unity and common origin.[4] It has led them to treat what they cannot but see as Foucault's 'totalising logic', 'remarkable synthetic powers' and typological concepts as unfortunate but occasional 'lapses' in which he inexplicably failed to live up to his own principles.[5] And it has led at least one critic to accuse Foucault of contradiction: 'He announces the death of man and proceeds to fight for him, the death of philosophy and continues to philosophise, the death of language and he writes or delivers inaugural discourses'.[6]

Foucault, understandably, found such accounts of his work positively 'bewildering'. He protests in one interview that: 'In the new edition of the *Petit Larousse*, it says: "Foucault: a philosopher who founds his theory of history on discontinuity". That leaves me flabbergasted. . . My problem was not at all to say: "*Voilà*, long live discontinuity, we are in the discontinuous, and a good thing too"' (PK, 111, 112). This should be accepted. And not only because absolute discontinuity would also be absolute incoherence and thus perfectly useless for historical work of any kind, much less for historical work that has 'political meaning, utility and effectiveness' (PK, 64). In Foucault, discontinuity, differentiation and dispersion serve a precise and clearly delimited methodological function. They serve as a tool which is 'not made for understanding but for cutting' (LCP, 154). Their function is atomising: to break down the familiar units, categories, continuities and totalities through which history, society and the symbolic order are traditionally interpreted, and to permit the historical analysis of the complex specificity of events without precluding the establishments of new Foucaldian historical formations. Foucault was attempting to 'reconstruct generative processes' and to 'make visible' heretofore unseen relations among apparently disparate phenomena (PK 50); he was not attempting to subvert all relation and all process. After 1968, for reasons which will be explored below, discontinuity, differentiation and dispersion also take on a more concrete political and strategic significance.

Moreover, contrary to those commentators who argue that there was a break or discontinuity in Foucault's work between *L'Archéologie du Savoir* and *Surveiller et Punir*, Foucault insists on the continuity of his thematic concerns throughout his writing and on the essential continuity of his method. Foucault often indicates that there have been local corrections and 'self-criticisms': that his use of 'experiment' in *Histoire de la Folie* showed that he was still too close to admitting a general subject of history; that the structural analysis in *Naissance de la Clinique* threatened to overwhelm the specificity of the problem he was exploring; that *Les Mots et les Choses* lacked methodological signposting; or that in his early work as a whole he lacked a specific analytical field for power relations and tended to confuse them too much with systematicity (PK, 113, 115; AS). and after 1968 a new dimension – that of power – did appear in his work. But Foucault never revamped his 'instruments of analysis'. He refined and elaborated them. Foucault's frequent changes of theoretical vocabulary are likely to give those who still assume that words must stand for things grounds for arguing that Foucault's theoretical work is discontinuous. But here it is worth pondering an epigram of Nietzsche, who was probably Foucault's most important mentor: 'What is originality? To see something that has no name as yet, and hence can't be mentioned, although it stares us all in the face. The way men usually are, it takes a name to make something visible to them. Those with originality have for the most part also assigned names'.[7] From this point of view, Foucault's changes in terminology could be seen as a continually renewed attempt to make something he saw, which had no name before him, visible to us.

The most illuminating key to the methodological continuity of Foucault's work is provided by his friend and colleague, Gilles Deleuze. Deleuze observed that although Foucault is concerned with 'differentiations, dispersions and mutations . . . the fact remains that, methodologically, it is possible to distinguish great types of statement (*énoncé*) and to find great dualities in the regulation of the multiplicities'.[8] For Foucault's 'instruments of analysis' throughout his work, consisted of two opposite but interlocking methods: one method is essentially synchronic – it describes a space occupied by multiple elements which are related among themselves and centred on typological identities, and it is very variously derived from Rieman, Heidegger, Bachelard and Canguilhem; the other method is essentially diachronic – it begins from the present, establishes historical continuities by the use of an ironical or inverted binary method, and is almost entirely indebted to Foucault's interpretation of Nietzsche. Together, these two methods constitute the 'instruments of analysis' that Foucault used for his topological and geological survey of the battlefield throughout his writings. And it is these methods that we must now look at.

INSTRUMENTS FOR A HISTORY OF THE PRESENT

Foucault has often reiterated in different words and in different ways that his aim has been to write a 'history of the present'.[9] This is a project that Foucault shared with Nietzsche, and its implications and methodological consequences are best understood by reference to Nietzsche.

For Foucault, to write a 'history of the present' is first of all to write a history of 'the fundamental duality of Western consciousness' (LCP, 230) because, as far as he was concerned, it is this fundamental duality which has made us 'what we are at this present moment'.[10] In *The Genealogy of Morals*, Nietzsche also began from this fundamental duality, defining it in objective, subjective and what might be described as 'functionary' terms, and asking three questions about it. These questions are also Foucault's questions, but Foucault reformulates them to make them applicable to his present. In France in the 1960s and 1970s, Nietzsche's dualities no longer moved in the shadow of the Church, but lived on, somewhat transformed, in the shadow of a centralised, secular state.

In objective terms, Nietzsche asked: 'Under what conditions did men construct the value judgements – good and evil?[11] Foucault points out from the point of view of his present in a secular, administratively orientated scientific or quasi-scientific society that 'when a judgement cannot be framed in terms of good and evil, it is stated in terms of normal and abnormal' (LCP, 230). Accordingly, it is in terms of normal and abnormal that Foucault frames Nietzsche's question. All of Foucault's books are devoted to an exploration of the conditions under which present-day judgments of normality and abnormality were constructed. Reason and madness or sanity and insanity in *Histoire de la Folie*, health and sickness in *Naissance de la Clinique*, truth and error in *Les Mots et les Choses*, the lawful and the unlawful in *Surveiller et Punir*, the sexually acceptable and the sexually deviant in *Histoire de la Sexualité* are all specific aspects or variants of present-day judgments of normality and abnormality.

With regard to the subject, Nietzsche pointed out that there is now an 'inner split' in the subject and that 'we perform experiments [upon ourselves] which we would never perform on any animal, cheerfully and curiously splitting open the soul while the body still breathes. . . We have no doubt today that sickness is instructive, much more instructive than health.[12] And he went on to ask: 'Does this not make us everyday more questionable, but also more worth questioning?' Writing in the 1960s and 1970s in a specifically French intellectual environment where psychoanalysis, Marxist sociology and political economy, and structural linguistics filled the firmament, Foucault pointed that that 'where religion once demanded the sacrifice of bodies, knowledge now calls for experimentation on ourselves, calls us to sacrifice the subject of knowledge' (LCP, 263). He asks what part psychiatry and psychoanalysis, the studies of wealth, of language and of man, played historically in constructing an inwardly divided self and in making the subject an object to himself. And is this not worth questioning?

Finally, Nietzsche asked about the functionary role of the 'ascetic priest' in elaborating and promoting the divisions which come to dominate men's minds. He asked: How was it done? What was the point of this process? What personal and social will or power-political interest did it serve? And above all, 'What is the meaning of its incredible power? Why have people yielded to it to such an extent?'[13] Writing from his experience of universities and psychiatric hospitals and from his involvement with French prisons, Foucault asked the same questions about the 'intellectual' – about the doctor and the psychiatrist, the scholar and the philosopher, the judge and the social worker. He asked: What role did they play in elaborating and promoting the social divisions between normality and abnormality and in constructing the 'dissociated self?' How did it happen? What will or power-political interest did it serve? What positions did the intellectual occupy in the process of establishing and maintaining these divisions and what is the secret of their incredible power?

For Foucault, to write a 'history of the present' is not only to write a history of the 'fundamental dualities of Western consciousness' which have made us 'what we are at the present moment'. It is also to write that history from within these dualities. Dualities are not merely the object of Foucault's historical studies; they are also an essential dimension of his method. Foucault's histories are written at the point of division between dualities, at the point where opposites mutually define and determine each other while remaining absolutely distinct. As Foucault points out, Nietzsche's genealogy is neither a genealogy of the energy of the strong nor a genealogy of the reactions of the weak; it is 'precisely that scene where they are displayed, superimposed or face to face' (LCP, 150). Similarly, Foucault's histories are neither histories of the normal nor histories of the abnormal, neither histories of reason, truth and law, nor histories of madness, error and punishment. They describe the scene where reason and madness, truth and error, the lawful and the unlawful are displayed in their complex

and changing interrelationships. Foucault used a variety of metaphors to describe the scene. In the 1960s, he described it in positive
terms as a limit, whose nature was illuminated for the historian at
those moments when it was transgressed. In the early 1970s, he
preferred the imagery of absence and referred to it as 'a space
which divides [opposites], a void through which they exchange
their threatening gestures and speech'. In the late 1970s, he turned
to the language of conflict, struggle and war: he spoke of 'strategies
of struggle in which the two forces are not superimposed and do
not lose their specific nature' but in which 'each constitutes for the
other a kind of permanent limit, a point of possible reversal'.[14] But
whatever the metaphor, the point is the same. Foucault is always
standing at the dividing line between the normal and the abnormal
and moving with it, to show us how it works and where and how
it changes.

For Foucault, to write a 'history of the present' is not merely to
write a history of the 'fundamental dualities of Western consciousness' from within these dualities. It is also to call the present into
question by problematising its self-evident truths, by 'reversing'
its accepted modes of analysis and by constructing a counter-
history which mocks and rocks the complacencies of the status
quo. Nietzsche subtitled *The Genealogy of Morals* 'an attack'. Foucault
subtitled this aspect of his history of the present a 'critique'. Both
proceeded on the assumption that 'all seeing is essentially a matter
of perspective, and so is all knowing', and therefore that to change
the perspective from which things are usually seen and known is
also to change *what* is seen and known.

Foucault's position on the dividing line between dualities offered
him innumerable possibilities for changing the perspective from
which things are usually seen and known. Standing on the dividing
line, he could do more than even-handedly follow the ping-
pong of the drawing and re-drawing of boundaries through the
confrontation and interaction of distinct but opposing principles –
although this in itself is no inconsiderable change of perspective.
Standing on the dividing line, he could pause to look in the
direction of the abnormal, in the direction of the mad, the criminal,
the sexually taboo, and study the various principles of exclusion
which were in force as well as what happened in the world of the
excluded, as he does in *Histoire de la Folie, Surveiller et Punir* and
Histoire de la Sexualité. Or he could pause to turn in the direction
of the normal and try to grasp it in its 'positivity': he could explore

the procedures used to delimit, transmit and impose social and sexual norms and the regularities which defined each norm, as he does in *Surveiller et Punir* and *Histoire de la Folie*; or, as in *Naissance de la Clinique* and *Les Mots et les Choses*, he could examine the ways various disciplines imposed their norms, how they delimited the truths that could be said, how they regulated and controlled the methods by which these truths could be determined and transmitted, and how they excluded as error all knowledge which did not conform to their paradigms.

But Foucault's favourite method for changing the perspective, which is also Nietzsche's, consists in what he calls a *renversement* – an inversion, reversal and overturning – of accepted values, modes of analysis and historical continuities, which is accomplished with 'studious cheek' (OD, 72).[15] On one level, this *renversement* consists in simply arguing the opposite of what is customary. On another level, it also involves showing that what are assumed to be clear-cut opposites are much more involved and interrelated than is usually imagined. Like Nietzsche, Foucault operates this *renversement* both within historical periods and by contrasting historical periods with each other. But it is worth noting before going on to explore Foucault's 'studious cheek' in more detail that whatever form *renversement* may take, it always remains within the dualities. It alters the imbalance of good over evil, reason over madness, truth over error, the norm over the abnormal and blurs their convenient boundaries. But it does not dialectically synthesise them or unify them in any way.

In *The Genealogy of Morals*, Nietzsche performs a *renversement* of traditional assumptions by arguing that what Christianity has taught us to accept as 'good' virtues are in fact havens for the poor, the weak and the fearful, and masks for malice and selfishness; while what we have been taught are vices and evils are in fact the virtues of the strong, the brave and the free. And as Walter Kaufman has pointed out, in *The Gay Science* and elsewhere, Nietzsche goes beyond this simple contrast of good and evil, to explore the complex modalities of their operation.[16] Foucault performs a similar operation. For instance, in *Surveiller et Punir*, Foucault explores the methods of punishment and surveillance which have been used on those outside the law who have been imprisoned, to show that these methods of surveillance and punishment are also the law of the factory, the school and the institutions which control the lives of supposedly free, law-abiding

citizens. In *Naissance de la Clinique* and *Les Mots et les Choses* Foucault
shows that if knowledge is not precisely error, it is at least a fragile
and transitory construct which cannot live up to its own claims to
truth. And in *Histoire de la Folie*, he shows that those excluded by
the norms of reason are not always the mad, that reason has had
more than its measure of folly, that it has at different times and in
different ways drawn on what it has defined as madness, and that
the division between reason and madness is ultimately a partition
within reason itself.

Foucault performs the same *renversement* in relation to the
accepted modes of historical analysis: those which describe history
in terms of continuities, like tradition, influence or the genetic
origin and development of phenomena, and those which describe
it in terms of continuous teleologies like evolution or the progress
of man towards some future golden age; those which give history
an anthropological subject, describing it in terms of human intentionality, the way man has 'made himself', or the way great
historical figures have changed the course of events or the contents
of knowledge; those which give history a transcendental subject,
like the development of spirit, the progress of knowledge, or the
cunning of reason; those which synthesise people, ideas and events
into movements, classes, or visions of the world; and those which
claim to find behind the mass of historical documentation, some
hidden and privileged essence, truth or fundament. Foucault
reverses and overturns all these traditional modes of historical
analysis by treating history as a series of specific and concrete but
changing events which occur by chance and exist in their own
right, according to their own regularities and with their own
interrelationships. Men's lives, actions and discourses figure in
Foucault's histories as specific and local events which relate in
specific and local ways to other specific and local events. Above
all, Foucault preserves the separateness, distinctness and concrete
specificity of the things he relates to each other. This particular
renversement, which owes more to Heidegger than to Nietzsche, is
perhaps Foucault's sharpest tool for 'cutting' up the continuities,
syntheses and unities of traditional historical analysis. For Foucault,
history does not lack its coherences, its regularities or even its
systems; but unlike other historians, Foucault goes to great lengths
to describe the regularities formed by the interrelation of events
without obliterating the singularity or fudging the boundary of
those events. This is what he means when he speaks of describing

systems in their dispersion, differentiation and multiplicity.

It might be useful to concretise Foucault's difference from traditional historians here by comparing the way each might describe the furniture in a room. The traditional historian might see a shabby three-piece suite, a worn carpet, freshly painted walls and a DIY unit with an expensive bar, TV and music centre, and an empty space awaiting a video which is still in its packing case on the floor. He might say that the owners of this living room were in the process of gradually improving the room, and describe their acquisition of each object as a stage in the perfectionment of the room; or he might treat the room as an instance of living rooms or of the history of technology in Western societies. Alternatively, he might describe the way the inhabitants of the living room had discovered that they must throw out the old, worn-out bits of furniture to make the room what it should be in its ideal future state. And he might reveal what the room demonstrated about its creators – how it reflected their world view, their social class and the economic conditions of society. Foucault would do none of these things. He would not see a living-room or a three-piece suite, but specific items of furniture in a particular space. He would describe the precise circumstances in which each item was introduced into that space; show how the positioning of the settee, each armchair, the coffee table, the TV, the music centre and the bar in relation to each other constructed a recreational area which made certain activities possible – like conversation, drinking, viewing and listening – and excluded other activities – like cooking or washing. He would show what the positions people could occupy within the area, and how its organisation imposed on them certain postures of the body, certain forms of behaviour and certain attitudes of mind. He would show how the principles governing this recreational area made it possible to accomodate a mixture of old and new items of furniture, to change individual items and to add new items, like the video or a dining-table, without changing the character of the space. And he would show how the different items within the room related to other items in other spaces within the same house.

Foucault's *renversement* of traditional assumptions and conventional modes of historical analysis changes the perspective from which things are seen and makes it possible to see them in a new way. The same effect is achieved by setting off the present from the past. As Foucault pointed out: 'To diagnose the present is to say what the present is, to say how the present differs from all that is not it, that is from our past'.[17] This does not mean, as is sometimes supposed, that Foucault is writing from a position outside the modern age. It means that he is showing what the present is by contrasting it with a past period when things were thought and done very differently, but with a logic and justification no less binding, no less coherent, and no less valid *in its own terms* than our own. Nietzsche used the Greeks and the aristocratic Teutons to subvert the confident assumptions of the Christian era. Foucault usually used the Renaissance. The study of a past period in its specificity and internal coherence is a *renversement* of historical analyses which either subordinate past periods to some supra-historical schema of development or treat the past in terms borrowed from present usage or modern day value systems. And the discovery that completely different values and ways of doing things make sense in their own very different configurations of truth is a *renversement* which problematises our modern notion of truth. It changes the question from: 'What is the surest path to truth?' to 'What is the history of truth itself?' (PK, 66; LCP, 144).

But in Foucault the past is not only different from the present; it is also intimately connected with the present. The ways in which it is connected will become apparent now as we turn to the fourth and last dimension of Foucault's history of the present.

For Foucault to write a 'history of the present' is not merely to write a history of the 'fundamental dualities of Western consciousness'. It is also to break down the great overarching abstractions of which these dualities are composed into their component elements and to show how each of these components emerged in the course of history. Again, Nietzsche gave Foucault the lead here. He pointed out that 'all terms which semiotically condense a whole process elude definition . . . however, at an earlier stage that synthesis of 'meanings' must have been more easily soluble, its components more easily dissociated'.[18] He showed how the 'meaning' of punishment could be broken down into at least eleven component elements and suggested that the historian conceive of 'the whole history of a thing, an organ, a custom' as 'a continuous *chain* of reinterpretations and rearrangements which need not be causally connected among themselves, which may simply follow one another'.[19] Nietzsche brought out the relationship between interpretation and power: 'The lordly right of bestowing names is such that one could almost be justified in seeing the origin of language itself as an expression of the rulers' power. They say: "This *is* that or that"; they seal off each thing or action with a sound and thereby take symbolic possession of it'.[20] And he suggested that the historical chain of interpretation and rearrangements ought to be seen in power-political terms on the assumption that 'everything that exists, no matter what its origin, is periodically reinterpreted by those in power in terms of fresh intentions' and that 'all outstripping and overcoming means reinterpretation and rearrangement in the course of which earlier meanings and purposes are necessarily either obscured or lost'.[21]

As is clear from his Résumés of the courses he gave at the *Collège de France* while he was preparing *Surveiller et Punir*,[22] Foucault proceeded by breaking down the great duality of the lawful and the unlawful into more specific elements like 'judicial knowledge' and 'punishment'; and then by breaking these down again into components which could be explored independently as they operated in society in different historical periods. In 1972–73, for instance, he taught that the concept of punishment in the Classical Age combined four major forms of punitive strategy which had different historical origins and had, in different historical periods, been the exclusive or privileged form of punishment. In 1971–72, he taught that juridical knowledge involves three components which are also combined in many modern forms of 'scientific' investigation – measure, inquiry and examination – and that these had come into being for different power-political purposes in different historical periods. Inquiry with its centralising function and associated strategy of punishment and examination with its function of control, selection and exclusion and its associated strategy of punishment became the organising principles of the two historical periods Foucault dealt with in *Surveiller et Punir* in 1976. As is clear from a paper Foucault gave at a conference in 1964,[23] *Les Mots et les Choses* is constructed in the same way. The three historical periods described in *Les Mots et les Choses* are each centred on a principle – of correspondence, representation or binarism – which Foucault shows operate in combination in modern human sciences like philology and literary criticism, psychiatry, sociology and economics.

This presentation of history as a 'historical succession of models' of interpretation (PK, 74) permits Foucault to show 'what the present is' both by setting it off from the past and by holding up component elements of the present for inspection and reevaluation.

The description of the operation of each principle of interpretation within its own historical configuration brings out the differences between the past and the present, since many of the meanings and purposes of earlier configurations have been obscured or lost. But it also establishes a troubling continuity, a continuity not merely of particular principles of interpretation which have persisted into the present, but of interpretative function. For each principle of interpretation 'governs' the statements that can be made, the truths that can be found, the behaviour which is permitted or proscribed, and the forms of treatment and control which are in force in the historical period of its ascendancy, just as the combination of these principles governs what can be known, said and done in the judiciary, in the asylums and in the human sciences at the present time. Centralisation, domination, control and the power of selection and exclusion are built into Foucault's historical method from the beginning, not added to it artificially after 1968. From *Histoire de la Folie* onwards, Foucault treats history as a 'series of reinterpretations', describing 'the principle and single law of [their] apparition' and the play of forces in each 'system of subjection' (LCP, 152, 150).

Foucault went beyond Nietzsche, however, in also finding the means to describe each system of interpretation or 'discursive formation' in its complexity, specificity and concrete mode of operation. What Foucault called archeology in *L'Archéologie du Savoir* was precisely this: a way of describing 'the law of what can be said, the system which regulates the appearance of statements (énoncés) as singular events . . . which differentiates the multiple forms of existence of specific discourses and specifies the duration proper to each' (AS, 170–1). In other words, archeology is a way of describing the successive laws of successive interpretative systems without any *Aufhebung*, without any obliteration or transcending of the singularity and particularity of events; it is a way of discussing the regularities which govern different discourses, different disciplines, different practices and the different modifications and transformations within these discourses, disciplines and practices without losing sight of their specific differences and without unifying them. Archeology is a way of achieving generality without sacrificing specificity, continuity without sacrificing discontinuity, form without sacrificing dispersion, and focus without sacrificing multiplicity. As such archeology occupies the same position as Foucault does within the great dualities of Western consciousness; it is a systematic 'rewriting' of history (AS, 183) at the point of division where opposites mutually determine and define each other, while remaining distinct.

In the *Genealogy* Nietzsche had argued that morality needed to be studied 'as it has actually existed and actually been lived' and that interrelationship and change needed to be viewed differentially as 'a series of more or less profound, more or less independent processes of appropriation, including the resistances used in each instance, the attempted transformation for purposes of defence or reaction, and the results of successful counter-attacks'.[24] But Nietzsche himself generally ignored the precise and differentiated ways in which interpretations were actually lived and changed, confining his analyses to the more general and typological level of principles of interpretation and their interaction. Foucault had to look elsewhere for a way of displaying the complex and changing interrelationships among large numbers of distinct, differentiated and constantly changing phenomena. And he had to find a way of discussing the interplay between 'discursive' and 'non-discursive practices' without falling into the traps and impasses associated with discussions of the relations between thought and reality, theory and practice, or superstructure and infrastructure.

As Pamela Major-Poetzl has demonstrated, Foucault found his model for describing the space where the elements of each interpretative system interact and change in the field concepts of modern physics and in historians of science like Bachelard and Canguilhem, who had evolved methodologies inspired by field theory and quantum physics.[25] But, as Foucault explains, to explore the relations between discursive and non-discursive practices, he also had to part ways with the historians of science:

If concerning a science like theoretical physics or organic chemistry one poses the problem of its relations with the political and economic structure of society, isn't one posing an excessively complicated question? . . . But on the other hand, if one takes a form of knowledge (*savoir*) like psychiatry, won't the question be much easier to resolve, since the epistemological profile of psychiatry is a low one, and psychiatric practice is linked with a whole range of institutions, economic requirements and political issues of social regulation? . . . Medicine certainly has a much more solid scientific armature than psychiatry, but it too is profoundly enmeshed in social structures (PK, 109).

In other words, Foucault's solution to the problems of the sociology of knowledge was to choose objects of study which themselves inhabited the division between thought and reality, theory and practice, knowledge and the political, social and economic structures of society, and to show how, in these particular objects of study, apparent opposites intermeshed. Having once chosen such objects of study, Foucault could explore the ways in which psychiatric, medical or penal practices, institutions, and the political policies and economic constraints associated with them governed the generation of new knowledge, new theory and new thought; and conversely, how the generation of knowledge and technology governed psychiatric, medical or penal practices, what happened in institutions like the hospital, the asylum and the prison, and the generation of political and economic policies about them. This exploration of the intermeshing of knowledge, policy and practice was not conducted in terms of causality, but in terms of conditions in one part of the system which make possible the emergence and insertion and functioning of something in another part of the system (AS, 211). And it worked very well as long as Foucault confined himself to fields of knowledge which were already obviously enmeshed in social structures. But as *Les Mots et les Choses* shows, when once Foucault changed the object of study to disciplines like grammar, biology and the study of wealth which have less immediate and less obvious links to 'a whole range of institutions, economic requirements and political issues of social regulation', the problem of the relation of knowledge to social structures remained beyond his grasp.

There are other difficulties with Foucault's instruments of analysis, and Foucault himself was aware of some of them. For instance, in *L'Archéologie du Savoir* he tried to defend himself against the charge that archeology seems to freeze history, describing discursive formations and seeking general rules which are valid for all points of time but neglecting temporal series within these formations and reducing chronology to the moment of rupture when one discursive formation is substituted for another. But Foucault's defence is not very convincing, because it consists of admitting that temporal successions have to be suspended to a large extent, first because the rules do not change with every statement, and secondly to make visible the relations within a discursive formation.

'Archeology', he says, 'takes for its model neither a purely logical schema of simultaneity; nor a linear succession of events; but it endeavours to show the interlacing between relations which are necessarily successive and others which are not' (AS, 219). Foucault is obviously trying to occupy the middle ground between opposites again, but it is doubtful whether this satisfactorily answers the objection that he is in some ways freezing history.

Another objection to Foucault's instruments of analysis of which he was aware is that they make his histories extremely difficult to follow. They make them difficult to follow not, as is sometimes supposed, because he was playing post-structuralist games or parodying history, but because his mode of analysis required him to pursue so many threads at the same time and to encorporate so much specific detail that the reader is in constant danger of missing the wood for the trees, branches, twigs and texture of the bark. Foucault tried to counter these objections in two ways. First, he increased the methodological signposting – he gave lectures on Nietzsche; he wrote *L'Archéologie du Savoir* which is entirely devoted to methodological explanation; and he produced a multitude of articles and gave innumerable interviews to try and clarify what he was doing and what he meant by such terms as power, discursive formation, genealogy, archeology, signification or archive. Secondly, he changed his style. The rhetorical and poetical richness of the early books gives way in the later ones to a much more sparse, straightforward and down-to-earth style, in which imagery is used much more sparingly for essential analogical purposes. But, despite these attempts to deal with objections that his histories are hard to follow, Foucault has not been entirely successful here either. For one thing, his explanations often generate even more confusion. For instance, he declares in one interview that archeology 'owes more to Nietzschean genealogy than to structuralism so-called' and in another speaks of archeology and genealogy as separate aspects of a single method.[26] One source of his difficulty in defining terms may be that, like Nietzsche, he saw them as 'pockets stuffed with meanings' which could only be disentangled, as he does in his histories, by giving each separate meaning, content and definition in its own historical context. But this does not overcome the difficulty or make his terms seem stable and easily comprehensible. Readers and commentators have found *Surveiller et Punir* and *Histoire de la Sexualité* more accessible than his earlier books. But they have also found *L'Archéologie du Savoir* either irrelevant to Foucault's histories or completely bewildering. And the succession of different terms and images Foucault has used to try to clarify what he was doing, has generated intense debate about how his work has changed over the years.

Foucault has also been criticised for historical inaccuracy and for neglecting to define either his own position in relation to the matter he discusses or the role and power of his own discourse. These criticisms seem to me to be unjustified. Foucault is writing in a long, but possibly not yet respectable, tradition of 'critical history' that goes back at least as far as Bayle. According to this tradition, there are no 'accurate' histories and can be none, because all history is narrative, and narratives, whether literary or historical, inevitably select from the mass of possible materials and order them according to a logic they lack in life. By the time Foucault came on the scene of critical history, historical narratives had been further fictionalised, first when it was perceived that all the possible points of view or views of the world embodied in them were ideologically and politically suspect, and then when the system of interpretation within which they were written was perceived not as a reflection of reality, but as an artificial construct or network which created the objects it described and determined how they might be seen. Foucault makes it clear that he is speaking in this tradition of critical history. He does not pretend to write a history either of things as they were or of things as they were perceived at any given historical moment; and he does not pretend to be either exhaustive or final. He explains that the discursive formations he describes govern individual discourses and individual non-discursive practices without necessarily being perceived to do so; rather they operate as a sort of 'positive unconscious' or as an 'a priori' of thought speech and action. He explains that he is not writing *the* archeology of the human sciences, but only *an* archeology, and also that had he picked a different group of human sciences both the underlying formation and the interrelations to be described would be quite different (PK, 65). He makes no secret of the point of view from which he is writing: his histories were to be 'scalpels, molotov cocktails, or minefields' as well as 'an instrument, a tactic, an illumination'.[27] And he repeatedly referred to his books as fictions: 'I am fully aware that I have never written anything other than fictions'; 'my book is a pure and simple fiction; it is a novel. . .' (PTS, 75).

At the same time, in a context where all systems of interpretation, however fictional, govern the knowledge and practices of society, the fact that a book is a fiction does not preclude it from having real effect and from being a form of practice. This is why Foucault could say: 'It seems plausible to me to make fictions work within the truth, to introduce truth effects within a fictional discourse, and in some way to make discourse arouse, 'fabricate' something which does not yet exist, thus to fiction something. One 'fictions' history starting from a political reality that renders it true, one 'fictions' a politics that does not yet exist starting from a historical truth' (PTS, 75). This is an echo of Nietzsche's observation in *The Gay Science* that 'it is enough to create new names, new estimations and probabilities in order to create in the long run new things'. And it is a perfectly logical consequence of a view where, to borrow Lacan's phrase, 'words create things', where things are unknowable and unthinkable outside language, and where there is no longer any 'real' recall against fictions. But it should be noted that it once again makes man the creator of his world. As Nietzsche said: 'We can destroy only as creators'.

Similarly, in a context where all systems of interpretation, however fictional, govern the thoughts, knowledge and practices possible within them, historical narratives are both projections into the past of a system of interpretation and projections of the historian's position within them. Thus Foucault can write histories where 'knowledge is allowed to create its own genealogy in an act of cognition' and where narrative becomes 'the vertical projection' of his own position within the fundamental dualities of Western consciousness (LCP, 157). And he can say that although he may be writing a novel, 'it is not I who invented it; it is the relation of our epoch and its epistemological configuration to a whole mass of utterances. So that although the subject is in effect present in the totality of the book, it is an anonymous "someone" who speaks in everything that is said'.[28] Foucault is thus far from neglecting to define either his own position in relation to the matter he discusses or the role and power of his own discourse. Foucault always views individuals as subjects who occupy certain positions within discourse, arguing that the same position can be occupied by a series of different, and otherwise anonymous subjects. And he views himself no differently. If he shrugs off all questions which seek to locate him as a psychological subject, if he warns his readers not to make him a subject in the civil or bureaucratic sense, if he tells his readers not to expect him to remain always the same, and if he refuses to define the position from which he speaks, it is not because he hopes to figure as an absent subject or to play hide and seek with his readers. For all Foucault's histories are explorations and projections of the discursive formation and of the position within them from which he speaks. As he points out very early in his career, 'the principle of interpretation is nothing but the interpreter, and this is possibly the meaning that Nietzsche gave the word "psychology"'.[29] The interest of his interpretation lies, he would claim, not in its reflection of him as an individual, biographical or psychological (in the conventional sense) subject, but in its attempt to show us that the divided place from which Foucault speaks is also our place, and that we have never seen it in quite the same way before.

Foucault's instruments of analysis make his histories both highly structured and extremely detailed. It is impossible to do justice in a few pages to their wealth of detail and to their full dispersive range. But it is possible to bring out their underlying historical structure and their principal points about our present-day divisive practices. This is what is attempted in the sections which follow, which are organised according to Foucault's three questions: about the divisions of men from each other produced by judgments of normality and abnormality; about the inner divisions produced by judgments of error and truth; and about the role of the intellectual in promoting or superseding these divisions.

ALIENATION, SOCIAL EXCLUSION AND MENTAL INTEGRATION

At the end of the Middle Ages, leprosy disappeared from the Western world. On the fringes of the community, at the gates of the towns, it was as though great shores were opening up, shores that the ill no longer haunted, but left sterile and uninhabited for a long time to come. For centuries, these areas would belong to the inhuman. From the 14th to the 17th century, they would wait, soliciting by strange incantations a new incarnation of the ill, a different grimace of fear, a renewal of the magic arts of purification and exclusion (HF, 13).

These opening lines of *Histoire de la Folie* outline the structure and continuity of the book. Synchronically, they indicate the division between the towns or communities and the spaces of exclusion once occupied by lepers which Foucault will follow down the centuries. Diachronically, they indicate a division in time, a period of difference: the centuries of the Renaissance during which these spaces lay fallow, no longer inhabited by lepers, nor yet inhabited either by the heterogeneous group of paupers, vagabonds, criminals and 'alienated minds' (HF, 16) who took their place in the Classical period, nor by the insane and mentally deranged who replace them today.[30]

But as Foucault suggests in these lines and subsequently makes clear, these divisions are not ruptures, any more than the metaphorical spaces are either empty or meaningless. The excluded are not banished to some outer realm of darkness; the spaces of exclusion are from the first riddled with institutions. In the Middle Ages, there were 19000 leper-hospitals in Christendom, 2000 of them in France. Many of these same institutions later became the locations for the enclosure or incarceration of the paupers, vagabonds, criminals and madmen of the Classical and Modern periods. Throughout history, the excluded in these institutions were in some way funded by the community and governed by decrees, by policies, and by practices of purification and exclusion which bound them to those who excluded them. And they in their turn fertilised first the minds and imaginations and later the science of the community by holding up to it, as in a mirror, the image of what it was or was not. At the gates of the town, where they could be seen and known, the excluded in their institutions were a factor that the community had to integrate in its mental world. In this sense, the excluded occupy a boundary position 'on the fringes of the community'; they are a shore-line, a 'threshold', 'on the inside of the outside and vice versa' (HF, 22), through which and in which the town and the community come to definition. Thus, despite the Renaissance centuries when madness was folly and fools were dealt with in a very different way, the excluded who came to occupy the place of the lepers in the Classical and Modern periods also took over their functions. 'Albeit with new meaning and in a very different culture, the forms subsist – essentially this major form of rigorous partition, which is social exclusion but also mental integration' (HF, 16).

Moreover, despite the fact that the Renaissance represents a break in the history of institutionalisation, Foucault shows that it produced two opposite strains of thought about madness which have persisted, in varying forms, to the present day. Of all the types of exclusion practised in the Renaissance, Foucault concentrates on one which, in his view, most captured the minds and imaginations of Renaissance painters, writers, philosophers and mystics: the practice of putting the deranged on boats and sending them off on a pilgrimage to a holy shrine, thus at once purifying the towns of them and exposing them to the possibility of a miraculous cure. Foucault shows dispersively where and how the 'ship of fools' appeared in the literature, art, mystical imagery and philosophical texts of the fifteenth and sixteenth centuries, and then brings these diverse strands together in what he calls 'the tragic folly of the world', and 'the critical consciousness of folly' (HF, 38, 39). The tragic folly of the world, he argues is predominant in the art of the period – in the work of Bosch, Brueghel and Dürer among others. It consists of a cosmic vision where disturbing dream figures and grotesquely impossible animals reveal the madness at the heart of man and an extreme of disorder which heralds the apocalyptic end of the world in a 'delirium of pure destruction' (HF, 38). In this tradition, madness is also inseparable from wisdom: it represents the threatening dangers of knowledge beyond the permitted limits, and therefore a necessary experience of the questor after wisdom. The critical consciousness of folly, on the other hand, predominates in the 'universe of discourse': in the period's moral satires, comedies and farces and in the humanist texts of Flayder and Erasmus. Here folly reveals the truth about man. Taking centre stage and holding discourses about itself or about the world, folly is the mouthpiece of a deeper wisdom which criticises man's follies and the worldly foolishness of presumption or greed, ambition or curiosity, and of all manners of vice. This partition in the view of folly in the Renaissance parallels the partition between the towns or communities and the spaces of exclusion with which Foucault began, and he also follows this mental division down the centuries.

At the same time, in so doing, Foucault operates a *renversement*, an inversion and overturning, of present day assumptions. He argues that after the Renaissance the 'critical consciousness of madness and its philosophical or scientific, moral or medical forms' became predominant, leading 'rational thought to the analysis of madness as mental illness' (HF, 40). It all but submerged the tragic consciousness of madness, without ever quite obliterating it. The tragic consciousness re-emerged periodically in the work of people like Sade, and it persisted through the centuries as a lack which delimits the boundaries of the critical consciousness and defines the constraints of its meanings and its forms. 'Beneath each of its forms', says Foucault, '[the critical consciousness of madness] masks, fully and perilously, the tragic experience which it has not succeeded in entirely reducing' (HF, 40). In our time, however, in the work of Nietzsche and Van Gogh, Freud and Artaud, the tragic consciousness begins to burst through, questioning the adequacy and completeness of the critical, rational consciousness of madness. Foucault lends his voice to this post-Nietzschean attempt to 'liberate subjugated knowledges' (LCP, 196). And he does so by showing up the limitations of the practices and discourses of 'critical consciousness' in the Classical and Modern periods.

Foucault dates the Classical policy of internment from the edict of 1656 which founded the Hôpital Général in Paris to accommodate what seems to us today to be a motley band of paupers, criminals, unemployed people and madmen. What these groups had in common in the Classical period, however, is that they were all either unable or unwilling to work. And by the middle of the seventeenth century, idleness and indigence had become a major problem. Able-bodied victims of the mid-century economic crisis, peasants who had been driven off their land, casualties of the wars, deserting soldiers and madmen roamed the towns in ever increasing numbers, begging or stealing for a living and threatening to disrupt the social order. When Henry IV came to Paris, there were 30000 beggars in a population of 100000; a few years after the establishment of the Hôpital Général, it contained 6000 people or about 1 per cent of the population. Internment in the Hôpital Général and in the thousands of institutions like it which sprang up in France and all over Europe, had therefore, in the first instance, nothing to do with medicine or mental illness. It was aimed at 'an indistinct mass: a population without resources, without social attachment, a class which found itself abandoned or which had been made mobile for a time by the new economic developments' (HF, 77). Internment was a measure designed to put an end to vagrancy, indigence and agitation, by excluding and confining all those who threatened the bourgeois social order. And as such, it was a measure which changed the boundary line between the towns and the spaces of exclusion. As Foucault says: 'In the classical world, work and idleness fashioned a line of partition which substituted itself for the great exclusion of leprosy' (HF, 84).

Foucault repeatedly refers to the motley collection of internees in the Classical period as 'the alienated' (HF, 59ff). He uses the terms alienated and alienation in three allied senses. The first derives from the Latin root *alienare*, which simply means 'to make other'. The second is that preserved in the English term 'alienist', and refers to mental illness or insanity. The third is a complex *renversement* of the Marxist use of the term. These three uses of the term govern Foucault's description of the emergence of madness as mental illness. He often uses the term in two or more senses concurrently, and to preserve this ambiguity, I will translate the words as 'alienation' and 'alienated' whenever it appears, even if this sometimes sounds a bit unusual in English.

Thus Foucault begins by arguing, in opposition to Marxist historians, that internment was neither a spontaneous elimination from society of 'asocial elements' nor a stage in the process by which society became conscious of a pre-existing phenomenon – madness – and made it an object of medical study. He grants that eighteenth-century internees resemble those whom we now consider 'asocial' and distribute among prisons, asylums, houses of correction, psychiatric hospitals and psychoanalysts. But he argues that 'asocial elements' were the result and not the cause of 'the gesture of segregation'. It was the gesture of segregation which defined what was asocial and inhuman in the Classical period; and by banishing what was defined as asocial or inhuman, segregation created the 'other'. Segregation made figures who had heretofore been familiar parts of the social landscape strangers by shutting them away, by placing them out of reach and beyond the pale of the normatively human and social. And in the process, it also cut off from us and placed beyond our ken certain aspects of ourselves embodied in these figures. Using the term alienation in its Latin sense of 'making other', therefore, Foucault explains that 'this gesture [of segregation] created alienation' and that 'the decree by which modern man designates the madman as the bearer of his own *alienated* truth has meaning only in so far as the field of alienation – to which the madman was banished along with so many others who no longer have any kinship with him – was constituted long before he came to monopolise and symbolise it for us' (HF, 94).

In an argument which preempts his later insistence on the

relationship between knowledge and power and which operates a *renversement* of the Marxist view of alienation exclusively as a product of economic processes, Foucault shows how socially held ideas and socially conceived policies created the social reality of alienation, which eventually became an object of knowledge in its own right. He explains that poverty and idleness were conceived in the Classical period very variously as manifestations of divine punishment or displeasure, as obstacles to the social order and potential focuses of revolt, as moral transgressions against the bourgeois work ethic, and as states which traditionally required some form of public charity. And he shows how these ideas were translated into practices in the institutions. The houses of internment, he says, were set up to assist the poor by giving them food and lodging in return for their work. But since the poor and the idle were also viewed as antagonistic to the social order and as morally culpable for not working, they were also set up as places of punishment, repression and reformation where the poor's moral shortcomings and tendency to disorder could be corrected by forced labour, ruthless constraint and a rigorous convent-like order. And since poverty was itself seen as a divine punishment, this regime of constraint and repression could be administered with the comfortable conviction that it was God's will and perhaps some remission of the sinners' pains in the afterlife.

Preempting his later emphasis on the 'positivity' of knowledge and power, Foucault argues that, once established, 'internment played not only a negative role of exclusion, but also a positive role of organisation' (HF, 96). Turning his attention to alienation in its second sense of mental illness, he argues that much of what we now consider intrinisic either to madness or to the unconscious derives from the internal organisation of institutions of internment in the Classical period. For the mad were interned in a single space with homosexuals, sodomites, prostitutes, debauchees, pro-digals and others who had transgressed against the interests or morals of the bourgeois family; with blasphemers, suicides, sorcerers, magicians, diviners and alchemists, who had transgres-sed against the norms of belief; and with libertines and freethinkers whose championship of the passions set them against the norms of reason. Foucault claims that this conflation of certain kinds of internees within the houses of internment homogenised them and led to a blurring of distinctions in the perception of madness. For, like the poor, this apparently heterogeneous group of social, sexual and spiritual deviants were viewed as morally culpable and 'measured by their divergence from the social norm' (HF, 117), but, unlike them, their particular forms of divergence and moral culpability were conceived as forms of error or Unreason. The madman, who stood out clearly as an autonomous figure in the Renaissance, now came to be identified in significant ways with other internees in this excluded field of 'unreason'; so there was no longer any 'separation between madness and transgression, between alienation and wickedness' (HF, 152) or even between 'madness and crime'. If the madman was distinguished from the others at all, it was only as an exemplum of the way the bestiality of unreason robbed man of his humanity. And this, Foucault argues, has left us with a troubling legacy today. 'By annexing sexual prohibitions, religious interdicts and liberties of thought and of the passions to madness in the realm of Unreason, classicism formed a moral experience of unreason which serves as a basis for our own "scientific knowledge" of mental illness' (HF, 121). In the 'scientific' study of mental illness, the prohibitions and interdicts of the classical period became neuroses; sexual deviancy, religious illusions, unregulated passions, and abnormal or arcane conceptions came to be viewed as properties of the unconscious and characteristics of the insane; the theme of animality was preserved in the view of mental illness as a 'pathological mechanism of nature' (HF, 177); and madness became a pastiche of transgressions against the norms of bourgeois society of which the madman was not originally guilty. In this sense it can be said that internment positively created mental illness.

Once the positive organisation of the houses of internment came into play, therefore, the initial partition of good and evil in terms of Work and Idleness came to be doubled by another partition of good and evil in terms of Reason and Unreason, with all that that implied. Work, Reason, Morality, Good Order and the Norm were now firmly ensconced in the towns and communities; Idleness, Unreason, Immorality, Disorder and Deviation from the norm were banished and alienated in the spaces of exclusion. And Foucault devotes the second part of *Histoire de la Folie* to showing how this affected medical and philosophical thinking about madness in the eighteenth century.

There is no question here of any theory of reflection or of any division between theory and practice. For Foucault, internment was a practice which had its moral, theological, political and economic theory, and medicine was a theory which had its practices. Foucault only claims to show that there are 'structural analogies' between the perception of the mad in philosophy and medicine and the partition of Reason and Unreason concretely implemented in the internment of the alienated.

The first such analogy is that mad people were 'non-beings' for doctors and philosophers, as they were non-beings for the community. They were non-beings first in the sense that they were really absent. Medicine and philosophy lacked any real contact with the mad in the Classical period. Doctors were not required to assess the madness of internees or to treat them until the Assembly's decree of 1785. Internment in the Classical period was a decision taken not by doctors, but by magistrates, ministers, kings and chiefs of police in the interests of public order or at the request of the internee's family, neighbours or local priest. And within medicine itself, there was 'social fragmentation' between medical theoreticians about madness and the lay practitioners who actually saw the mad: mad people who were not interned were more likely to be treated by apothecaries, surgeons, herbalists, quacks and nuns than by doctors. With the exception of a few hospitals where some of the mad were treated for a relatively short time, the doctors who theorised about madness had virtually no contact with the mad. The same is true of the philosophers who remained within the towns and within the confines of the rational critical consciousness. The mad were also non-beings in the second sense that they were associated with all that is not: with error, which is not truth; with illusion, which is not reality; with vacuity, which is not sense; with deviancy, which is not morality; with unreason, which is not reason.

The second analogy is that as in the towns reason and order were responsible for banishing and enclosing the mad, so in philosophy and medicine, reason and order were given the task of understanding and explaining them. In philosophy, it was held that, although madness was a negation or absence of reason which could not be defined in positive terms, a madman could be immediately recognised by any rational man by his departures from normal and rational behaviour. The madman thus became 'the other in relation to others: the other – in the sense of the exception – among others – in the sense of the universal' (HF, 199). And the rational man became the judge and diagnoser of the madman's madness. Medicine assumed that madness was, like other illnesses and like nature itself, governed by a concealed rational order that could be discovered by reason, and it attempted to classify madness and its subdivisions among the other illnesses on the basis of its most superficial and manifestly visible symptoms. But the system of classification used was modelled on the deductive organisation and division of species in botany, where the form of each species and sub-species was determined logically in relation to the forms of all the other species and sub-species. It was a logical and theoretical, rather than an empirical system of classification, in which reason reproduced its images of morality, truth, reality and being. As a result, it bore very little relation to actual madmen and had to be abandoned in the nineteenth century.

Foucault shows, however, that before it was abandoned, it produced ideas about the passions and the imagination and about the causes and therapies of madness, which have remained with us to this day.

Unlike the philosophers of the classical period, who separated the body from the soul and argued about which was the cause of madness, the doctors treated body and soul as a unity and madness as a phenomenon which affected both simultaneously and in a similar fashion. This meant, on the one hand, that they sought the proximate causes of madness in some alteration of the brain or nervous system and embarked upon anatomical research. And it meant, on the other hand, that they looked for the secondary causes of madness in anything that might affect either the body or the soul; the climate, the over-luxurious life of certain people in society, the effect of novel-reading or of the theatre on the imagination, perturbations of the passions, feelings of anger, fear, sorrow and scorned love, or excessive studying. Madness thus became 'the sign of a particular sensitivity of the human organism', and, at least in part, the result of 'the influence of the environment' (HF, 243).

Consonant with this view of the unity of body and soul, delirium was seen in the classical period as affecting both: it manifested itself in the silence of gesture, in the strangeness of conduct, in the violence of language, in disturbances of the organs of sense and in unreal or irrational imaginings. Like the philosophers, eighteenth-century doctors measured madness against the norms of the rational man. Delirium was madness because it was error, a form of blindness to truth and reality. A man was not mad because he saw images, but because he was so caught up in them, so convinced by them that he failed to do what a rational man would do: stand outside them and measure them against something which is not an image, something real, true or rational. The mechanisms of delirium were understood to be the same as those of dreams, but what distinguished dreamers from madmen was that they woke up: 'Delirium', said Pitcairn in the eighteenth century,' is the dream of people who are awake' (HF, 258). In the Renaissance, dreams were thought to borrow the qualities of madness to show reason its limitations and its frailty; in the Classical period, reason was given the task of showing dreams and madness their limitations and their frailty. For the Classical period, 'madness began where man's relation to truth becomes disturbed or obscured' (HF, 259); in the Renaissance, truth began where reason confronted the tragic consciousness of madness.

Foucault's description of the way classical theorists defined different forms of madness is a *renversement* of this modern view of the function of reason in relation to madness and dream. With consummate irony, Foucault details and elaborates the complex descriptions eighteenth-century doctors gave of different categories of madness – dementia, mania, melancholy and hysteria – and shows that each description was governed by a single image. Everything about melancholy, for instance, was heavy and dark: it was governed by the humid and cold humours, it made the body fluids languid and the blood viscous and slow-moving, it sent dark vapours to the brain, and made the mind sad, fearful and solitary. Everything about mania on the other hand was heat and movement: it was governed by the hot and dry humours, it manifested itself in lunacy, fury and audacity, in a continual agitation of the spirits and vibration of the senses, and in an extreme tension of the bodily fibres. Dementia was pure negativity, the reverse of reason: it was disorder, mental distortion, illusion, error, non-reason and non-truth. And hysteria was pure sensibility: a sensitivity of the nervous system and irritability of the mind so excessive as to prevent the body from communicating its sensations to the brain. If madness is to be so caught up in one's images that one takes them for truth and reality, then the rational doctors of the classical period who conceived and painstakingly elaborated these images of non-being, of heaviness and darkness, of heat and movement, of humours and vibrating fibres, were surely mad. 'The essential point,' says Foucault, 'was that the work was not done from observation to the construction of explanatory images; that, on the contrary, the images ensured the initial synthesis, that their organising power made possible a structure of perception in which the symptoms acquired their significance and organised themselves as the visible presence of truth' (HF, 296). And Foucault argues that these images are still with us, translated into the 'neutral' language of psychology, psychiatry and psychoanalysis.

Finally, the Classical period made its contribution to modern psychiatry through its therapies. Some of these, like immersion and purification, or like the use of opium, derived their logic from the old idea that there is a panacea for every ill, that somewhere in nature there is an antidote for every disease and that to cure someone, one has only to use nature against itself. Other therapies owed more to the concept of madness as a dream state of withdrawal from the world and its truth, in which the madman was imprisoned in error, illusion and moral fault. For instance, doctors tried to awaken madmen from their imaginary world and to bring them back to reality, first by the administration of rude physical shocks, and later by constraining the mad to live a highly ordered and moral life under surveillance. Or, because they assumed that the mad discourses and illusions of delirium must, like any illness and like nature itself, conceal a meaning and a logic, they used theatrical illusion to answer the madman's underlying logic. For example, the madman who thought he was dead and who was really dying because he refused to eat, was answered by a group of actors dressed up in winding sheets eating and drinking in front of him and persuading him that the dead eat and drink just like the living. Foucault argues that these two groups of therapies were the basis for the later split between the medical and psychological treatment of madness. From this point of view, Freud's 'art of discourse' and of 'bringing [mentally disturbed people] back to the truth' was not a discovery, but a rediscovery, a return to a classical approach to madness which was lost and obscured in the nineteenth century.

But then, the end of the eighteenth century and the beginning of the nineteenth century produced a new partition between the towns and the spaces of exclusion, which radically changed both the perception of madness and its treatment. The determining factors here seem to be first, an enormous increase, in the course of the eighteenth century, in the numbers of alienated minds, not all of whom could be accommodated in extant houses of internment; and secondly, the spread in the community of a haunting fear of madness and contagion. In the third part of *Histoire de la Folie*, Foucault shows how intellectual responses to these problems and the practices growing out of them separated madness from poverty and unreason, drawing poverty and unreason back into the community and leaving madness and crime to divide the space of exclusion between them.

The separation of madness from unreason was a by-product of the attempt to explain the startling increase of 'alienated minds' and especially the growing numbers of sufferers of 'disorders of the nerves'. It was argued that this increase was due to the social milieu and to changes in it resulting from the historical progress of civilisation. Madness, it was said, was due to excessive liberty in a commercial society, where men were exposed to so many contradictory opinions that they could no longer find truth; where their pursuit of calculating self-interest distanced them from the satisfaction of their immediate needs and desires; and where religion, which had once helped to exorcise their guilts, had lost its hold. And it was due to the growing artificiality of a civilisation whose material progress encouraged people to live unhealthy and unnatural lives, detaching them from their dependence on the seasons, turning night into day, and providing excessive leisure, which promoted indulgence in the passions, disgust with life and boredom. Where the classical period saw madness as a negation of *the* truth, therefore, the late eighteenth and early nineteenth century saw it as a loss by man of *his* truth in the unhealthily and degenerately artificial milieu of society.

Foucault describes this complex of ideas as 'a very rudimentary concept of alienation which defines the milieu as the negativity of man and views it as the *a priori* of all possible madness' (HF, 397). And in a *renversement* of Marxist assumptions, he argues that this is where 'the alienation of the doctors and the alienation of the philosophers originated in an obscure kinship' (HF, 392). These two 'alienations' only became distinct from each other later in the nineteenth century when 'the philosophical concept of alienation acquires historical significance by the economic analysis of labour, while the medical and psychological concept of alienation abandons history to become a moral critique in the name of the endangered well-being of the species' (HF, 399). In other words, the separation occurs when Marxism attributes the loss of man's truth in society exclusively to his labour relations, while psychology and psychiatry attribute it to processes of guilt and repression occuring exclusively in 'Man'.

Already at the beginning of the nineteenth century, the notion of man's alienation from himself and from nature in the social milieu began to separate madness from unreason. For while madness became man's detachment from his truth, unreason remained the immemorial expression of this truth. In the form of the 'delirium of the heart, the madness of desire, the extravagant dialogue of love and death in the boundless presumptuousness of appetite', (HF, 381) and in the work of poets and philosophers from Sade to Holderlin, Nerval and Nietzsche, the old forbidden images of unreason lived on and took their place once more in the imagination of the community.

The poor began to be distinguished from the mad in the industrial phase of capitalism when poverty came to be seen as an economic problem and when population began to be seen as the source of a nation's wealth. For then it was considered more beneficial to the community to release the poor from confinement and to let them wander free in the towns, because it was assumed that their numbers would bring down wages, and that lower wages would both reabsorb them into the economy and increase the wealth of the nation by making its products more competitive on the world market. Instead of being an unnecessary financial charge on society in houses of internment, the poor could thus help themselves and help the community by supporting themselves through their work in the open market. This perception of the poor as the source of a nation's wealth rehabilitated the poor morally and reintegrated them socially and economically in the community. But it also produced a new division between the able-bodied poor, who were socially useful, and the ill who were unable to work and remained a charge on society. 'For the first time in the Christian world', says Foucault, 'illness found itself isolated from poverty and from all the forms of affliction' (HF, 439).

The new partition which brought poverty and unreason back into the towns and left madness, crime and illness in confinement came into force with the Declaration of the Rights of Man at the height of the French Revolution in 1790. The Declaration decreed that all prisoners were to be released except for criminals and madmen judged by doctors to be a threat to themselves or to others; that special asylums were to be set aside for the mad; and that no man might be imprisoned or confined except by due process of law. The Declaration thus brought medicine and the courts into the picture for the first time; and it created a space of exclusion which belonged exclusively to madness in which, as Foucault goes on to show, madness was gradually objectified, internalised and judged.

According to Foucault, medicine was from the first given a judgmental role. Its first task was to protect the community from the mad and from unnecessary expenditure by deciding who was genuinely likely to harm himself or members of the community, who was mentally deranged but not a danger to himself or others, and who was only simulating madness in an attempt to hide in the asylums from the revolutionary furies of the Terror. The decision was taken within the asylums by interrogating the interned and by freeing them from their chains and observing their behaviour. Under the supposedly neutral gaze of the doctor, who was supposedly untouched by considerations of government or by the self-interest of families, madness was to reveal its truth. And for the first time, records were kept about the mad with the intention of adding to what was known about man. Foucault argues that in this process, 'madness was alienated from itself by being given the status of object' (HF, 463); and that, as an object which instructed man about himself, madness 'became the first of the objectifying forms: those [forms] by which man could get an objective grasp of himself' (HF, 481). Here Foucault is using the term alienation primarily in the sense of 'making other'.

Medicine's attempts to cure the mad in the asylums were no less judgmental. Different as they were in many respects, both Tuke's Quaker Retreat in England and Pinel's Bicêtre in France (once a house of internment and before that a leper-hospital) used a system of rewards and punishments administered by the doctor and his wardens to force the mad to become conscious of their madness and to assume responsibility for their behaviour. Tuke proceeded on the assumption that madness was caused by the unnatural and immoral life in society and that it was curable by a return to nature, the simple life and the primeval values of religion and of the patriarchal family. He therefore built his Retreat on the great plain of York, where the mad could be isolated from the evils of society, exposed to the healthful influences of nature and of simple physical labour, and placed in an environment which practised the morals and injunctions of religion. He organised the Retreat not only as a natural and moral society, but also as a substitute family, where the mad were treated as children and the wardens exercised benevolent but judicious and unsparing parental control. The wardens used fear of confinement or of the strait-jacket and the 'need for esteem' and affection to get the mad to control at least the outward manifestations of their madness and to learn to behave according to the norms of nature and religion. Under the watchful gaze of the wardens and through their punitive or approving reactions, the mad were made to become conscious of their madness, to assume responsibility for their behaviour, to develop 'self-restraint' by internalising guilt for misbehaviour, and thus to return to nature, religion and truth. As Foucault points out, this curative method was based on a myth about what is fundamental, natural and inalienable in man: madness was seen as a state of alienation from an inalienably reasonable natural and religious fundament, and the cure was conceived as a return to this fundament by way of recognition and mastery of one's own alienation.

Pinel did not share Tuke's assumptions about nature and religion. At a time when the Revolution was running the full gamut of violence, wickedness and vice, he thought that madness was caused by the immorality and degeneration of the lower classes of society and that it was curable by a return to conformity to traditional social types of virtue. But, like Tuke, his curative methods were designed to bring madmen to a sense of their madness and to get them to conform to the behaviour he expected by making them internalise guilt and develop self-control. To make the mad judge themselves to be mad, he taught his wardens to react to their delusions either by absolute silence, or by getting them to recognise and condemn their own madness in other internees, before being shown that the madness they first saw mirrored in others was also objectively their own. To get the internees to conform to the behaviour he expected, Pinel used fear and unexpected, unpleasant punishments, like sudden douches of icy water accompanied by references to the fault committed. Foucault explains that repression of the fault by the madman after repeated punishment represents a recognition and internalisation of the judgment, which also created remorse. Those who could not be brought to see their own madness, or who did not respond to punishment or fear, were locked up in cells and excluded from the asylum community, so that in effect a second seclusion was operated within the asylum community itself.

In a *renversement* of the accepted view of asylums as benevolent, curative places, Foucault insists that both as a place where the decision about internment was made and as a place of cure, the asylum was – and remains to this day – an essential juridical institution. It judged alone, immediately and without appeal; it developed its own methods of punishment and used them at will; and while it imagined it was liberating the mad by releasing them from their chains, it was in fact 'enslaving them' by turning them into helpless objects under the pitiless and controlling gaze of the wardens.

> The asylum in the age of positivism which Pinel is so much praised for founding, is not a free sphere of observation, diagnosis and therapy; it is a juridical space where people are accused, judged and condemned, and from which they are freed only by a translation of this process into the psychological depths, that is to say by repentance. Madness is punished in the asylum even if it is excused outside. It was for a long time, and is still today, imprisoned in a moral world' (HF, 523).

This view of the asylums at the end of the eighteenth and beginning of the nineteenth century is the foundation for Foucault's analysis of the prison and of the 'disciplinary society' in *Surveiller et Punir*.

More disturbing even than his view of the asylum as a place of judgment and punishment, perhaps, is Foucault's argument that in the course of time 'the situation [of madness in the asylums] became its nature; the constraints [of the asylum] took on a deterministic meaning . . . what had been a social reform of internment became faithfulness to the fundamental truths of madness; and *the manner in which the madman was alienated* was forgotten, to reappear as the *nature of alienation*' (HF, 458). So, for instance, the asylum made the madman a child in a patriarchal bourgeois family situation, in which his madness was constantly pitted against the authority and truth of the rational warden. Psychoanalysis later treated this family situation and the incessant conflict with the authoritative Father both as inherent to mental illness and as characteristic of the whole history of Western culture, if not of civilisation itself. The doctor's authority and curative power in the asylums derived not from his knowledge of madness but from his status as a man of reason and from his assumption of the roles of 'Father and Judge, Family and Law'. This was perfectly clear to both Pinel and Tuke, who stressed that the doctor's effectiveness did not depend on his scientific competence. In modern psychiatry, Foucault argues, the source of the doctor's authority and curative power is the same as it was in Pinel and Tuke's asylums; only their origin has been forgotten, and they have been overlaid by the myth that the doctor is applying objective scientific knowledge. Moreover, according to Foucault, the institutional form designed by Tuke and Pinel, where the madman must 'recognise his guilt and rid himself of it, allow the truth of his illness to appear and suppress it, and resume his freedom by alienating it in the demands of the doctor' (HF, 547) remains an a priori of medical perception and practice.

With the birth of the asylum and the decree that people might only be imprisoned after due process of law, madness began to be mentally integrated in the community in new ways. The new public trials not only made public shame 'the most redoubtable form of alienation' (HF, 468); it also made certain kinds of immorality and unreason familiar to ordinary people. The introduction of juries, who represented the conscience of the community and who decided on the partition between the socially acceptable and what must be socially excluded, also had its effect. For the first time, juries excused crimes of passion: blinded by the madness of passion, criminals were not held to be responsible for their crimes. This meant, in the first instance, that madness and unreason were seen not only as psychological motives of action, but also as psychological determinants for which men were not responsible. And it also meant the erection of a new partition within madness between 'good forms' like jealousy, irrational love or blind fidelity which bourgeois society recognised but proscribed and which were held to mitigate crime; and 'bad forms' of madness which were unrecognisable in bourgeois terms, and which were condemned as vice, perversion and inexcusable wickedness. Some forms of madness and unreason were thus brought back into the community as an internalised, psychologised form of determinism.

Moreover, from the time when the asylum turned the madman into an object of knowledge, the community studied the mad with a view to obtaining 'objective' knowledge about man and his truth. 'From that day,' Foucault points out with biting irony, 'man has had access to himself as true being; but this true being has been given to him only in the form of alienation' (HF, 548). On one level, this resulted in the logical absurdity of 'positive' psychology which has sought the truth about man in his negation: to seek knowledge of the personality in dual personalities, knowledge of the memory in amnesia, knowledge of language behaviour in aphasia, or knowledge of the intelligence in mental deficiency is, Foucault argues, to assume that the truth about man appears when it has disappeared and become 'other than itself' (HF, 545).

But, on another level, the fact that man's true being is given to him only in the form of alienation results in the conscious absurdity of Foucault's study of madness. For, as Foucault is careful to point out, his history of madness is not in fact a history of a psychological type: the madman (HF, 548). It is a history of other kinds of madness. It is a history of the process by which the community alienated certain values and certain types of thought, certain forms of behaviour and certain types of people by excluding them and making them 'other', and then characterised them as the 'alienated' – the mentally ill, the asocial elements, the disaffected, the outsider, the other. It is a history of the alienation of the rational critical consciousness of madness from the tragic vision of madness; and of the conditions which led to the emergence of a psychology which alienates man from his truth by making him seek it in an 'other', who is, yet is not, like him, and which alienates the madman from his unreason by making him speak the language of reason, order and morality. In so far as all these alienations and exclusions are still with us today, superposed one on top of the other, the strata in which they originated buried in the depths of history, Foucault's history of madness is an 'archeology of alienation' (HF, 94). It is a history of some of the 'dividing practices' by which 'the subject is either divided inside himself or divided from others' today.

Two events intervened between *Histoire de la Folie* and *Surveiller et Punir* which slightly changed the emphasis and added a new dimension to Foucault's historical analyses. The first was the publication in 1967 of Gilles Deleuze's book *Nietzsche et la Philosophie*; the second was the French student uprising of 1968 and its consequences.

Foucault payed tribute to Deleuze's work both in *Surveiller et Punir* and in a review of 1970, where he said that because of Deleuze, 'new thought is possible; thought is again possible' (LCP, 196). In his case, this was certainly true. For, by interpreting Nietzsche's *Genealogy of Morals* in the light of his *Will to Power*,

Deleuze showed that force, or the will to power, underlie every aspect of Nietzsche's genealogical and critical philosophy, so that history as a series of interpretations and reinterpretations must be seen as a history of the will to power; and he emphasised the affirmative aspect of Nietzsche's concept of power.

Beginning with Foucault's view of critical philosophy, Deleuze explained than in Nietzsche, meaning or interpretation is conceived as a 'force which appropriates the thing, which exploits it, which takes possession of it, and expresses itself in it';[31] and that in so far as every word, phenomenon or event is conceived pluralistically by Nietzsche as having multiple meanings or interpretations, each of these must be seen as the locus of the multiple forces competing for possession of it. This view of meaning as force dissolves the apparent solidity and fixity of such 'things' as reality, event, milieu, fact and experience. It does so because it denies that these phenomena exist prior to or separate from interpretation – 'the fact is an interpretation' – and because it means that reality as a system of interpretations and reinterpretations is also reality as a system of competing forces – 'There is no quantity of reality; all reality is already quantities of force . . . in relations of tension to one another'.[32] Deleuze used the term 'body' to describe such systems of forces: 'Every relation of forces constitutes a body: chemical, biological, social, political . . . the body is a multiple phenomenon, being composed of a plurality of irreducible forces'.[33]

The will to power is integral to this view of interpretation as force in two very different ways. It is integral to it first as a relation of domination and submission. Nietzsche, Deleuze says, conceives of the relation of forces as a hierarchy where some forces rule over others. And relations of domination and submission appear again when 'the history of a thing' is conceived as 'a history of the forces which take possession of it and the coexistence of the forces struggling to take possession of it',[34] because the forces which succeed in taking possession of the thing necessarily dominate and repress those they replace or displace. The will to power is also integral to the view of interpretation as force in a second sense which is inseparable from the act of interpretation itself. For, according to Deleuze, the will to power is also the force which interprets, 'that which *gives* meaning and value'.[35] Every meaning or interpretation, every concept, belief or proclaimed truth expresses a will: it raises the question of *who* wills precisely this concept, truth or interpretation and *what* exactly is being willed by it. According to Deleuze, the fundamental question in all of Nietzsche's work is: 'But what do they really will, these seekers of truth, who say: "I seek the truth"?' And Nietzsche's method is to treat all concepts, sentiments, beliefs, ethical systems and sciences as 'symptoms of a will which wills something'.[36] Power is inherent in this will, but not in the sense that power is the goal of the will or its primary characteristic; this will does not want power. Power is something that it has as a meaning-giving, appropriating force: it is 'that which wills in the will', and it is the will's 'genetic and differential element'.[37] In other words, power is what makes interpretations what they are and affirms them in their difference. It is the source of the positive quiddity of each interpretation, that which affirms it in the fullness of its being and differentiates it from every other. In Deleuze's reading of Nietzsche, therefore, the will to power – as the will which wills something and as positive affirmation of being – is inherent in all meaning and interpretation. Nietzsche's 'genealogical and critical method' consists in 'taking each concept (or feeling or action) back to the will to power so as to make it the symptom of a will without which it could not even be thought (or felt or performed)'[38] and Deleuze can say: 'genealogy, that is to say, the philosophy of the will to power'.[39]

Deleuze's reading of Nietzsche made it possible for Foucault to add the dimension of power to his instruments of analysis. It made it possible for him both to see the will power as inherent in systems of interpretation and to distinguish it from systematicity. Power and truth, power and knowledge, power and interpretation could be intimately interlinked as concepts which implied one another in so far as all truth, knowledge and interpretation implied a will which willed something and represented a positive affirmation; and this could be done without precluding an analysis of power in its other sense of hierarchical relations of domination and submission. By dissolving such thing-like terms as 'experience', 'reality' and 'consciousness' which he had used in *Histoire de la Folie*, and by seeing things as 'bodies', Foucault could show that history as a series of interpretations and reinterpretations was history as a series of competing and coexistent forces, and also that force — and the will to power in both its meanings – penetrated every level of social life and every aspect of history. As Foucault now said: 'Power is coextensive with the social body' (PK, 55). Deleuze's analysis of Nietzsche's will to power made it possible for Foucault to add 'genealogy' to archeology in 1967. But Foucault did not speak of power until 1971. Deleuze provides the probable reason for this delay when he points out that 'thought depends on the forces which take possession of it' and for thought to be active, affirmative and creative, the thinker needs 'extreme places, at extreme moments, where the highest and profoundest truths emerge and live'. If Foucault came to speak of power, it was, as he said, because 'for us it was not only a theoretical question, but part of our experience'.[40]

The extreme moments and the extreme forces which took possession of Foucault's thoughts and made power part of the history of his present were the uprising of French students and workers in May 1968 and the government's subsequent imprisonment of students, worker-militants and leading leftist intellectuals.

The spectacle of the suppression of the students by the police and the military on the streets of Paris was a spectacle of naked force. But repression, the use of power to suppress and control, was also integral to the thinking of the students: it was that against which they had rebelled. As the resolutions of the action committees and debating groups during the uprising show, the students equated the repressive force they found in the streets with repression in the universities and schools, repression in the factory and workplace, and repression by control of the access to knowledge and by ideological and psychological techniques. Here are some examples of what they were saying:

This civilisation is the disguise that permanent repression assumes in order to conceal and perpetuate itself; because as a rule this repression has not the obvious shiny appearance of a helmeted gendarme, but of less shocking, more acceptable uniforms, ones that are often even desired, such as the doctor's gown or the professor's cap and gown.'[41]

Monopolisation of capital is accompanied everywhere by monopolisation of power and of the news media . . . [the students' revolt] attacks those who pretend to be the custodians of authority and knowledge. It attacks those who, in their collective practice, teach obedience and conformism along with general knowledge . . . the same structures are in force everywhere with slight variations, and they are supported everywhere by the same mental structures that forbid the creativity of individuals and groups.[42]

If our situation leads us to violence, it is because all society commits violence against us . . . reducing us to slavery by depriving us of our humanity. . . We must reject the creation of a *hierarchy* of *values* and *authorities*, so that each one becomes the informer of another in order the better to direct all the workers in the most complete liberty.[43]

Examinations seemed to students the very essence of these hierarchical structures of repression and imposed conformity: they 'kept culture in confinement for the benefit of the few' by rigorous elimination all the way up the educational ladder; they made possible the 'private property of knowledge' and turned people into sheep.[44] In opposition to all this, the students demanded *autogestion* (self-management), a sharing of power in which power hierarchies would be abolished and everyone, workers and students alike, would be free to participate both in knowledge and in the decisions affecting them; they demanded 'recognition of the plurality of tendencies and schools of thought, as a law of democracy';[45] and having found themselves allied during the events of May with the subproletariat, the unemployed and other marginal and excluded groups, as well as with manual and technical workers, they rejected the idea that 'only workers are revolutionary', arguing that 'the revolutionaries are all those who are crushed and excluded by an inhuman system', and conceiving of revolution in the image of May 1968, as permanent *'contestation'*, 'permanent guerrilla harassment from key zones by active minorities'.[46] Foucault and most of the 'New Left' said and wrote much the same things after 1971.[47]

By 1970, there were more than a hundred students, militant workers and left wing intellectuals in prison, many of whom had been given heavy prison sentences and deprived for life of all civil and family rights. In October 1970, the Maoist Alain Geismar, a former General Secretary of the National Union of University Teaching Personnel and at that time leader of the *Gauche Prolétarienne* group was imprisoned. The *Gauche Prolétarienne* group was sharply anti-authoritarian, criticising not only employers and official bourgeois authorities, but also the 'little bosses' in the factories, in the unions and elsewhere whom they considered 'undercover agents' of power.[48] In 1971, after prison riots and a hunger strike among leftist political prisoners, Foucault and a small group of intellectuals started the *Groupe d'Information sur les Prisons* (GIP) to make it possible for the prisoners to be heard and to enable them to speak about what was happening in the prisons. And Foucault explained that, like the Maoist prisoners, GIP allied itself with the common law prisoners as well as with the political prisoners in the belief that 'ultimately the prison's elimination of common law prisoners was part of the system of political elimination of which [the political prisoners] were themselves the victims'; that 'that fringe of the lower class, at the outset under the domination of police pressures' must be 'reintegrated into political struggles'; and that 'ultimately committing a misdemeanour, committing a crime, questions the way society functions in a most fundamental way'.[49] Foucault's lectures at the Collège de France in the academic year 1971–72 were devoted to penal theories and institutions and to the relations between knowledge and power.

Surveiller et Punir, which appeared in 1975, incorporated all these themes into a schema taken over from *Histoire de la Folie*.[50] To make this clear, Foucault opens *Surveiller et Punir* with what can only be described as a double introduction. The first introduction picks up from *Histoire de la Folie*: it describes two essentially different modes of punishment which Foucault had either touched on or dealt with reasonably extensively in the earlier book. The first, in force between 1670 and the French Revolution, punished crimes by public execution and protracted physical suffering; it made judgment a secret process and punishment a public spectacle. The second mode of punishment, which was introduced at the end of the eighteenth and beginning of the nineteenth century, at the same time as the asylums, and which is still in force today, makes judgment a public spectacle and punishment a secret process. It conceives of the criminal as a psychological individual who has to be 'corrected' or 'cured' by deprivation of freedom and the judicious application of discipline; it gives the 'expert' – the psychiatrist, psychologist, social worker or warden – the same judgmental role as is performed by doctors and wardens in the asylums; and it turns men into objects of knowledge. From this point of view, *Surveiller et Punir* is a 'genealogy of the present-day scientifico-juridical complex' (SP, 27). It is a history of the process by which this modern, 'scientific', psychological and juridical mode of punishment came into being.

The second part of the introduction addresses itself to the relation of power and knowledge. Here power is viewed in both Deleuzian senses: as political relations of domination and subjection and as something intrinsic to the act of interpretation. In the first sense, power is a positive political technology geared to producing productive and subjected bodies; it is not a privilege possessed by someone, but 'a network of relations, always in tension, always in movement' (SP, 31), and it penetrates the entire 'body politic'. In the second sense, the sense in which 'Power and knowledge directly imply one another' (SP, 33) what is in question is the series of interpretative systems which create the knowing subject, the objects to be known, and the modalities of knowledge, and which make man an object of knowledge to himself. Foucault argues that the two are connected in so far as 'a specific mode of subjection gave birth to man as an object of knowledge for a discourse with scientific status' (SP, 28–9), and in so far as the modern 'soul' (variously and 'scientifically' discussed in terms of the psyche, the personality, subjectivity or consciousness) is something that 'exists' as a result of a particular technology of power and subjection. Since, by definition, this technology of power penetrates the entire body politic, its effects extend beyond the prisoners of the scientifico-juridical complex to all those who are disciplined, controlled, corrected, drilled and watched in society: 'the mad, the children, pupils, the colonised and those fixed in an apparatus of production who are controlled throughout their existence' (SP, 34). From this point of view, *Surveiller et Punir* is a 'genealogy of the modern soul', a history of the way it came into being as a result of a particular technology of power and control which extends throughout society. This aspect of genealogy presents society as the students saw it in 1968: as a system of permanent repression and control, where the same mental and physical structures appear with slight variations in the policing institutions, in the educational institutions, and in the factories, and it uses the prisons to 'question the way society functions in a most fundamental way'.

In the first two parts of *Surveiller et Punir*, Foucault combines these different elements of his two 'genealogies' by his positioning of the system of judgment and punishment. Judgment and punishment, now viewed as the power to judge and to punish, and as processes which are productive of some sort of truth, are positioned on the dividing line between the towns or communities and the spaces of exclusion. As a result, the truths they manifest or proclaim and the practices they are empowered to adopt look both ways – to the community and to the criminal excluded from it – and have implications for both.

In the first system of punishment, in force up to the French Revolution, the establishment of the truth about the crime was the absolute right and exclusive power of the sovereign and of the judges to whom he delegated this power. The multitude had no say in the matter. This is why criminal proceedings up to sentencing were kept secret both from the public and from the accused. There were rules about how the truth about the crime was to be established and the judge was a specialist in so far as he alone understood the rules about the different kinds of admissible proof and the arithmetic of their addition into appropriate penalties. But he was also an administrator of the full force of absolute power, since he was entitled to extract confessions from the accused by torture. Torture was perceived as a truth-producing ritual: it was connected to the old trials by ordeal or by duel in which victory was thought to manifest the judgment of God. In the inquisitorial process, torture was perceived as a confrontation between accuser and accused in which the accused could manifest the truth of his innocence by holding out against the physical ordeal. Confession, on the other hand was seen as a victory for both power and truth: it represented the strongest possible proof of the truth of the accusation and also a complete victory over the accused, since it forced him to participate in the proceedings against him and made him acknowledge the truth of the accusation and of the punishment.

Confession and torture were also essential elements in the public execution of criminals, but here they were directed not to the criminal, but to the community. In an elaborate ceremonial, the criminal paraded through the town, carrying on his body a placard proclaiming his crime and confessing his guilt, to make visible to the populace both the truth of the judgment and the validity of the punishment. In the elaborate ritual of torture, in the 'exquisite anguish' suffered by the victim in the long, drawn-out process of dying, in the cutting up and crushing of his body after death, another kind of truth was made manifest to the populace: the truth of the king's absolute power over the people and of his right to take revenge on those who, in infringing his law, affronted his person. The disymmetry between the punishing violence done to the body of the victim and the original crime reactivated the power which had been put in question by the crime and manifested the vast superiority of the king's power over that of his subjects in order, quite simply, to terrify the populace into submission. The function of punishment in the community, therefore, was to implement what Foucault calls a 'politics of fear' (SP, 52) and it had to be all the more impressive to make up for the inadequacies of the mechanisms of crime detection and law enforcement in general.

According to Foucault, several circumstances led to the abolition of public executions and to the substitution of more 'humane' forms of punishment. First among these was the fact that 'the politics of fear' stopped working. Instead of being awed and cowed by public executions, the populace in the second half of the eighteenth century began to rebel against them, snatching victims from the scaffold, turning them into popular heroes, and making the ceremonial of punishment an occasion for public riot and disturbance. It was at this point that theorists began to argue that the sovereign power manifest on such occasions was a demonstration of tyranny which provoked revolt and did nothing for the criminal at all. No less important, was a change in the attitude to 'illegalisms'. As a result of a new capitalist order in which wealth was tied not to land but to property, a whole series of illegal practices, especially those involving theft, which had been widespread and acceptable during the *Ancien Régime*, came to seem a threat. Raw materials, tools, manufactured goods in ports, depots, factories and warehouses were hard to guard, and widespread petty theft could amount to a considerable loss of wealth for the entrepreneur. The new methods of judgment and punishment were therefore designed 'to make punishment and the repression of illegalisms a regular function coextensive with society; not to punish less, but to punish better; to punish with reduced severity, perhaps, but to punish with more universality and necessity; to insert the power to punish more deeply into the social body' (SP, 84). Instead of a few brutal and dramatic punishments to offset a general tolerance of illegalisms and a general inability to enforce the law, there was to be a chequer-work of mechanisms of prevention and enforcement to check and punish all crime, however petty, wherever it occurred.

The first such mechanism was preventive and aimed primarily at the community. Unlike the public executions, it operated 'no longer on the body, but on the soul' (SP, 103). It consisted, as one contemporary pointed out, of 'binding people with the chain of their ideas' (SP, 105) by creating a mental association of crime and punishment and a habitual union of the idea of the criminal with the idea of a traitor and outcast. To associate the possible benefits of crime with the greater disadvantages of punishment, a code of all possible infractions of the law and their corresponding punishments was drawn up and publicised. A centralised system of police vigilance was developed to ensure, as far as possible, that no crime escaped justice, and that no idea of improbability disturbed the association of crime and punishment. And the trial, the process of judgment, was made public, but made public in such a way as to ensure that the logic of crime and punishment and the nature of their association was understandable to all. The obscurities of scholastic 'proofs' which were comprehensible only to experts were therefore replaced by manifest common sense, sensible evidence, 'scientific' demonstrations and the magistrate's explanatory 'summing up'. The criminal, on the other hand, was placed 'on the other side' of the line between the communities and the spaces of exclusion: he was presented as a creature who had broken and betrayed the social contract on which community life was based and who had thus disqualified himself from citizenship; he was portrayed as the enemy of all, as 'a villain, a monster, a madman perhaps, a sick person and eventually as someone "abnormal"' (SP, 104). A criminal was someone whose character, *milieu* and history made him likely to repeat his offence and who therefore represented a danger to the community. Because considerations of prevention were paramount, one-off crimes of passion were treated with relative leniency and punishment was conceived as a process of 'correcting' the criminal so that he would not offend again.

According to Foucault, two 'objectivations' of crime and the criminal were produced by these tactics of prevention. The exclusion of the criminal to the 'other side' of the boundary line made possible the scientific objectivation and treatment of the criminal by psychologists, criminologists and social workers, as the exclusion of the mad in *Histoire de la Folie* made possible the scientific objectivation of mental illness. And the codification of crime and punishment and the nature of the trial established crime as a fact to be determined according to common norms, and made the criminal an individual to be known by specific criteria, such as milieu, character, history, likelihood of further offences etc.

By 1810, imprisonment was no longer conceived as mere detention of the criminal, but was viewed as a positive process of correction. An attempt was made to give prisoners the habit of discipline by forced labour, by a strict timetable which determined what they must be doing at every moment of the day, by a system of obligations and interdicts, by isolation in cells, and by continual surveillance. Like the cure of madness in the asylums, correction of prisoners in the prisons depended on the relationship established between the prisoner and the wardens who subjected to surveillance, drilled, controlled, corrected, penalised and rewarded him. Punishment became a secret process because, like the doctor as the agent of cure in the asylums, the warden as the agent of punishment in the prisons needed to exercise absolute power over the inmates, without distraction or interference from the outside. At the same time, as the surveillance of the mad in the asylums produced a whole body of knowledge about madmen, so the surveillance of prisoners and the prison's task of correction produced a whole body of 'knowledge' about the criminal: reports about his history, the circumstances of his crime, about what was said during his interrogation and during his trial, about his behaviour before and after sentencing, about his daily behaviour in the prison. As a technique of punishment with its own rules, method and knowledge, which fixed its own norms and was empowered to decide when prisoners were 'ready' to be released, the prison became relatively autonomous from the judiciary.

In the third part of *Surveiller et Punir*, Foucault attempts to show why this form of imprisonment became the almost exclusive form of punishment at the beginning of the nineteenth century, and why it has remained so to this day. He describes the early nineteenth century as he had described the Classical period in *Histoire de la Folie*: as a period obsessed with order which excluded and endeavoured to control everything that smacked of disorder. But he adds that the nineteenth century saw the threat to order as coming not only from floating populations unable to integrate with the community (the poor, the vagabonds, the unemployed, the criminal and the mad), but also as coming from the demographic growth of the population and from the new 'multiplicities' of soldiers, pupils, ill people and workers. He argues that the early nineteenth century developed 'disciplines' in all areas of life to 'order human multiplicities' (SP, 219), to neutralise resistance, agitations and revolts, to nullify everything which makes a multiplicity unmalleable, and to turn people into 'docile and useful bodies'.

'Disciplines', as they evolved in the early nineteenth century, were detailed techniques to subject and utilise the forces of the mind and the body, to transform and perfect them for the productive tasks they must perform in the schools, the factories, the army or the hospitals, and to ensure the conformity and 'good behaviour' of all elements of the population by constant surveillance and control. Disciplines 'individualised' people the better to subject them to surveillance and to control them – they separated and distinguished people from each other, they classified them, giving each his place in hierarchies of competence, ability, class and behaviour, and they collected knowledge about each of them.

If the prisons became disciplinary institutions with their drilling, their training, their rigid timetables, their prescribed obligations and interdicts, their cellular structure and their constant surveillance by wardens empowered to reward and penalise, therefore, it was because these disciplinary 'fretworks' were developed in the community and 'projected . . . onto the confused space of internment' (SP, 200–1). At the end of the eighteenth and beginning of the nineteenth century, the prison was recreated in the image of society; or, alternatively, society became like a prison. While criminals and madmen were being enclosed in corrective prisons and curative asylums, the army was being interned in barracks for the first time; students were being interned in colleges; the ill, who had previously been treated at home, were being interned in hospitals; and workers, who had previously occupied dispersed workshops, were being enclosed together in factories. Not only were the same disciplinary techniques used in all these institutions; but they all came to be characterised by a 'binary division and stamping (mad–non mad, dangerous–harmless, normal–abnormal)' (SP, 201). In the prisons and the asylums, in the schools and factories, in the hospitals and in the army, the dangerous were separated from the harmless, the academicaly able from the less able, the skilled from the unskilled, the ill from the contagiously ill, the well-behaved from the badly behaved. In factories and in schools, in prisons and in the military, people were classified and organised serially according to their abilities and the tasks to be performed: in the schools, there were now classes and positions within each class, there was a timetable and a syllabus of graduated studies; in the factories, workers were positioned according to their skill in the different phases of manufacture; in prisons, there was classification according to crime and according to behaviour; and everywhere there were hierarchies of skill, of behaviour, of responsibility and authority. Supervisors, foremen, drill sergeants, wardens, teachers and overseers were empowered to surveille everyone constantly, to make sure that each person did the exercises or performed the tasks required of him according to the timetable and according to specific norms of performance and behaviour, without waste of time, distraction, or 'unnecessary' communication with others. They were also empowered to constantly 'examine' the performance and behaviour of the prisoners, pupils, workers, madmen or soldiers in their charge, and to reward or penalise them accordingly. 'At the heart of all disciplinary systems,' says Foucault, 'there is a small penal mechanism. . . the disciplines establish 'infra-penalties' in a space left empty by the laws' (SP, 180). Lateness, absences, interruptions of work, inattention, carelessness, lack of zeal, rudeness, disobedience, chit-chat, insolence, immodesty, and any other departure from the required conformity were penalised and 'corrected'.

From the nineteenth century on, therefore, the prison with its high walls and secret work of drilling, training, control, correction, punishment and surveillance was no longer at the gates of the community; it was 'built in the midst of nineteenth-century towns' as a 'material and symbolic expression' of what Foucault calls 'the disciplinary society' (SP, 118). It was also built in the hearts of men, in so far as, knowing himself to be constantly watched and examined in his performance and behaviour, the subject of this disciplinary strategy of power began to watch, examine and control himself, thus becoming 'the principle of his own subjection' (SP, 204). From this point of view, the prison, and most notably Bentham's Panopticon, with its central tower for surveillance surrounded by a ring of cells in which each prisoner was individually visible to the tower, becomes 'a generalisable model for the functioning and a manner of defining the relation of power to men's everyday lives' (SP, 206–7). For the tower does its work whether or not there is actually anyone in it watching and whoever is assigned to do the watching, because the prisoner in his cell cannot actually see who is watching or indeed if there is anyone watching him at all. The tower is a visible but unverifiable symbol of power which makes the internee behave as though he is being watched and examined even when he is not. This system of surveillance precludes the need to constrain the prisoner to good behaviour, the madman to calm, the pupil to application, the worker to work. And as power begins to operate automatically and impersonally in the subject who supposes himself watched and examined and who begins to watch and examine himself, 'real subjection is born mechanically from a fictive relation' (SP, 204). As the placing of criminals and madmen on the 'other side' of the boundary line made them objects of observation, which in turn made possible the development of psychological, psychiatric, criminological and statistical knowledge about them, so the constant surveillance and examination of pupils, workers, patients, and soldiers transformed the population into observed and classified individuals and made possible the accumulation of enormous amounts of documented information about each individual as well as the development of the human sciences. The examination of pupils by teachers, of patients by doctors and psychiatrists, of clients by social workers, of prisoners by wardens, of workers by managers and foremen, produces a documentary archive about each individual and turns him into a 'case'. The human sciences could build on this and within this, by treating the individual as a describable and analysable object with its singular traits, particular evolution and peculiar capacities in an attempt to acquire total and permanent knowledge of him. Or they could treat individuals comparatively, describing groups or collective facts, measuring norms and departures from the norm, in an attempt to acquire total and permanent knowledge of the population. Either way, the individual is objectified; he is turned into an object and viewed as an other by an other. Produced in the first instance by the disciplinary techniques of a power which made multiplicities docile and useful by separating them into manageable units and by keeping subjects distinct from each other, the subjected subject became an object of knowledge to the human sciences and to the institutions of power. Subjection, subjectivation and objectivation, Foucault argues, are inseparable from one another.

The transformation of the community into a disciplinary and 'carceral' society does not, for Foucault, preclude the continued existence of spaces of exclusion. These spaces, now occupied by delinquents 'fabricated' by the prisons, differ from earlier spaces of exclusion in so far as their occupants, too, are transformed into docile and useful bodies. Foucault argues that the disciplinary society substitutes for the uncontrollable mass of vagabonds and occasional criminals 'a relatively closed and limited group of individuals over which it is possible to maintain constant surveillance' and that 'delinquency, that other, dangerous and often hostile world, blocks or at least maintains the current illegalist practices at a relatively low level (small thefts, small acts of violence, embezzlement)' (SP, 283). Some delinquent milieux, he says, like prostitution, are actively controlled by the disciplinary forces of society (health checks, the establishment of houses of prostitution etc.). And delinquents are useful to the police as spies, informers, *agents provocateurs*, and strike-breakers.

The presence in the towns of the prisons, the schools, the hospitals, the factories and the barracks, each with its high walls and hidden mechanisms of surveillance and discipline makes Foucault's title for this book – *Surveiller et Punir: Naissance de la Prison* (Surveillance and Punishment: The Birth of the Prison) – as ironical and as much of a *renversement* of our expectations as *Histoire de la Folie*. Foucault pointed out that *Histoire de la Folie* was not in fact a history of a particular psychological type, the madman; and he pointed out that *Surveiller et Punir* was not in fact a history of the 'prison-institution', but of the 'practice of imprisonment'.[51] In *Histoire de la folie*, Foucault explored the madness of the community in alienating certain people, certain truths, and certain aspects of itself. In *Surveiller et Punir*, he explores the imprisonment of the community in its own surveillance and punishment, the way the 'programming of conduct' has alienated the subject from control over the forces of his own mind and body, and the way the mechanisms of power and knowledge have alienated subjects from each other by making them objects of surveillance, control and knowledge to each other. If the prison was originally conceived as a deprivation of liberty, and if the deprivation of liberty was originally considered a punishment, then the disciplinary society which deprives its members of freedom by imposing conformity, by defining 'normality' and by exercising unrelenting control over all aspects of men's institutional lives is also a society in which life is constant punishment. Foucault reverses our current assumptions about the liberty, equality and democracy of Western society by showing that discipline is the 'substratum of formal and legal liberties', that it acts as a sort of 'counter-legality', and that it creates dissymmetries as insurmountable as those of absolute sovereignty by subordinating people, by qualifying and disqualifying them according to their docility and usefulness, and by normatively classifying them in hierarchies in relation to each other (SP, 224). The pattern of surveillance and punishment which the community supposes it has reserved for the spaces of exclusion is thus shown by Foucault to have been materially and mentally integrated in what Foucault calls 'the carceral town' all along. And as in *Histoire de la Folie*, the excluded and alienated 'other' turns out to be ourselves.

THE DIVIDED SUBJECT AND THE DEATH OF MAN

Les Mots et les Choses, the book which established Foucault's reputation in 1966, is an account of the birth of the divided being we call man and an argument for his demise. It is a description of 'the great caesuras, the furrows, the divisions in the Western *episteme* which chiselled out the profile of man and expose it to possible knowledge' (MCH, 390); and it is its *renversement*, the outline and model of a form of knowledge which would erase the divisions, flatten out the furrows, and allow man to merge once more into the substance from which he was hewn.

In some respects, *les Mots et les Choses* is the methodological counterpart of *Histoire de la Folie*. Like *Histoire de la Folie*, *Les Mots et les Choses* deals with three historical periods – the Renaissance, the Classical and the modern – each of which is shown to have its own *ratio* and coherence. Where *Histoire de la Folie* approached the boundary line between the community and the spaces of exclusion from outside the town walls, through all that the community made Other to itself, *Les Mots et les Choses* approaches the boundary line from within the town, through the different ways in which the community positively constituted its space of inclusion. Foucault calls the principles governing a space of inclusion an *episteme*. Epistemic principles determine what objects can be identified by the community, how they can be marked, and in what ways they can be ordered; they make certain perceptions, certain statements, certain forms of knowledge possible, others impossible; and by regulating diverse aspects of the community's mental activity, they stamp these diverse activities with a certain fundamental Sameness. Where *Histoire de la Folie* could be described as a 'history of the Other', therefore, *Les Mots et les Choses* may be described as 'a history of the Same', and these are, in principle, but two sides of the same fence (MCH, 15–6).

In fact, in practice they are not exactly two sides of the same fence, and history in *Les Mots et les Choses* is no more than a distant echo of history in *Histoire de la Folie*. For in *Les Mots et les Choses* Foucault reconstructs history to support an argument: the argument that the divided figure of man 'invented' at the beginning of the nineteenth century is responsible for the antinomies and impasses of contemporary thought, and that these can be overcome by effacing the figure of man and by using a new *episteme* modelled on the Renaissance and Classical periods when man, in his present form, was not. This argument leads Foucault to narrow his field of interest to three purely theoretical areas of knowledge which, in his view, form the pre-history of the modern vision of man as a living, working and speaking being. And it leads him to give the *episteme* of the Renaissance and Classical periods an artificial unity and an unproblematical simplicity they lacked both in *Histoire de la Folie* and in the periods in question.

Thus, for instance, in *Histoire de la Folie* the Renaissance was a period which knew the complexities both of the 'tragic folly of the world' and of the 'critical consciousness of madness'. In *Les Mots et les Choses*, the Renaissance is centred entirely on the figure of Resemblance. It is a period when all things were conceived as fundamentally similar to each other. Whether by virtue of proximity (like body and soul) or by reflection (as the human intellect reflects God's wisdom or the eyes, the stars), whether by analogy (the stars are to the sky as the grass is to the earth) or by the call of sympathy, all things in the world mirrored each other. Nature was a book read by using surface resemblances as the visible signs of hidden correspondences. Man appeared in nature as a privileged focus for such correspondences: he was a microcosm which mirrored the macrocosmic order of the earth, sky, stars, winds and storms; he was like all things and all things were like him. And language, too, was seen as a thing of nature. In grammar, letters, syllables and words were studied for their essential properties and fundamental affinities. Words were thought to be signs of things, linked by a profound similitude to the things they designated, so that discourse was fundamentally the image of what it stated. But language as a thing of nature had also, like nature, fallen from its first pristine transparency, and like nature too, it now both manifested and hid its truth. Texts, therefore, had to be interpreted to reveal their secret discourse and hidden truth. The Renaissance was the age of commentary and of the esoteric text.

Interpretation, then, was the Renaissance's characteristic form of knowledge. In a world where all things were held to secretly echo one another and where everything called for interpretation, the task of interpretation might at first sight appear to be infinite. But Foucault points out that these characteristics of the Renaissance world in fact define the limits of interpretation. Because all things echoed and repeated each other, interpretation was 'condemned to always know the same thing', albeit by a process of indefinitely extensible analogy (MCH, 45). Because nature and language were both writings to be deciphered, interpretation made no distinction between what was seen and what was read, between what had been observed and what reported. For instance, a Renaissance natural history of the serpent would assemble information about the serpent's feeding habits, habitat, physical characteristics and prescriptions for the cure of bites with mythology, legends, miracles and the etymology and synonyms of the word serpent. Finally, as graphically demonstrated by the correspondence between microcosm and macrocosm, far from being infinitely open and extensible, interpretation was in fact enclosed within the well-defined perimeters of the world: 'Nature as a play of signs and resemblances closes itself up upon itself in the duplicated figure of the cosmos' (MCH, 46).

In the Classical period, when the epistemic centre shifted from Resemblance to the perception of Identity and Difference, Resemblance came to occupy the outer perimeters of knowledge. It was viewed as the indistinct and unreliable basis for the serious work of establishing clear identities and differences among things. And it became the property of the madman (who finds resemblances everywhere) and of the poet (who explores the hidden affinities and secret truth of things). Resemblance thus came to be identified with two figures who, according to Foucault, occupy a position 'at the outer edge of our culture and close to its essential divisions, a position "at the limit" – with a marginal posture and profoundly archaic silhouette which gave their speech its strangeness and its power of contestation' (MCH, 63–4).

For, in the classical period, the central task of knowledge was no longer to link everything together; it was to distinguish things. Knowledge now endeavoured to discern things clearly: it compared them in ordered successions proceeding from the simplest to the most complex; it organised the system of their identities and differences in the simultaneous space of a 'table'. Succession and classification did not reflect the order of things – in nature, things are not found beside each other either in graduated series or in classificatory groupings. Succession and identification reflected an order of thought – a sequence or structure of representations in the mind. Language was accordingly separated from things. It was no longer a thing of nature linked to things by a fundamental similitude and containing hidden depths. Language was now conceived in a new way as a representation of the representations in the mind. Words were signs marking thoughts. They were neutral instruments, ideas of things conventionally used to represent the ideas of other things. As the Port Royale Grammar put it: 'The sign enclosed two ideas, one of the thing which represents and the other of the thing represented, and its nature consists in exciting the first by the second' (MCH, 78). And Foucault points out that Saussurian binarisim begins here.

The separation of words and things and the preoccupation with ordering things according to their identities and differences was characteristic of the Classical period as the resemblance between words and things and the preoccupation with interpretation had been characteristic of the Renaissance *episteme*. And in the Classical period, according to Foucault, nature, wealth and language itself were all reformulated in terms of representation and systematically ordered.

General grammar, for instance, classified parts of speech according to the different ways they represented ideas. It argued that the verb, which represented judgments and attributions of being differed from the noun, which named or designated specific representations. Like the noun, the adjective designated representations, but unlike it, it only designated traits never found on their own. Like the verb, prepositions, conjunctions and other syntactical signs represented relations among representations, but unlike the verb, these had value only within the proposition and did not represent an attribution of being. At the same time, general grammar placed parts of speech in graduated series: all verbs for instance came down to the simplest and most fundamental verb, the verb to be, which was inherent in more complex verbs, and which represented both a judgment of being and the affirmative nature of language; and nouns were thought to move, like representations themselves, from the individual to the species to the genre and the class in graduated sequences of increasing generality.

But while language was conceived as identical with thought, it was also perceived as differing from thought: for instance, language presents what appears simultaneously to the mind in a linear order, one word after another, and this linear order differs in different languages. According to Foucault, this discrepancy opened up a critical dimension in the classical *episteme* lacking in the Renaissance, when all commentary was interpretation and all interpretation was a restatement of the discourse hidden beneath the discourse being interpreted. Where commentary 'sacralised' the text, the classical critique of texts judged the adequacy of its images, figures and order of discourse to the ideas being represented. Similarly, the classical critique of grammar judged the adequacy of different grammars (declensional or prepositional, fixed or free) to the representation of ideas. And the classical critique of words showed the impossibility of building an adequate science and philosophy with ordinary words which confuse what is distinct and separate what belongs together, and it argued the need for an adequately analytical language. Consequently, Classical discourse was preoccupied with the task of naming represented things and of naming them in such a way as to indicate their being. When Classical discourse named the being of all representations in general, it became philosophy: the analysis of ideas and the theory of knowledge. When Classical discourse gave each represented thing an appropriate name and covered a field of representations with a network of appropriate words, it became science: labelling and classification.

According to Foucault, the separation of words and things made possible the separation of what was observed and represented in the mind from what was read or believed without observation, and it thus made possible the creation of a science based on observation. But because mental representations were conceived as being essentially visual, and because names were signs of mental representations, scientific observation was confined to the field of visibility. 'To observe', says Foucault, 'was to content oneself with seeing. To see a very few things systematically. To see in the somewhat confused wealth of representations what could be analysed, recognised by all and given a name everyone could agree upon (MCH, 146). Classical science labelled and classified only what was immediately visible. Excluding functions and invisible inner tissues, botanists described plants in terms of four surface phenomena: the form of elements, their number, their proportion and their distribution in space relative to each other. These surface phenomena defined what botanists called a 'structure', and this structure made it possible to classify plants according to their identities and differences. The extension of these methods to minerals and animals made life little more than a classificatory characteristic in the table on which all natural things were ordered in a continuum.

As everything in nature was now representable by the analytical language of science, so wealth was now representable by money. In the Renaissance, money had been a real mark of wealth, because it was itself a precious metal (gold or silver); like words, it had the same reality as what it said. But in the Classical period, money derived its value not from its substance but from its function as a sign. Money became a sign which represented the need or desire of the people exchanging goods or services for the goods or services being exchanged. It varied in value according to the quantity of merchandise available, according to the quantity of coin in circulation and according to peoples' needs and desires. In the Classical period, therefore, the analysis of wealth concentrated on trying to determine the quantity of money that must be in circulation to represent things in such a way as to ensure that the price of goods and services did not rise too fast, that the balance of trade remained favourable, and that the population remained at subsistence level at least in the numbers required by the work force.

The Classical *episteme* began to break down, Foucault argues, when things began to be perceived as having an internal organisation of their own which did not correspond to the order of representations in the mind. General grammar, natural history and the analysis of wealth began to move behind immediate visibility into an architectural space where relations between parts were determined by function rather than by identity and difference. Thus, in natural history, the surface structure of animals and plants began to be referred to the vital functions of organs hidden deep within the body. Life, with its functions of reproduction, growth and nutrition and its inevitable proximity to death now determined the organisation – and the ordering – of natural beings. And it constituted a field where things occurred in their own way, according to their own laws, and 'in a space other than that of words' (MCH, 243). By the same token, wealth ceased to be a question of how people represented by money their need or desire for what was being exchanged. It began to be measured in terms of work, the function of which was productivity. And this productivity was seen as depending on the organisation of conditions like the division of labour, the progress of machinery, and the accumulation of capital which had their own laws and necessities and which were deployed in a space that was not the space of the mind. General grammar, too, shifted its emphasis from the study of grammar as a representation of the order of ideas in the mind to the study of grammar as a formal organisation of elements grouped in a system which imposes on words and syllables their signification in a regime which is not that of representation. At the turn of the nineteenth century, then, language, life and work began to be seen as having their own organisation, as occupying their own space, and as 'defining an internal space which, for our representation, is on the *outside*' (MCH, 252).

From this point on, Foucault argues, 'the epistemological field breaks up into pieces, or rather, it splinters in different directions' (MCH, 357).

The effect of seeing things in terms of their own proper organisation was to make them discontinuous from each other. The possibility of modern psychology arose, according to Foucault, when the mind came to be seen as having an organisation distinct from that of things. Modern philology was born when language became an autonomous phenomenon, with an organisation different from that of thought and that of things. Economics replaced the analysis of wealth when work and productivity came to be perceived as processes unfolding independently of representation. And modern biology and geology carved up natural history when the organisation of living beings was viewed as separate and distinct from that of 'dead' inorganic matter.

The effect of seeing things in terms of their own organisation was also to historicise them, for, unlike the timeless tables of identity and difference in the Classical period, organisations were perceived as unfolding in time. History became to the modern *episteme* what order had been to the Classical, 'the mode of being of all that is given to us in experience . . . that in our thought which cannot be circumvented' (MCH, 231). And in the nineteenth century, economics, biology and philology gave work, life and language an origin and development in time. Ricardo, for instance, argued that the need to work derived from an original shortage of products of the earth which made work necessary to provide enough food for the population. Men worked under the threat of death, in an attempt to survive, and the more men there were, the more they would have to work to find new resources and new lands to exploit until the time when the population became stagnant and the lands sufficed. Cuvier linked the organisation of living organisms to the external phenomena each used to maintain and develop its own structure and to the conditions which made its existence possible. He thus laid the groundwork not only for the notion of evolution, but also for the temporal notion of life as an organism's struggle to stave off death and to maintain itself, however briefly, in its conditions of existence. With Bopp, philology began to root language not in a judgment of being but in the expressive needs of acting subjects. And once changes in language were seen as manifesting changes in the fundamental activity and 'will' expressed by people who spoke, languages could be studied historically as manifestations of the 'spirit' of peoples.

The modern epistemic concept of organisation thus fragmented the smooth, well-ordered plane of classical knowledge by making the organisations and histories of different things discontinuous from one another and discontinuous within themselves. In the process, it shattered the classical continuum between words, representations and things; it produced the modern situation in which, on the one hand, there are things with their own organisations in space and, on the other, there are representations which succeed one another in time and only partially convey things to a subjectivity; and it created modern man as a being who is divided both from things and from himself.

For once things had their own internal organisation which was external to representation, the mind could no longer, as in the Classical period, fully encompass things; something always escaped its representations. Life, language and work were functions which made it possible to describe the inner organisation of empirical forms of production, of empirical natural beings and of empirical languages. But they themselves did not exist except in the empirical things they made it possible to explain; they had no independent empirical existence, and what they were in themselves could therefore not be known. By the same token, once the order of representations in the mind no longer corresponded to the order of things, representations had to be conceived as having their own organisation and their own laws. And the coherence of this organisation could only be grounded, as the coherence of natural, economic and linguistic things had been grounded, in a function which could provide principles of organisation, but which itself had no empirical reality – the function of Subjectivity. Subjectivity on the side of the subject and Work, Language and Life on the side of the object were 'transcendental' in the Kantian sense: that is to say, they were purely a priori concepts or principles which provided the structure necessary to organise what is given empirically in experience. The concept of organisation thus produced a double division: a vertical division between Subject and Objects, each of which had their own inner organisation; and a horizontal division within these organisations, between an empirical level and a transcendental level.

The division between subject and object not only divided man from things, it also divided man from himself. For man appeared on both sides of the divide: he appeared both as an object of knowledge and as the subject who knows. Philology, biology and economics studied language, life and productivity as organisations with their own laws; but they also placed man in the midst of these organisations and in the midst of these laws. Man was the one who spoke to express his will and his activity in different ways at different times, and he was the one whose words derived their signification from the prior organisation of language. Man was an organism governed by its vital functions, struggling to stave off death and to maintain itself in its conditions of existence. Man was the being who worked to survive, to offset the deficiencies of nature and to produce enough food to live; and he was the one subject to the division of labour, the progress of machinery and all the conditions of productivity. In philology, economics and biology, man was a speaking, working and living being. But as a speaking, working and living being, he was also bounded and finite; he was a creature circumscribed by death and dominated by the conditions of his existence and the laws of his language, who could only be known via his words, his organism and the things he produces. On the subjective side of the divide, where he figured as the subjectivity trying to know himself via his words, his organism and the things he produces, man appeared as equally finite and bounded. He experienced himself as living within the confines of a body which occupies a space among things, as having 'speaking thoughts' which he threads into a line of words, and as driven by desires which determine the value of all things for him and make the economic conditions of his existence a burden. Thus on both sides of the Subject–Object divide, 'finiteness echoes itself' (MCH, 326). Modern man is finite, as Renaissance and Classical man were not: in the Renaissance when man was the microcosmic centre of all correspondences, he was like the whole world and the whole world was like him; in the Classical period, when the representations of his mind were the locus for the synthesis of all words and all things, his representations potentially opened onto infinity. Only in the modern period, Foucault insists, is man bounded to the comparatively narrow and finite spheres of Life, Work and Language.

The horizontal division between an empirical level at which things are given and a transcendental level which provides the a priori principles for ordering what is given also split man off both from things and from himself. It split man off from things by creating two distinct levels of scientific knowledge and the continuing problem of how to relate them. On the empirical level, it created the 'positivist' inductive sciences, which describe the organisational laws of phenomena, but not their fundamental rationale. And on the transcendental level, it created the purely formal deductive a priori sciences based on mathematics and logic which are supposed to give the empirical sciences their structure and coherence. The empirical–transcendental division split man off from himself in the same way. It divided him into an empirical part – the life he lives, the thoughts he has, the words he speaks, the work he does – the logic of which escapes his immediate experience, and a transcendental part – the act of thought by which he grasps and structures this 'unthought' level of being. To Foucault, then, the unconscious, in all its senses, is not something discovered when scientific thought started treating man as an object to be known. The unconscious is the unthought. It is all that has not been structured by the *cogito*, whether in man's mind or in his experience of life, work and language. It is the product of a specific *episteme* which separates man's empirical existence from the *cogito* which attempts to grasp it and give it coherence. Man could not conceive of himself as an empirical–transcendental being 'without thought discovering at the same time – both in itself and outside itself, both at its edges and interlaced in its own weave – some part of night, some apparently inert depth which engages it' (MCH, 337).

The figure of man in the modern *episteme* is therefore both finite and fragmented. Man is a living, working and speaking being, but his speech has an organisation and a history which separates it from his work, and his work has a history and organisation which separates it from his organism. Modern man appears, moreover, on both sides of the divisions between Subject and Object, on the transcendental and on the empirical levels, in the *cogito* and in the Unthought. All modern thinking has consequently been an attempt either to reunite man with himself and his world or to reunite the discontinuous subdivisions of his knowledge. And in the the last part of *Les Mots et les Choses*, Foucault shows how modern thought has tried to do this, why it has failed, and what it ought to do instead.

To bridge the Subject–Object divide, Foucault argues, modern man has made his experience of himself as a finite being living in his body, speaking through his words and valuing things by his desires, the ground and limits of his knowledge. In other words, he has conceived of himself as capable of knowing Life, Work and Language by virtue of the fact that he is a living, working and speaking being; and he has conceived of the limits of knowledge as being constituted by the full repetition in the Subject of what is in the Object. When man has full knowledge of the organisation and history of Life, Language and Work and of the way he figures in them and they figure in him, he presumably has full knowledge of himself and his world, and all divisions are overcome. To have full knowledge means that the *cogito* has grasped all the 'unthought', that nothing remains either on the empirical level of man's subjective experience or in Life, Work and Language which has not been structured and organised by the mind. For to have full knowledge means that man has become conscious of all that has heretofore remained silent and unconscious both within the Subject and within the Object. This is why, Foucault argues,

all modern thought is spanned by the law of thinking the unthought – reflecting in the form of the For-Itself the contents of the In-Itself, disalienating man by reconciling him to his own proper essence, explicating the horizon which gives experiences their backdrop of immediate obviousness, lifting the veil of the unconscious by absorbing oneself in its silence and listening to its indefinite murmur (MCH, 338).

But Foucault shows that this attempt to overcome division and alienation by 'thinking the unthought' and by trying to show 'how the Other, the Distant, is also that which is Closest and the Same' (MCH, 350), is both doomed to failure and completely unnecessary. It is doomed to failure because the Other appears in the modern *episteme* as the necessary and inevitable accompaniment of the modern figure of man. For the Other is not, as far as Foucault is concerned, some mysterious abyss at the heart of man or the world man once made and can no longer recognise as his own. The abyss at the heart of man and the unrecognisable world are aspects of the 'unthought', and 'the unthought . . . is the Other in relation to man' (MCH, 337). Epistemically, the unthought is both a stranger and man's twin brother. It appears strange and distant because it is what escapes the forms of man's knowledge, what fails to echo modern man's finiteness, what man has failed to imprint with the Sameness of his familiar anthropological face. But the unthought is in fact his twin, his double, because it is nothing but the shadow he unknowingly casts as he thinks. The mysterious abyss at the heart of man, the alien and unrecognisable dimensions of existence are products of the empirical–transcendental divide; they are constituted by the very shape of man's thought as what is outside thought. And they should be allowed to remain there. Instead of trying to turn the Other into the Same, Foucault suggests, we should allow the unthought to retain its Otherness and leave it where it is, outside thought. For here it can be used to define the limits of thought and to delineate the configuration of knowledge. The unthought, the Other can be used as the blind spot from which we can see what is being seen and as the position from which we can reassemble the picture of man and see him in his truth. This is how Foucault used the Other in *Histoire de la Folie*, and it is how he has been using the unthought in *Les Mots et les Choses*. For instance, the unlike was the unthought in the Renaissance; the invisible in the Classical period; and Foucault would argue, difference is the unthought in the modern period. The absence of unlikeness makes Renaissance thinking emerge as a network of resemblances; the absence of the invisible makes classical thinking emerge as a representation of visible surfaces; and the absence or intolerance of difference makes our thought emerge as a perpetual movement towards 'the unveiling, which is always yet to be accomplished, of the Same' (MCH, 351).

As modern thought has centred on man as a finite, thinking subject and has endeavoured by 'thinking the unthought' to reunite man with himself and with his world, so the human sciences have centred on man as a finite empirical being and endeavoured to reconstitute his empirical coherence by bringing to light the unconscious processes which govern his life, his work and his speech. The human sciences deal with man in so far as he lives, works and speaks, but, unlike biology, economics and philology, they are not concerned with the inner organisation of Life, Work and Speech. The human sciences are concerned with what men empirically think of themselves, their lives, their work and their language. Psychology, sociology and the study of literature and myth analyse the way men represent to themselves their individual lives, the world in which they live and work and the possibilities of their language. The proper object of the human sciences, therefore, is representation. But the human sciences also go beyond representations into the realm of the unthought by seeking the unconscious determinations of men's representations. To this end, they have borrowed models from biology, economics and linguistics: as in biology, they have conceived of man as having functions to discharge in a given milieu and within given conditions of existence and have sought the norms of adjustment which permit him to discharge his functions; as in economics, they have conceived of man as having needs and desires which bring him into conflict with others and have sought the rules which regulate or exacerbate this conflict; as in philology, they have assumed that man's behaviour, rites, discourses, habits and traces have a meaning and that they form a coherent system of signs. The functions men exercise and the norms which determine them, the conflicts men develop and the rules which regulate them, the significations men give and the linguistic systems which govern them are largely unthought. For men representing their lives and their language to themselves are largely unconscious of the rules, the systems and the norms which predetermine what they say, think and do.

Foucault thinks that in the concepts of function and norm, conflict and rule, signification and system, the human sciences have laid the foundation for a possible form of knowledge. These concepts seem valuable to him in two ways. They seem valuable first in so far as significations originate in and derive from linguistic systems which precede them and show themselves indistinctly through them, and in so far as functions and conflicts derive from norms and rules which precede them and show themselves indistinctly through them. This makes the linguistic system, the rules and the norms unthought or unconscious in relation to the significations of language, the conflicts of men or ideas, and the functions of things, and it reopens the possibility of knowledge as exegesis or interpretation. For it makes the task of knowledge that of discovering the unconscious system, the unthought rules or norms which govern conscious thought, speech or behaviour. And this is precisely what Foucault has been doing in *Les Mots et les Choses*. He has been trying to determine what unconscious epistemic principles, norms and rules have governed the thinking of the community.

The concepts of unconscious system, rule and norm seem valuable to Foucault for another reason too: they make it possible to unify the human sciences' field of knowledge. As long as the human sciences analysed men's representations from the point of view of function (Durkheim, Lévy-Bruhl), of conflict (Marx, Comte) or of signification (Freud), they failed to unify their fields, and they failed to unify the human sciences, because each of their concepts created division. Function created a dichotomy between the normal and the pathological; signification created a dichotomy between the significant and the insignificant; and conflict produced the false alternative between overcoming conflict or being annihilated by it. The concepts of system, norms and rules, on the other hand, allow the human sciences to give each field its own proper coherence, while leaving room for diversity and conflict, or even for dichotomies of value. As it is possible to accommodate the fact that different or opposite things are said within a linguistic system, so it is possible to accomodate the fact that diverse things were thought and that conflicts arose within the set of rules or group of norms which govern an episteme. Similarly, in the field of the human sciences as a whole, the concept of an unconscious governing system makes it possible to unify the field while allowing for pluralism. It makes it possible to treat individual fields of knowledge in isolation as coherent but different systems without detracting from the unity of the system as a whole. This is what Foucault has been doing throught *Les Mots et les Choses*. He has allowed the study of language, the study of money, wealth and productivity and the study of nature their own coherence their own rules, their own concerns and their own history. But he has also brought out their 'unconscious' unity, by showing where they all shared the rule of interpretation, of classification or of organisation, the norm of similitude, or of order or of history, the system of resemblance, of identity and difference, or of empirico-transcendental doubling.

The shortcoming of the human sciences, as far as Foucault is concerned, is that they have not managed to circumvent the primacy of representation and that they have not been properly critical. Because they have remained within representation, they have remained trapped in the empirical–transcendental bind of perpetually trying to go behind representations – their own and those of the men they study – to more and more fundamental, grounding and a priori representations. As a result, they are always trying to show man his 'real conditions', to 'unveil' man's true form and original contents; and they are always trying to demystify themselves. This is also what prevents them from being properly critical – because all that they find at bottom and a priori to set against conscious representations is man in his finitude, man as a living, working, and speaking being who is subject to death, desire and language as law.

The third way in which modern thought has tried to reunite man with himself and his world is in and through history. The problem here is to reconcile two kinds of history or, as Foucault prefers to put it, two kinds of origin. On the one hand, there are the histories of Life, Work and Language, each with their own proper organisation and development. These histories logically require an origin, but its nature remains shrouded in obscurity. On the other hand, there is men's history, which only ever appears against the backdrop of Life, which began long before he came on the scene; he appears historically as a working being only in the context of the most rudimentary forms of work in a society and in a time which have already been 'institutionalised'; he appears as a speaking subject not at the first cry or the first word which can be imagined to have given rise to a language, but in a language that already exists. Man, therefore, is always finite in relation to time; he always originates where something has already begun, is always laden with forms and contents which have preceded him and are outside his control. Modern thought has tried to overcome this dichotomy of histories and origins in two interconnected ways. The first is to try to bring man and things together within human time, by making history the history of man's knowledge and experience of things, and by creating a moment in that history when things are seen for the first time in their full and ineluctable truth. This is to reproduce, in historical terms, the modern *episteme*'s assumption that division will be overcome when everything in the object is repeated in the subject. The other way of overcoming the dichotomy of histories and origins is to project an original moment when man, life, work language were one into the future. This made history from Hegel to Marx and Spengler circular and repetitive – it made the end of history a return to and repetition of an original unity which had retreated into the mists of time. And like modern thought, it made history a perpetual movement towards the unveiling of an essential Sameness, the sameness of all things to man.

These historical modes of reuniting man with himself and his world are therefore unacceptable to Foucault for the same reasons that modern thought's attempts to repeat all things in the Subject and to imprint the same familiar anthropological figure of man on everything were unacceptable to him. But they are also unacceptable to him because they create new divisions on the empirical–transcendental axis. Three divisions are created by the historicisation of man's knowledge and by the creation of a moment in that history when things are seen for the first time in their truth. The first is the division between the empirical, imperfect and developing knowledge of men in history and the stable, definitive 'transcendental' knowledge which shows it up for what it is; the second is a division between illusion and truth, between the ideological chimeras of empirical men and the transcendental truth which shows the historical conditions of these chimeras; the third, and most fundamental, is the division between the positivist empirical analysis of the historical conditions of knowledge and the philosophical analysis of the way true knowledge develops and ultimately emerges in history.

The modern *episteme* is therefore always falling back into its original divisions. Centred on the finite figure of man as an empirical and transcendental being and seeking to unite all hints in and through that figure, modern thought is always moving between two poles: Division and Sameness, the Otherness of things or the repetition of all things in man and of man in all things, the Unthought and its absorption in the *Cogito*. And as Foucault has endeavoured to show, there is no possibility of doing otherwise as long as thought is centred on man. The only way out, as far as Foucault is concerned, is to learn the lesson that the history of knowledge *can* teach: in showing that man's knowledge was empirically grounded in historical conditions, the history of knowledge also showed that its validity was limited to a particular historical episode. It thus undermined any knowledge's pretension to universality and made the relativity of knowledge its absolute.

The way out of the impasse of modern thought is therefore to relativise: to cease to see the anthropological figure of man as the necessary condition of all knowledge and the only possible locus of unity, and to begin to see it as a chronological episode in the history of thought. This, of course, is what Foucault has done in *Les Mots et les Choses* by juxtaposing Renaissance, Classical and Modern forms of thought.

Once modern thought has been relativised, it becomes possible to do two things. It becomes possible to question its basic assumptions – to ask whether the anthropological, empirical and transcendental figure of man is really a necessary condition of knowledge, and whether he really exists. Foucault observes that man in this sense did not exist in the Classical period and that classical knowledge got on perfectly well without him. Once modern thought has been relativised into a chronological episode in the history of thought, it also becomes possible to conceive of history as moving on to another episode and to do what one can to help it along. This is why Foucault argues in *Les Mots et les Choses* for the imminent death of man, why he insists that 'nowadays it is impossible to think only in the empty space produced by man's disappearance' (MCH, 353) and why he endeavours to fill that space with the model and outline of an alternative form of thought. For if, as Foucault has endeavoured to show, man's division from things and from himself is a result of man making his *cogito* the condition and himself the centre of all things, then these divisions can never be resolved as long as man remains in place trying, without success, to straddle all divisions and to turn all Others into himself. The only way out of division and alienation is to erase man, to turn the page and to start thinking from somewhere else.

According to Foucault, the somewhere else that modern thought has begun to think from is Language. The modern preoccupation with language takes three forms: formalisation, interpretation and literature. The value of formalisation for Foucault lies in the fact that it seeks 'the laws of what it is possible to say' (MCH, 312) and endeavours to make the universal and abstract forms of language the epistemological ground in which philosophy, the human and empirical sciences and mathematics can meet. Unlike formalisation, modern interpretation analyses 'what is said in the depths of discourse' (MCH, 311). It treats language as a 'thick and consistent historical reality . . . the locus of traditions, of silent habits of thought and of the obscure spirit of peoples' (MCH, 310), which govern men's speech unbeknownst to themselves. Interpretation is the modern form of critique because, in bringing to light this unconscious and determining level of language, the myths, the assumptions, the traditions which bind men to think and speak in certain ways, interpretation seeks to break these constraints and to loosen the chains of history and language. Modern literature also seeks to loosen the bonds of language, but it does so in such a way as to take language to its limits, to the point where language designates nothing but itself and manifests the finiteness of man through the finiteness of what language enables him to say.

These different aspects of the modern preoccupation with language are all of value as far as Foucault is concerned, but like everything else in the modern *episteme*, they are divided from each other. In modern thought, formalism appears to be the opposite of interpretation, analysis the opposite of literature. The urgent problem for Foucault is to overcome these divisions, 'to find a single space for this great play of language', because he believes that to do this 'could be to take a decisive step towards a completely new form of thought and to close off the mode of knowledge constituted in the last century' (MCH, 318).

Foucault brings the different aspects of the modern preoccupation with language together in the single space of the *episteme*. The *episteme* is a 'group of formal structures which make discourses significant, give the rules which regulate needs, their coherence and their necessity, and ground the norms of life elsewhere than in nature or in purely biological functions' (MCH, 391). The *episteme* is therefore a formal model which defines the 'law of what it is possible to say', but it is a formal model which is unconscious in relation to the people whose speech and thought are determined by it. It is a structure which gives reality its thick and consistent historicity, and one which brings out the finiteness of man by showing the limits within which he must think and speak in any given historical period. The *episteme* treats language as something which designates nothing but itself, but it designates itself as a form which structures its contents and makes objects perceptible in certain ways. Finally, the *episteme* is an abstract form in which philosophy and the human and empirical sciences can meet: it allows each its own proper coherence and necessity, while giving all a common epistemological ground.

Foucault's notion of *episteme* may be a 'decisive step towards a completely new form of thought', but it is not yet outside modern thought. It is, if anything, on the boundary line between the modern and the post-modern. Foucault's epistemic method accepts many of the assumptions of modern thought as he presents them. Like modern history, the *episteme* assumes that men's thoughts originate in something that has 'already begun' outside them and that they are therefore determined by forms and contents which are outside their direct control. It relies heavily on the modern view of history as the mode of being of all things; it relativises knowledge, makes it discontinuous and seeks its organisation in an unconscious system, norm or set of rules. In the *episteme*, finiteness still governs men's minds, even if finiteness is now historicised. Knowledge is still in pursuit of the unconscious and the unthought, even if it is now presented as capable of structuring them. In so far as the formal structures of the *episteme* represent a priori organising principles in relation to what men actually think and say, the transcendental–empirical duality continues to reign. And one could argue that, like Lacan, Foucault merely restructures received ideas by reorganising them around an absent subject – the death of anthropological man.

But there is a little more to it, as Foucault tries to indicate when he characterises his thinking as 'positive'. And it is partly a question of attitude. Foucault can accept Otherness, Division, Discontinuity, Repetition, man's determination by language and culture, the dictation of the unconscious, the finiteness and historicity of man and of his thought, and the death of the Romantic subject as Lacan, for instance, could not. To him they are not evils to be overcome – marks of alienation or negations of true being – but extant elements of modern thought. This means that he can turn them to good use as tools of thought and yet discover an area of freedom within them. In Foucault, the alien Other becomes the Limit and the blind spot from which it is possible to see; Division and Discontinuity become configurations to be included and allowed for in the formal structure of the *episteme*; man is determined by language and culture, but within his determination, there is an area of choice – as Foucault says, 'at every moment, the structure proper to individual experience finds a certain number of possible choices (and of excluded possibilities) in the system of society and inversely, social structures find a certain number of possible individuals (and others who are not) at each of its points of choice, as in language the linear structures always permits a choice at any given moment between several words or phonemes (and excludes others)' (MCH, 392). Foucault has demonstrated this measure of freedom in *Les Mots et les Choses* by the extent to which his thinking is lodged in modern epistemic structures and by the way he chooses to combine and invert them to arrive at something new. In Foucault, moreover, repetition has its rules, the unconscious its system, which are the object of a *critique* which has learned from Freud's 'talking cure' that, to escape the unconscious dictation of our speech and actions, we have only to bring what is unconscious to consciousness. As Foucault indicates when he calls his revelation of the modern anthropological figure of man a *critique*, to make us aware of its recurrence and role in our thought and speech is to free us from its domination. In Foucault, the finiteness of man's thought is not a tragic fate, but a comic celebration of the ridiculousness of human pretensions to universal knowledge and universal truth. It is what permits us to move from one finite and temporary 'set' of knowledge to another, equally finite and temporary one, so that 'the face of man dissolves in laughter and the masks return' (MCH, 397). In Foucault, the Romantic subject, creator of the world and knowing centre of the universe, is dead, but man is reborn as the subject of language. He occupies the space between Nietzsche's question: 'Who is holding speech?' and Mallarmé's answer: 'It is the Word'. For, as Foucault has shown throughout *Les Mots et les Choses*, it is through a study of the Word, through an analysis of the language of Life, Work and Language, that it is possible to reconstitute the changing figure of the speaker, of man as he constitutes himself and his world through his speech. Foucault's *episteme* is thus both a demonstration that formal structures govern our words and thoughts, and their overthrow.

La Volonté de Savoir, the first volume of *Histoire de la Sexualité*, published ten years after *Les Mots et les Choses*, continues this project. Like the latter part of *Les Mots et les Choses*, *La Volonté de Savoir* explores the modern division between thought and the unthought and the *cogito*'s attempts to obtain knowledge of man by grasping the unconscious and the unthought. In *La Volonté de Savoir*, however, the question is posed more specifically as a question about how 'the will to know' came to seek the truth of man in that 'fragment of ourselves' which is our unconscious sexuality. Like the latter part of *Les Mots et les Choses*, too, *La Volonté de Savoir* seeks to bring to light the formal structures which determine this modern chase after the secrets of the unconscious in an attempt to overthrow these formal structures and to 'take a decisive step towards a new form of thought'. But *La Volonté de Savoir* goes beyond *Les Mots et les Choses* by resolving two of the major unresolved problems of that book.

The first of these unresolved problems concerns the unconscious nature of the *episteme*. The *episteme* was basically a very simple logical structure – like resemblance, or identity and difference, or the division between the thought and the unthought – which is repeated and continually elaborated in a period's different fields of knowledge and which conditions or shapes men's actual empirical thinking and speech unbeknownst to themselves. As an attempt to bring to consciousness the fundamental structure of this cultural collective unconscious in any given period, the epistemic method is essentially a cultural and historical form of psychoanalysis. Foucault himself described it as a cross between ethnology and psychoanalysis (MCH, 391). This may have resolved some problems, but it created another. For Foucault's failure to detach his object and method from those of psychoanalysis resulted in a failure to detach himself from psychoanalysis's anthropological and man-centred assumptions. However implicitly, *Les Mots et les Choses* still unfolds in the mind of man; it is still a history of man's representations. Despite Foucault's attempts to focus on language and ideas and to avoid a presentation which would attribute changes in thinking to the work of major individual thinkers, man remains as a sort of transcendental collective abstraction, the locus of thought and of its unconscious constraints. To achieve his object, which was to erase man and to think in a space where he was not, Foucault had to subject psychoanalysis itself to a critique; he had to overthrow its assumptions and distance his method from it. This is the first thing that Foucault undertakes to do in *La Volonté de Savoir*.

The second unresolved problem in *Les Mots et les Choses* derives from the extent to which the *episteme* is still rooted in the transcendental–empirical duality of modern thought. The *episteme* was conceived as the unconscious structure of conscious thought, as the a priori organising principle of what men empirically think and say, as a constraint upon men's thinking which, within certain limits, they are compelled to obey. The epistemic method may try to include or to straddle divisions, but it cannot erase them, because it is itself rooted in a division. It reproduces the binary logic of modern thought and cannot conceive of a space which is not divided into outside and inside, finite and infinite, conscious and unconscious, version and inversion, subjection and domination. Yet if Foucault was really to 'close off the mode of knowledge constituted in the last century' and to find 'a single space for the great play of language', he had to break free of the binary structure of modern thought and to replace it with something else. This is the second thing he undertakes to do in *La Volonté de Savoir*.

Foucault opens *La Volonté de Savoir* with a *renversement* of the psychoanalytical assumption that our sexuality has been repressed since the birth of capitalism and the bourgeois order. On the contrary, he argues, the history of Western societies since the inception of capitalism and of the bourgeois order has been marked by a steady proliferation of discourses about sex. Instead of accepting the psychoanalytical duality of consciousness and the unconscious, and instead of taking it for granted that our sexuality has been repressed, therefore, we should go 'behind' repression, interdiction and exclusion, and seek to explain this steady proliferation of discourses about sex, asking ourselves how the notions of repression, interdiction and exclusion arose within them.

According to Foucault, there are three factors responsible for the proliferation of discourses about sex in Western societies: the Christian practice of confession, eighteenth-century attempts to order and control the population and nineteenth-century medical science. If the great explosion of discourses about sex is contemporaneous with the birth of capitalism and of the bourgeois order, Foucault argues, it is because in the Classical period people were institutionally incited to speak about sexuality so that sexuality could be known, classified and used as a means of social control.

In the Classical period, population studies began to observe and register peoples' sexual behaviour, the age of marriages, the numbers of legitimate and illegitimate births, the use of contraception and so on, in order to be able to intervene to increase or decrease the birthrate according to the needs of the labour market. Boarding schools were built to contain and control childrens' sexuality by means of suitable sleeping arrangements, constant surveillance and moralising instruction. A whole literature grew up around childrens' and adolescent sexuality, a literature of precepts and advice to parents, teachers and headmasters, a literature of clinical cases, schemas for reform and plans for ideal institutions. In medicine, psychiatry and the law, the sexuality of children, mad people and criminals was questioned and classified. For the first time, the different varieties of sexual behaviour were distinguished and ordered, the different perversions of the instincts named, the different implicit and explicit sexualities within the family (between parents, between parents and children, with domestics) were differentiated. 'Lines of penetration' were thus established for knowledge and power to reach every segment of the population. Discourses on sex multiplied in the classical period, Foucault argues, not outside power or against it, but where it was exercised and as a means of exercising it. Power did not seek to forbid or exclude sexuality; it sought to produce and multiply it to use it and to extend its utility. Discourses on sexuality gave teachers, doctors and legislators, judges and the police in general power over peoples' lives. And if sex was, at the same time, presented as a taboo, this was only a mechanism to get them to talk about it. Sex was made to appear a hidden secret which it was vital to discover to incite people to think and talk about it all the more.

The constraint to tell oneself and someone else as often as possible everything concerning one's sexual behaviour, sexual pleasure, sexual thoughts, sexual dreams and profoundest sexual desires originated in Church confessionals. In the confession, desire was turned into discourse with the aim of affecting desire by discourse. The effects sought were effects of mastery and detachment, of spiritual development and of turning back to God, but the effect produced was one of subjection of the individual to the Church. For, according to Foucault, the nature of the confessional relationship is such as to give the one who requires the confession, who judges it, punishes, orders, reconciles and consoles, who purifies, saves or liberates, power over the one who submits by confessing. With the Protestant Reformation, the practice of confession spread outside the Church into relations between parents and children, mentally ill people and psychiatrists, delinquents or criminals and experts. And in the nineteenth century, the practice of confession as a means of revealing a hidden truth and liberating the subject from it was integrated with medical science. Confession became a form of examination. To justify the demand for total confession and the need for the doctor-confessor, an inexhaustible causal power for the most varied effects throughout life was attributed to sex; and sex was presented as something obscure and clandestine, hidden from the subject himself, which could only be brought to light by the team work of confession. The beneficial and liberating effects of confession were medicalised and recoded as a therapeutic operation and 'sexuality' in the modern sense was born.

Foucault regards this development with considerable distaste. We have, he argues, become a confessing society; we confess our sins, our crimes, our guilt, our thoughts, our dreams, our desires, our childhood, our past, our illnesses, our unhappiness; we confess in public and in private, to our parents, our teachers, our friends, our priests, our experts, our doctors, to those we love and to ourselves. Our literature, no longer heroic, has become confessional, and our philosophy too. Individualisation in modern society has become inseparable from the confession of our truth. Sex has become the universal key to this truth and the reason for everything. Everything about us – our selves, our bodies, our souls, our individuality, our history, has been subjected to the logic of sexuality and desire. And this has produced a double subjection: a subjection to 'normalisation' and control; and a subjection to subjectification, to the perception of ourselves as subjects who are divided from ourselves.

Foucault performs a *renversement* of the subject as a being who is divided from his own unconscious by insisting that this division 'does not result from some natural property which is inherent in sex itself, but from the tactics of power which are immanent in our discourses (VS, 94). Man is not 'by nature' divided from himself; the subject is not 'by nature' separated from his unconscious truth. The subject as a being who has within him a knowledge of what he does not know, whose truth is to be sought in a sexuality which perpetually makes him elude himself, whose unconscious has to be deciphered and interpreted by an other – this elusive and internally divided subject is exclusively a product of our discourses about sex and of the tactics by which power has sought to know, to control, and to 'normalise' us. Foucault frees the subject from his internal divisions, therefore, by telling him that the truth about what he is does not lie in his unconscious. It lies in his language, in the manifest exteriority of discourse. Man's truth is therefore not hidden in the depths of himself, it is not an unfathomable secret; it does not need to be confessed, and it is not fatally and eternally the same. For what has been produced in and by discourses can be seen, and once seen, it can be overthrown and replaced in and by different discourses.

Foucault also performs a *renversement* of the juridical notion of power as law which is immanent to the divided subject in our discourses. Whether in the theory of repression or in the Lacanian notion of the law as creating the lack which constitutes desire, whether in theories about the sovereignty of the state over its subjects, in the family or in the law courts, power always appears as a law of prohibition and interdiction which subjects the subject (or part of him) and makes him submit. Foucault overthrows and replaces this juridical notion of power as law, and in the process he demonstrates that it is possible to transcend the limitations both of the *episteme* and of binarism.

For Foucault now conceives of power in a space which is not centred on a single point – be it a dominant structure of thought or a sovereign power – and which is not divided into above and below, outside and inside, conscious and unconscious, domination and subjection. Foucault conceives of the space of language, culture and society as an open, mobile and dynamic 'field' of interrelations in which power is everywhere and comes from everywhere. Power is immanent to all interrelations, be they economic or scientific or sexual, in the realm of knowledge or of practices, on the level of particular local interactions or on the level of the 'global strategies' which emerge from the repetition of particular power relations. Power, with its inherent disequilibrium and instability and its concomitant forms of resistance, is immanent to the family and to apparatuses of production, to small groups and large institutions; it is within the relations between parent and child, teacher and pupil, doctor and patient, psychiatrist and madman, social worker and client, expert and subject. Power is immanent in every domain of knowledge, it organises all discourses including those about truth, sex, power and history, and including Foucault's own discourses. And it is often 'tactically polyvalent' – in other words, it can be doing several things at the same time.

Foucault's own discourse about power occurring everywhere in a mobile and unstable field of interrelations is a good example of the tactical polyvalence of a discourse. One tactical dimension of his discourse has to do with showing that what has been produced in and by discourse can be overthrown and replaced by discourse. Thus Foucault's discourse about power relations eliminates the subject by focusing on interactions and discourses which occur in the space between subjects; it eliminates the unconscious by indicating an area of the unthought which, once named, can be visible to all; it all but erases binarism by replacing it with multiplicity; and it enables Foucault, and others who may be so inclined, to think and speak in a new way.

Another tactical dimension is more properly political. The notion of power occurring and meeting resistances everywhere in personal and professional relationships as well as in civic and economic relationships reminds us that none of us is as powerless as we have been taught to imagine. Set against the totalising, normalising, disciplining and all pervasive operation of power in the modern world, Foucault's discourse on power reminds us that, while we are subjected to power, each of us is also a power-point at which multiple power-relationships intersect (personal, professional, economic, legal, civic etc.) and that even where we appear to be subjected, we have a local power of resistance. Set against the juridical notion of power as a law of interdiction and prohibition to which everyone is subject and which can only be overthrown by a mass uprising against repression, Foucault's discourse on power opens the possibility of multiple forms of local resistance and action for each individual in his own specific place within the field of discourses and power relations. As Foucault says: 'as soon as there is a power relation, there is a possibility of resistance. We can never be ensnared by power: we can modify its grip in determinate conditions and according to a precise strategy'.[52]

Another tactical dimension of Foucault's discourse on power is to show that, while discourse may be 'an instrument and an effect of power', it can also be 'a point of resistance, a starting point for an opposite strategy' (VS, 133). This means that discourse itself becomes a form of action, and one proper to those who find themselves at a power-point of knowledge and discourse.

La Volonté de Savoir should not be viewed as an introduction to *Histoire de la Sexualité*, but as part of a continuing argument. In *Les Mots et les Choses*, Foucault determined that the divided subject who rules the modern *episteme* should be erased; in *La Volonté de Savoir*, he succeeded in erasing him by turning the subject into a power point at which multiple power relations intersect; in the three further volumes of *Histoire de la Sexualité* which Foucault managed to write before his death, Foucault pursued the problem of the subject and the forms of his subjectivation back into the ancient world and to the first centuries of the modern era; and in his article, 'The Subject and Power', Foucault described his work as as attempt 'to create a history of the different modes by which, in our culture, human beings are made subjects' and his study of sexuality as a study of 'how men have learned to recognise themselves as subjects of sexuality'.[53] Given Foucault's taste for *renversement*, given his desire to take a decisive step towards a new form of knowledge and his insistence that we 'have to promote new forms of subjectivity through the refusal of the kind of individuality which has been imposed on us for several centuries',[54] and given the direction of Foucault's argument in the volumes of *Histoire de la Sexualité* which he completed – given all this, it is not too much to suppose that, had *Histoire de la Sexualité* been completed, *La Volonté de Savoir* would have appeared as a bridge between the projected death of man in *Les Mots et les Choses* and his projected rebirth in a new, non-humanistic, undivided and unsubjected form at the end of *Histoire de la Sexualité*.

THE SPECIFIC, POSITIVE INTELLECTUAL

Foucault's presentation of the modern intellectual as a figure who is both determined and determining is a *renversement* of traditional views of the intellectual.

The intellectual appears in Foucault's writings as a subject who is always determined by specific events. Foucault shows that the doctor in his modern form was created by the birth of the clinic, and the psychiatrist by the Assembly's decision to establish separate asylums for the mad and to give psychiatrists the role of judge of who is to be confined and for how long. Foucault shows that the sociologist and the statistician emerged with the policy of collecting information about the population, the better to control it and that the 'expert' witness – the criminologist, psychologist or social worker – appeared with the law courts' requirement for specific information about the criminal's personality and history. Foucault presents the modern intellectual – magistrate, doctor, psychiatrist, teacher or technocrat – as determined also by the fact that he works within a carceral institution – a law court, hospital, asylum, school or factory – which imposes on him roles of surveillance and control and gives him the power to discipline and punish. At the same time, the intellectual in Foucault's writings is himself determined by certain forms of exclusion and control. Since the beginning of the modern era, he is shown to have been subject to specific qualifying (or disqualifying) examinations, and to the decrees of controlling bodies like the medical council, the psychoanalytical association or the university. These constitute the intellectual as the 'expert – the one who has the exclusive right to speak about specific subjects in specific circumstances. Finally, the intellectual in Foucault's writings, is always determined by a specific 'regime of truth'. He speaks within a specific *episteme* and a specific 'discipline', within certain modes of separating error from truth and within certain intellectual practices. Foucault describes the modern intellectual as the heir to the confessional, to disciplinary practices and to the transcendental–empirical divide. He is a subject who thinks, works and speaks within an order where consciousness is divided from the unconscious, the *cogito* from the unthought, where individuals are incited to speak of themselves, their histories, their dreams and their secret desires; where their behaviour and performance is scrutinized, subject to surveillance, registered, filed and preserved; where truth is documented, reported, classified, examined and organised in specific ways.

This is why Foucault argues that the modern intellectual can no longer be viewed as a 'representative of the universal', as 'the conscience/consciousness of everyone', as a spokesman for a 'universal' class like the proletariat or as a 'free-floating' master of justice and truth. As magistrate or psychiatrist, doctor or social worker, laboratory worker or sociologist, teacher or data processing expert, nuclear physicist or geneticist, pharmacologist or technician, intellectuals work 'in specific sectors, at precise points where they are situated either by their professional conditions of work or by their conditions of life (housing, the hospital, the asylum, the laboratory, the university, familial and sexual relations)'.[55] And in these specific sectors of society where they are situated, intellectuals 'encounter problems that are specific, "non-universal", often different from the proletariat and the masses'.[56] Foucault's first *renversement* of traditional views of the intellectual, therefore, consists of showing that the intellectual is as firmly grounded in the social and historical order as everyone else; that if he is 'other', he is other only in so far as he has different specific problems from other sectors of the population which grow out of his different specific conditions of life and work; and that instead of viewing himself as a disinterested searcher for truth or as a social outcast, intellectuals should view themselves in their specificity, in terms of their domain and conditions of work, in terms of their place of employment, in the hospital, the university or whatever.

But in the midst of these specific determinations, Foucault shows that the modern intellectual also has a determining role. For instance, he describes how specific intellectuals created the regimes and curative practices in asylums and psychiatric hospitals, how doctors determined hospital practices, how intellectuals have run schools and laboratories. He shows where intellectuals have administered the power of exclusion, judging who is normal and who abnormal, who is healthy and who sick, who is sane and who insane, who is qualified and who unqualified. He describes how intellectuals have collected information about the population, and how they have produced a group of disciplines, a body of literature, a configuration of ideas, precepts and case histories, which facilitate certain forms of surveillance and control and permit the 'normalisation' of the population. And he shows that through their discourses, intellectuals have created, among other forms of 'truth', both the alienated subject who is the object of their study and the inwardly divided subject with his subjected subjectivity and unconscious desires.

Because modern intellectuals have acted throughout as 'agents of power' – judging normalities and administering exclusions, collecting and organising information about the population and creating the divided and subjected subjects they know – their truths can no longer be considered 'outside power or deprived of power'. This is why Foucault argues that truth is manifestly 'of the world', that it 'induces the regular effects of power',[57] that knowledge is formed wherever power is exercised and that every piece of knowledge permits and ensures the exercise of some form of power.[58] Moreover, Foucault argues, the power of knowledge has become even more extensive since 1960 because 'experts' have become increasingly important to the development of the 'technico-scientific structures' of contemporary society and because truth itself has become an increasingly important commodity. Centred on the form of scientific discourse, and produced and distributed by a few dominant institutions (like the university, the laboratory, the writing media, the mass media), truth today is 'subject to constant economic and political incitation'; it is 'the object of immense diffusion and consumption', and it is 'the stake of a whole political debate and social confrontation'.[59]

Foucault's second *renversement* of traditional views of the intellectual, therefore, consists in showing that the intellectual is not the weak, harmless, unwordly and rather derisory figure who has retreated into writing and speech because he is incapable of action. Foucault's *renversement* consists of showing that knowledge and truth are essential to the structuring and functioning of modern societies and that intellectuals are essential to the production, administration and distribution of this essential knowledge and truth. Moreover, in so far as discourses have the power to create objectified and divided subjects, to produce and impose exclusions, and to affect lives – discourse is action. Whether he acts in conformity with the current regime of power and truth in society or against it, whether he acts as an agent of power or as a point of resistance, the intellectual in his specific domain of work, in his specific conditions of work and in his specific place of work is always playing a positive, productive and powerful role within society and within its 'regime of truth'.

The specific, positive intellectual with his positive discursive power is at least a preliminary outline for a new kind of subject – a subject who is not alienated, not inwardly divided and not subjected. As a specific and positive subject, the intellectual is a power-point at which multiple power-relations intersect. He has a 'threefold specificity': he has the 'specificity of his class position (he is a petty bourgeois in the service of capitalism or an "organic" intellectual of the proletariat); he has the 'specificity of his conditions of life and work, linked to his condition as an intellectual (his domain of research, his place in a lab, in the university, in the hospital etc., the political and economic demands which he submits to or rebels against)'; and he has the 'specificity of the politics of truth in our societies'.[60] Because intellectuals have a privileged relation to society's 'regime of truth', discourse is their proper sphere of action. And because the specific intellectual is a point at which multiple specificities intersect, his discourse will also necessarily be 'tactically polyvalent'. It will have a bearing on all the dimensions of his specificity, whether he submits to the power relations inherent in them or rebels against them.

Foucault is not presenting specific positive intellectuals as a new privileged or ruling class. Nor is he pretending that they have a cohesion they lack. He conceives of specific intellectuals in their dispersion, each with his own 'local and regional' position within the class network, within the institutional network, within a field of knowledge, and within the regime of truth, and each with a correspondingly 'local and regional' possibility of speech and action. But as far as Foucault is concerned, this local and regional specificity is also the specific intellectual's revolutionary strength. For it means that each can work and 'struggle on [his] own terrain and on the basis of [his] own proper activity (or passivity)'. Each can 'engage in a struggle that concerns [his] own interests, whose objectives [he] clearly understands, and whose methods only [he] can determine' (LCP, 216). Each can engage in a 'specific struggle against a particularised power, the constraints and controls that are exerted against [him]'. And by 'mutual exchange and support', specific positive intellectuals can 'participate in a global process of politicisation of intellectuals'[61] and 'detach the power of truth from the forms of hegemony (social, economic and cultural) within which it operates at the present time' in order to 'constitute a new politics of truth'.[62] What has been created in and by discourse can be overthrown in and by discourse, and intellectuals have nothing to lose but the political, economic, institutional, cultural and epistemic chains which govern their production of truth.

The specific positive intellectual who is both determined and determining, yet free at the same time either to submit to particular-ised power relations or to rebel against them, is not merely a preliminary outline for a new kind of subject. He is also, at least potentially, a useful methodological tool, one that makes it possible to analyse an intellectual's social circumstances and contribution to knowledge in a new way. For once he is viewed as a power-point at which multiple power relations intersect, the intellectual can be described both in terms of his multiple specificities and in terms of the resulting 'tactical polyvalence' of his discourses, each of which may represent acts of submission or acts of resistance with regard to the status quo. This approach seems particularly applicable to Foucault himself. Foucault did, after all, ask not to be defined in more traditional ways as a 'psychological subject', a 'biographical subject' 'a subject in the civil or bureaucratic sense' or as a subject who remained always the same. And he can clearly not be described either as a subject who remained subjected to social conditions and intellectual influences, or as a subject with a one-dimensional form of discourse.

Foucault indicated the specificity both of his class position and of his conditions of work in the French university system in an interview he gave in 1971, when he characterised the university as 'an environment of exclusion' and university professors as 'part of the state apparatus'. The first function of the university, he explained, is 'a function of exclusion':

The student is put outside of society, on a campus. Furthermore, he is excluded while being transmitted a knowledge traditional in nature, obsolete, 'academic', and not directly tied to the needs and problems of today. This exclusion is underscored by the organization around the student of social mechanisms which are fictitious, artificial and quasi-theatrical (hierarchical relationships, academic exercises, the 'court' of examination, evaluation). Finally, the student is given a gamelike way of life; he is offered a kind of distraction, amusement, freedom, which again has nothing to do with real life.[63]

The university is not, however, exclusively a space of exclusion; like the prison or the asylum, the university, as Foucault presents it, is also a space which has the additional function of 'normalising' students so that they may later be reintegrated into society. After six or seven years in the artificial society of the university, Foucault continues, the student will:

insidiously . . . have received the values of his society. He will have been given socially desirable models of behaviour, types of ambition, outlines of political behaviour, so that this ritual of exclusions will finally take on the value of inclusion or recuperation or reabsorption.[64]

In Foucault's presentation, the university professor is the public official who presides over the university as a space of exclusion and performs the task of normalisation. He is 'part of the state apparatus'. It is his task to provide the upper-middle class with the professional cadres they require (technicians, engineers, teachers etc.); to form the 'docile bodies' who will conform to socially desirable models of behaviour, types of ambition and outlines of political behaviour; and to use hierarchical relationships, academic exercises and the 'court' of examination to discipline students, to punish non-conformity, and to judge and administer disqualifying exclusions. Like the psychiatrist in the asylum or the warden in the prison, therefore, the university professor is an 'agent of power'. He is the technician who 'maintains the transmission of knowledge required by the government, that is by the bourgeois class whose interests are represented by the government'.[65] Yet the university professor is himself a member of the lower-middle class, a class which Foucault says 'finds itself politically and socially more and more proletarianised' and 'in France is losing all control of the state apparatus'.[66] During the III Republic, Foucault explains, when there was a 'republic of professors', there was a direct link between universities, the professions and the political framework. This link has since been lost, and professors and professionals have been degraded to technicians who serve the upper middle class.

In describing university professors in France as people who work in a space of exclusion as officials of the state; as people who are part of the state apparatus but not part of the class which controls it and whose interests its serves; and as people who are lower-middle class technicians for an upper-middle class which excludes and proletarianises them, Foucault is describing university professors in France as people who are positioned on a series of dividing lines between exclusion and inclusion. And this is precisely the position from which Foucault wrote.

Foucault's view of the universities and of the position of university professors in France is not eccentric. It is not unique to him. Indeed his remarks about the universities and about the position of intellectuals within them touch on the major preoccupations of his contemporaries. Throughout the 1960s in France, academic and sociological writing like Serge Mallet's *La Nouvelle Classe Ouvrière* (The New Working Class) or Bon and Burnier's *Les Nouveaux Intellectuels* (The New Intellectuals) analysed and bemoaned the proletarianisation of those intellectuals who served the state as technicians, and described their loss of power and control to the upper-middle class technocrats who were allied with the Gaullist state and with its centralised and bureaucratic planning. A recurrent theme in academic analyses of the French educational system is the excessive authoritarianism of teaching methods, the resulting passivity of students, and the shortcomings of a system in which pupils are so ruthlessly weeded out all the way up the educational ladder that even university students have little assurance of finishing their studies and obtaining their degrees. The obsolete character of the traditional classical and rhetorical education transmitted by French schools and universities, its irrelevance to the needs of the new technocratic and scientific society, its 'academic' abstraction from life, and its failure to prepare students for jobs in the market place is another constantly recurring set of themes, from Pierre Naville's *La Formation Professionnelle et l'École* (Schooling and Professional Training) in 1948 to the deluge of writing by university professors about the shortcomings of French universities which followed the French student uprising of 1968. This sort of criticism produced a spate of essentially unsuccessful attempts in the 1950s and 1960s to reform the secondary school and baccalaureat programmes and resulted in a host of new technical colleges designed to train the technical cadres required by France's rapidly modernising society. But these attempts at reform left the university unreformed. Faculties of letters continued to teach the classical disciplines in traditional ways, leaving their students less well equipped than before to find jobs. And social science subjects continued to be distributed almost at random among the Faculties of Letters, of Law, and of Medicine, and in *Grandes Écoles* of Administration.

Foucault indicated the specificity of his condition as an intellectual in the university in his inaugural lecture at the *Collège de France*, when he described the various 'procedures for the subjection of discourses' (OD, 46) which constrained the intellectual in his discursive and non-discursive practices. Some of these procedures are forms of exclusion which are already familiar from Foucault's other writings, like the binary divisions between reason and madness or truth and error, which select and control what may and may not be said, or the exclusion of certain topics from discourse and of certain people from speech. Other procedures for subjection which Foucault describes are internal either to discourse itself or to the circumstances within which discourses may be held. For instance, the intellectual who is qualified to speak in the university is usually qualified to speak within the limits of a certain discipline. And a discipline, Foucault insists, 'is not the sum of everything true that can be said about something' (OD, 32). A discipline is 'a policing of discourse', 'a principle of control for the production of discourse' (OD, 37) because it requires that discourses address themselves only to specified objects in terms of specified conceptual instruments. Not unconnected with this is the fact that scientific or technical, medical, economic or political discourses are produced and circulated in closed 'societies of discourse' in such a way as to make them inaccessible to outsiders and unappropriatable by them. Within disciplines and within such 'societies of discourse', Foucault claims, doctrines are yet another source of subjection, for they turn discourses into indications of the speaker's orthodoxy or heresy and mark the speaking subject as belonging to a certain class, status group, race or interest group. Moreover, whether within the university or within closed societies of discourse, discourses can only be delivered in certain ways, according to specific rituals which define gesture, behaviour, the circumstances of speech, the effect of words, the role of the speaking subject and the proprieties which he must obey. 'What', Foucault asks, 'is an educational system, if not a ritualisation of speech; if not a qualification of speaking subjects and a fixing of their roles; if not the constitution of a doctrinal group however diffuse; if not a distribution and an appropriation of discourse with its powers and its knowledge? What is 'writing' (that of 'writers') if not a similar system of subjection?' (OD, 47).

Foucault's own discourses were attempts to resist all such subjections. And there were as many tactical dimensions to his discourse as there were specific conditions which constrained it.

Foucault's first and perhaps most fundamental discursive strategy was to resist the subjection of disciplines and to escape the confines both of doctrines and of 'societies of discourse'. Arguing that the lines of demarcation between disciplines like philosophy, history, literature, science and religion were nothing but principles of classification, normative rules and institutional types, Foucault created 'archeological formations which coincided with the delimitations of no discipline and which would not even be superimposed on the delimitations of disciplines in the periods under study'.[67] He evaded the confines of the various 'societies of discourse' by defining the intellectual's sphere as discursive practices in general. This qualified the intellectual to speak of anything and everything in language. It did not entirely obliterate the possibility of at least one closed 'society of discourse' – because it is hard to imagine the academically uninitiated making much sense of Foucault's writings, for example. But it did at least constitute all intellectuals as *one* society of discourse and make it possible for them to roam at will among different types of discourse, pulling things together and making what sense of them they could without conforming either to the delimitations or to the rules of any single type of discourse or any single discipline.

Foucault escaped doctrine and other cultural forms of preconception by *critique*. As we have seen throughout, Foucault's favourite critical tactic is to change the perspective from which things are usually seen by *renversement*. Of all his many *renversements*, perhaps the most tactically important is that which transformed history from a study of the past into a study of the present. For together with Foucault's obliteration of the divisions between disciplines and his definition of the intellectual's sphere as everything that is in language, this transformation of history into an analysis of the present represents a blow in the struggle to make what was taught in the university (particularly in the Faculties of Letters) less obsolete, less irrelevant and less removed from life. Once the humanities and social sciences were united in language and discourse, and once it became possible for Foucault as a university professor to draw different types of discourse together, it also became possible for him to provide students with a more complex and more integrated picture of culture and society, and of the subject's position within them. And once the purpose of historical scholarship was to bring out the constraints and delimitations of the present, it became possible for Foucault to use his scholarship to provide students with a critical perception of the norms and functioning of the technological and technocratic society in which they were to be reabsorbed. Far from subverting Faculties of Letters by undermining their traditional departments and traditional methods of teaching, this was a bold move to strengthen them by giving them a new role. In France, Letters had once been exclusively responsible for the education of France's homogeneous liberal élite, which had been characterised primarily by a certain style of writing and speech, and by shared classical and literary points of reference. But in the post-war years, Letters had become peripheral and increasingly irrelevant to the education of France's new technocratic and scientific élite. Faculties of Letters had lost influential ground to the newly created *Grandes Écoles* – polytechnics, schools of administration, colleges of science and engineering – which now produced most of the country's upper-middle class élite. Faculties of Letters could only make a bid to regain their importance in the training of France's intellectual élite by tying scholarship 'directly to the needs and problems of today' and by offering the future leaders of French society a more rounded, complex and critical view of that society. This is precisely what Foucault was attempting to do.

Foucault's *critique* was also part of a larger political and revolutionary tactic. Besides placing the university professor in the position of no longer having to transmit knowledge which served the state apparatus, *critique* also helped others to see where their particular battles needed to be fought. By presenting the modern individual as an essentially administrative unit which is programmed, classified and objectified by insidious disciplinary techniques which pervade knowledge, the prisons, the factories and the schools; by showing that modern man's subjectivity is subjected by the very voices which incite him to speak about himself, his history, his childhood and his unconscious desires; and by devoting his work to an identification of the exclusions and constraints which govern people's lives and to an analysis of the unthought structures which control their thought and speech, Foucault's *critique* showed students and intellectuals 'where the instances of power have secured and implanted themselves by a system of organisation dating back over a hundred and fifty years'. And it invited them to do something about it.

Foucault's critical discourse and his extension of the intellectual's sphere to the entire domain of language also constituted a tactic to change the positon of the university in society. For if the university could be brought to deal directly with the needs and problems of today; if it could offer students a complex but integrated picture of culture and society and of the subject's place within them; and if it could provide intellectuals with a truly critical perspective on the status quo, then it would no longer be a space of exclusion where people were taught to conform to the norms of traditional knowledge. It would become a power-house – 'the centre of a multiform ensemble of intellectuals who practically all pass through it and relate themselves to it'.[68] The university would become a centre where intellectuals were made critical and politicised and where critical and political intellectuals could later coordinate their local and regional battles against particularised powers. And this in turn would change the university professor from a mere technician of the upper-middle class into 'a privileged point of intersection', a point at which knowledge is power indeed.

Foucault's second major discursive strategy was to 'make fictions work within the truth'. He did this in many different ways.

Foucault 'fictioned' a space for power and knowledge and a 'politics' for intellectuals that does not yet exist, starting from a historical truth – the historical truth of the student uprising of 1968. The uncentred, unhierarchical space in which multiple relations intersect at multiple points, each of which has a local and regional power of action and resistance, was the space created in May 1968 by the interactions of innumerable students and university professors in innumerable different faculties and departments combining in their debating groups and action committees and working to change their own faculty, their own department, the way their own subject was taught and the constraints in their own place of work. After the collapse of the student uprising and of this new kind of space and the return of France to centralised hierarchical government, Foucault inverted the Marxist principle that 'being determines consciousness'. He allowed consciousness to fabricate a mode of being that does not yet exist, in which dispersed intellectuals, using the university as their point of intersection, and functioning on the basis of *autogestion* or self-management, act to resist and change the constraints, the disciplines and the regime of truth in the offices, factories, schools, hospitals and laboratories in which they work. But this fiction worked within the truth: the truth that most intellectuals do pass through the university or relate to it in some way; the truth that modern intellectuals work throughout society's key institutions; the truth that in France in the 1960s and early 1970s intellectuals expressed extreme dissatisfaction with their jobs on the grounds that they precluded creativity, initiative and freedom of action and required them to conform dully to the demands of their superiors; the truth that intellectuals do constitute a specific group in society with problems and interests different from those of the proletariat; and the truth that, were they all to act in their places of work and to coordinate their actions, intellectuals could change society.

Foucault also 'fictioned history starting from a political reality'. For instance, starting from the reality of a society and government which left-wing intellectuals found rigid, authoritarian, *dirigiste* and coercive, and from the reality of a technology capable of total surveillance, Foucault fashioned a historical version of George Orwell's *1984*. As Anthony Giddens has pointed out, Foucault's picture of society in *Surveiller et Punir* is somewhat one-dimensional: in epitomising the whole of society by the prison, Foucault ignores the difference between 'total institutions' in which people are confined all the time and institutions to which people have to travel from homes and leisure periods in which they are free to do as they will; and he ignores the fact that it is impossible to govern either workers or pupils without taking their will into account.[69] Foucault would answer that when he speaks of 'a disciplinary society' and of 'the diffusion of disciplinary methods', he is not speaking of 'a disciplined society' or saying that 'the French are obedient'.[70] Nor is he attempting to 'grasp a "society" in "all" of its "living" reality'.[71] He is merely trying to uncover the rationale behind certain disciplinary practices which emerged in France after the French Revolution and persist there to this day in order 'to contribute to changing certain things about the way things are said and done, and to take part in the difficult business of displacing forms of sensibility and thresholds of tolerance'.[72] Foucault's history works within the truth – the truth of authoritarianism, the truth of centralised information, the truth of the multiple daily disciplines that we all accept, the truth of the objectivation of people and of their manipulation in the social sciences, especially as these are used by governments and so on. It is because Foucault's history works within the truth that *Surveiller et Punir* has had the impact that it has. But it also fictions that truth by exaggerating it to make its point. How much the truth has been exaggerated, though, would probably be a matter of dispute between a left-wing French intellectual of Foucault's generation and an English or American scholar thinking in terms of his own society.

Foucault also went further than anyone else in fictioning a new 'regime of truth' – 'detaching the power of truth from the forms of hegemony (social, economic, cultural) within which it operates at the present time' and showing people that 'it is possible to constitute a new politics of truth' in which knowledge and truth are acknowledged as real powers and in which their positive economic, political, cultural and institutional roles begin to be explored.[73] Foucault did this not only by arguing that ideas are important to lives and that knowledge is power — this is something that all scholars and teachers know and that intellectuals who have been strongly influenced by an idea, a writer or a teacher immediately acknowledge. He did it not only by showing in his histories that knowledge was always developed where power was exercised, that knowledge often made it possible for power to be exercised and that intellectuals – doctors and psychiatrists, magistrates, teachers and 'experts' of all kinds – not only 'created truths' but also administered the powers of exclusion and control. He did it above all by personal example. Foucault 'fictioned' his own instruments for the analysis of the present; he fictioned a space for his discourse which coincided with the delimitations of no discipline; he fictioned a role for the intellectual and for the university professor; and in so doing, he showed more concretely than Nietzsche that interpretation has power, and that to change the perspective from which things are seen is also to change what is seen and to make it possible to think, speak and do things in a new way.

Strategically, Foucault's discourses were always attempts to 'show up, transform and reverse the systems which quietly order us about' and to 'show how one could escape'.[74] Foucault was allergic to the 'structuralism' of modern French society, and to all conscious and unconscious, explicit and implicit, forms of coercion or constraint, and he was careful to produce no dogma or revolutionary 'programme' which could, like Marxism or Freudianism or Structuralism, be used to condition and programme people in its turn. But there was one constraint he did not allow intellectuals to escape: the constraint of choosing whether to conform or to resist, whether to act as passive agents of the powers that be or as independent destroyers and creators of knowledge and truth. If knowledge is power and politics, then one had better choose one's side.

Important as this sounds, and influential as it has been on American thinking about the role of literary and cultural studies in recent years, it is worth asking whether this division between conformism and resistance is not, in fact, one of Foucault's few uncriticised and unoverthrown commonplaces. The opposition between conformity and resistance, submission and creativity, technocrats and technicians, has been a constant theme in French left-wing sociological writing in the post-war period. It is an opposition which is rooted, like so many of the myths that Foucault exploded, in the nineteenth-century conception of society as a place of conflict in which people are divided into antagonistic camps; and it is a view of society which constitutes something of a self-fulfilling prophesy. Instead of accepting this without question as a basis for thought, would the specific positive intellectual not ask, in more Foucaldian spirit, whether conformity versus resistance is not just another division of subjects and discourses which needs *renversement* and replacement by something else?

4

Derrida and the Wholly Other

'Vanity of vanities, saith the preacher; all is vanity. And because the preacher was wise, he still taught the people knowledge.'

Ecclesiastes

Where Foucault positioned himself between oppositions and Barthes inscribed oppositions in the same body, Derrida collapses all oppositions – and with them all the constructs of language, culture and rational thought – back into an originating unity which evokes that of the Jewish God: One, Sovereign, Incorporeal and wholly Other, at once transcendent and immanent, manifest and hidden, it can neither be described nor contained by the determinations of language and thought – including these. Deconstruction of the *constructi* – the concepts, structures and constructs – of language, culture and the philosophic mind is thus both less and more than a subversion of what Derrida has called 'the metaphysics of presence' which have governed Western language and logic from the Greeks to the present day. Deconstruction is a displacement of the human constructs that have displaced the originating unity. And it is an attempt to open out a metaphysic and a mind-set which have been closed to the wholly Other by carving out spaces or abysses in language and thought through which it can be glimpsed 'through a glass darkly'. At the same time, if what is glimpsed through the glass darkly is God, it is a de-constructed God, the Jewish God become pure *Ein Sof* and pared down to the mystery of his infinite Otherness.[1] Derrida's work could be described as an exploration of what it means to say that: 'God is *nothing* (determinate), is not any life because he is *all*, is therefore at the same time the All and the Nothing, Life and Death etc. Which means that God is or appears, *is named* in the difference between the All and the Nothing, Life and Death etc. In the difference, and at bottom as Difference itself' (ED, 170).

Derrida's language is difficult because he is trying to find new ways to say what language cannot say. Our language and the logos embedded in it, Derrida argues, are still fundamentally Greek. As such, they are foreign to the infinitely Other. The language and logos of the philosophers is not that of the prophets. But the prophets no longer have any language or logos other than that of the philosophers. If the prophets are still to speak, they must borrow the language and logos of the philosophers,[2] but they must also silence them. They must simulate the language and logos of the philosophers to give them sight of their own blindness to what is beyond them. 'If', says Derrida, 'we call this experience of the infinitely other Judaism, we must think about the necessity in which it finds itself and about the injunction enjoined upon it to produce itself as logos and to awaken the Greek in the syntax of his own autistic dream' (ED, 226).

Derrida's language is not only difficult because he is struggling to speak within an alien language and logos. It is difficult because he is struggling at the same time against language. If Derrida is enjoined to 'indicate' in his writings what he refers to in his early work as the 'sacred' or the 'divine', he is also enjoined to do while remaining faithful to the tradition that there may be no graven images of the divine. But language as we know it is always metaphorical, and writing in Western tradition is always an inscription, a representation, an engraving of language. How then is it possible to 'indicate' the divine without engraving images? According to a modern Jewish teacher, this was also a fundamental and recurrent problem for the prophets:

> The word is a sign or token; it appeals not only to the ear but to the eye; it sets forth an image and that image is in part mythical. . . From the time of Moses, men had known the commandment: 'Thou shalt not make unto thee a graven image, nor any manner of likeness of any thing. . .' But the very words that men used contained both image and likeness, and men had to strive to reach words that were full of life yet free of myth. The image in the word must not really be an image, but only a hint, a parable . . . it is a fascinating sight to see this battle taking place before our eyes in the pages of the Bible, to see the prophets fighting for a new language and fighting with it after they had attained it.[3]

This problem led Derrida to reconsider the whole place and

function of writing in Western tradition, and then, gradually, to develop his own alternatives, fighting for a new language and fighting with it after he had attained it.

These two aspects of Derrida's work – the awakening of the language and logos of the philosophers to the absurdity of their closure to the infinitely other, and the attempt to develop a writing – are intimately linked. They are aspects of Derrida's endeavour to 'hint at the glimmer of beyond-closure' (G, 25) and to re-deploy language and thought in the light of what cannot and may not be said. This is, if one wishes, the prophetic, apocalyptic or mystical dimension of Derrida's writings.

But, at the same time, Derrida is no traditional Jewish prophet. For Derrida, God is not, has never been, a *Shechina*, a presence. No vision, or dream, or voice from beyond-closure has ever presented itself to Derrida demanding to be translated into the imperfect languages of man. For Derrida, there has been no encounter, no journey, no meeting and no promise. If Derrida is a prophet, he is a prophet without a divine message, without a sacred meaning to give point and direction to the deeds and writings of men. In Derrida's work, there is 'no absolute referent. That is why they show nothing; they recount nothing; they represent nothing; and there is nothing they want to say' (Diss., 390). Derrida's meeting was not with the face of God, but with a body of writings, with 'a language [that] preceded my presence to myself', with *Tora, Kabbalah* and rabbinical exegesis (Diss., 379). But deprived of their 'absolute referent', *Tora, Kabbalah* and rabbinical exegesis are 'returned to a sort of atheism' (Diss., 383). Their structures, endlessly repeated and re-presented in what becomes a merely 'textual obsession', mark and re-mark the empty space of the God who 'is' not. Derridean writing alternates between attempts to penetrate the veil guarding the mystery and demonstrations of the absurdity – the reversibility – before the veil, of all human attempts to construct meanings and absolutes.[4]

RECONSTRUCTING THE TEXT

Derrida's early writings could be read as a prolonged 'supplement' – an addition to and substitution for – the first phrase of Genesis: 'In the beginning, God created the heaven and the earth'.[5] In what follows, I will retain the biblical words and underridean language until I have re-constructed Derrida's additions and substitutions.

Traditional metaphysics would read the creation of heaven and earth as an act that brought two determinate things into being and made them present. And it would do so despite the fact that, so far at least, the heaven and the earth can hardly be said to have been either determinate things or obviously 'present' since 'darkness was on the face of the deep' and 'the earth was without form and void'. In 'Reb Derrida', on the other hand, the act of creation would be read as an act of differentiation – as the introduction of difference between the heaven and the earth, and between God and the heaven and the earth. In the beginning, then, difference was introduced between the heaven and the earth and between God and the heaven and earth. And 'the origin of speculation becomes difference' (G, 55).

The emphasis in Derrida's reading would be on the idea that in creating heaven and earth, God 'divided the waters from the waters'. The Hebrew word *mavdil* standardly translated by 'divided' also means difference and separation. It is as though an original continuity of waters (or of God–heaven–earth) had been differentiated by a separation, a discontinuity, a distance. Derrida accordingly conceives a difference not as a demarcating line, but as a separation, a distancing, a spacing: 'actively, dynamically and with a certain perseverence in repetition, interval, distance, *spacing* must be produced between elements [which became/become/are to become] other' (M, 8).

Like the word Creation in English which describes both the generative act and what has been generated and is therefore both temporal and spatial, difference is at once 'genetic' and 'static', 'structural' and 'historical'. In traditional terms, difference would be 'the constituting, productive and originating causality, the process of scission and divisions, of which the differenced and the differences would be the products or the constituted effects' (M, 9). Difference is prior to the appearance of all that is and the condition for its appearance. Without difference there could be no determinate being and no oppositions: no objects and no subjects, no insides and no outsides, no presences and no absences. But difference is also the perseverance of such differences, the repetition of such divisions, the re-production of such fissures, the re-currence of spacing. If the difference between the heaven and the earth, for instance, did not recur, the difference between them and with it, the heaven and the earth themselves, would melt into each other and disappear. Scission and division thus repeat or re-produce or re-present themselves in time, each repetition or re-production or re-presentation being separated from the one before by a difference, an interval, a delay. This is what Derrida means by 'the becoming-time of space' and the 'becoming-space of time'. Space becomes time and structure history when the spacing which produced determinated being is re-produced in time, when divisions re-cur. Time becomes spatial when reproductions are separated by an interval, when re-currence is spaced out. Differ-ence, conceived as division and as a separating interval, is thus both spatial and temporal. In the language of the bible, God 'divided the waters from the waters' and He 'divided the day from the night'.

In reading the first words of Genesis, Derrida would take the unusual past tense of the verb *bara* (created) seriously.[6] In his view, the introduction of difference which produced the heaven and the earth and all that is occurred in the past, in a past so distant as to be irrecuperable. The differences introduced 'in the beginning' have merely been re-produced or re-presented ever since, in a temporal-ity in which every re-production or re-presentation is separated by an interval from every other. This has implications for what we consider the 'presence' of anything 'in the present'. For it means that there is no longer such a thing as the 'simple' or 'self-evident' presence of something in the present. Everything that is present *now* is always a re-presentation, a repetition of past presence. Because separated by differentiating intervals, every past present is also always other than and different from any present present, and the difference 'which makes possible the presentation of the being-present, never presents itself as such. It is never given in the present' (M, 6).

Derrida calls the spatial and temporal pattern of differences which produced all things and has been reproduced ever since, *l'archi-écriture* or the arche-writing. This pattern of difference is a writing, first because it is an inscription, an imprint – it leaves a mark and is not just a disembodied voice; secondly, because it involves spacing, as words on a page are spaced; thirdly, because it makes everything that is a sign – as Derrida says, 'The thing-itself is a sign' (G, 72); and fourthly, because just as there is no one-time language, so there is no one-time writing – to be a writing, signs and spacing have to be recognisable, and to be recognisable, they have to be repeated, re-produced. Perhaps to preclude any accusation that he is simply projecting a modern theory of language back onto creation, Derrida insists that the writing of which he is speaking precedes the writing we know and is in fact its precondition: 'If writing signifies inscription, and first of all the durable institution of a sign (and this is the only irreducible kernel of the concept of writing)', Derrida insists, then 'the very idea of institution is unthinkable before the possibility of writing and outside its horizon, that is to say, quite simply outside the horizon itself, outside the world as a space of inscription, as openness to the emission and spatial distribution of signs, to the regulated play of their differences. . .' (G, 65–6). Derrida also insists that the writing of which he is speaking precedes and is the precondition for speech. Indeed, in the bible, God introduced difference between the heaven and the earth and between Himself and the heaven and earth before he began to speak ('Let there be light'). In this sense, the pattern of differences which, according to modern linguistic theory, constitutes language and permits both speech and the recording of speech on paper, precedes both human language and human speech. Or to put it another way, God created writing (the system of differences inscribed in the world) and with it the possibility of language before He began to speak and before anyone wrote down what he might have said. Derrida's reversal of the accepted order of things – language, speech, the recording of speech by writing – also enables him to argue that he is not speaking metaphorically, that the writing of which he is speaking is not simply an 'image' or a 'representation'. 'It is proper to the sign', he says, 'not to be an image' (G, 67), and indeed of what can the heaven and the earth be said to be an image? And spacing can certainly not be described as an image or representation since it can neither be said to be really 'present' or really 'absent'.

In Derrida's reading of the first words of Genesis, God not only introduced difference between the heaven and the earth and between every subsequent re-presentation of the heaven and earth in time; He also introduced difference between Himself and the heaven and earth and between Himself and every subsequent representation of Himself. In other words, He made himself wholly Other. In Derrida, as in *kabbalah*, the world is only possible by virtue of a certain contraction and withdrawal of the deity, and the world is henceforth separated from the deity by an abyss. This means, in the first instance, that we can no longer ask 'What differentiates?' or 'Who differentiates?' and answer the question by defining God as a creative subject, as a Presence outside the world from whom the world proceded or as a being comparable to anything we know. The God who appears in Genesis as a creating subject ('God created the heaven and the earth') or as a speaking subject ('And God said: Let there be light') is already inscribed in a system of differences – in a system which divides God from God, God from the world, the intelligible from the sensible, inside from outside, above from below, the active from the passive and speech from act. God as subject is himself already a product of the system of differences which constitutes the arche-writing and the possibility of language. Moreover, the God who appears in Genesis as a creating and speaking subject appears in language; he is already a product of language. God as subject is 'inscribed in language, is a "function" of language, becomes a *speaking* subject only by conforming his speech, even in the said "creation" . . . to the system of prescriptions of language as a system of differences, or at least to the general law of differ[e]nce . . .' (M, 16). To think of God as a subject, as a Creator or Speaker, is to reduce his Otherness: it is to make him a subject like ourselves and to obliterate the difference between God and representations of God within the system of differences that constitutes everything within our ken.

The original difference between God and all that is and between God as Origin and God as Subject also means that God as Origin – or what God signifies transcendentally – always eludes us. 'The meaning is always out of play' (G, 367). We cannot work back from the world as arche-writing to some prior or transcendental signified because there is, by definition, no necessary resemblance between graphic images and what they signify. The graphic image is always 'arbitrary' and 'unmotivated' with regard to what it represents; there is always a difference between the marks used to signify something and what they are used to signify. The graphic images 't' or 'tea' no more resemble or reflect the sound or substance of what they signify than the oppositions inscribed in the world between the sensible and the intelligible, the passive and the active, the inner and the outer resemble God viewed as the original well-spring from which such differences emerged. Nor can we work back from the world as a system of differentiated signs, where the 'thing-itself' is understood to be a sign, for the sign is always separated by a difference and a delay from the signifier that comes to represent it – just as there has always already been a difference and a delay between the origin signified by the appearance of the heaven and the earth and the appearance of the heaven and the earth as signifiers of that origin. To put it another way, the origin is always lacking except in the form of the heaven and earth as signifiers of that origin. What is signified '*is always already in the position of a signifier*' (G, 108) and 'the meaning is always out of play' (G, 367).

Another way of saying this is that the world as a system of signs is a *supplement* for the missing signified, for the originating God who differentiated himself from the heaven and the earth and from representations of Him as a subject within the system of differences. 'The sign', says Derrida 'is always the supplement of the thing itself' (G, 208). A supplement is first of all that which is supplementary: it is that which 'seems to add itself as a fullness to a fullness' (ED, 314), that which heaps plenitude on plenitude and multiplies presence. The heaven and the earth, with their rivers, streams, and oceans with their greater lights for the day and their lesser lights for the night, with their host of growing, creeping and moving things, and with all their re-presentations are a supplement in this sense. 'The supplement *adds*; there is a surplus, a plenitude enriching another plenitude, a *plurality* of presence' (G, 208). But a supplement is also that which supplies a lack, that which replaces something which is missing, that which heaps plenitude on plenitude only to fill a fundamental void. A graphic sign is always a supplement in this sense because it always stands for something which is missing, always substitutes itself for the immediate presence of the thing, always shows itself in the stead of the thing itself. The heaven and the earth and all that is within our orbit show themselves instead of the God who has held himself in reserve; they 'take the place of the King' or of the father who has never been present in the world and who cannot be conjured into presence by that which has come to be in his place: 'In this play of representations, the point of origin becomes ungraspable. There are things, waters, images, an infinite reference of one to the other, but no longer any source' (G, 55).

The world as supplement is also what Derrida calls the *pharmakon* – at once the evil and the remedy. The supplement, the plurality of presence, is the evil in so far as it is not the king yet shows itself in the place of the king. But it is also the remedy for this evil, in so far as it can be used as a starting point for a return to the king. Not itself the origin of the world (in the sense of the originating source and the original unity), the supplement can nevertheless become 'the origin of the origin' (G, 90), the place from which to begin to think the origin, on condition that its difference from the origin is taken into account. Because the writing of the world is different from its Author, difference is the key to origin, and 'the origin of speculation is', once again, 'difference'.

Difference can help to recuperate at least some of the irrecuperable origin if it is conceived in an additional way: not only as a separating interval, but also as a linking interval. The word break (*brisure*) contains both these ideas. In English, as in French, break means a gap, an interruption in continuity, a separation between two things; but used of a hinge, it also means a joint or articulation of elements. 'Difference', says Derrida, 'is articulation' (G, 96). As articulation, difference means that each determinate thing or moment in time bears a relation, a connection, to something other than itself, preserving in itself the mark of the other. The present could not be a re-presentation if it bore no relation to a past presentation which is and remains other than itself, and if what had been marked out in that past presentation were not in some way re-marked in the present. A signifier could not signify if it bore no relation to a signified which is other than itself, and if it were in no way marked by the signified. The origin may be lacking except in the form of the heaven and the earth as signifiers of that origin, but the heaven and the earth nevertheless bear the mark of their origin; they bear a relation to what is other than themselves.

This is where the arche-writing as a system of differences inscribed in the space and time of the world becomes what Derrida calls the *arche-trace*. The arche-trace makes it possible to think both the original separation of god from the world and the world as a 'testament' (G, 101) to God. Unlike an inscription which can be considered without reference to its inscriber, a trace is *nothing* if it is not a sign or signal of something other than itself. A trace is a track, a path, a mark or a sign left behind by someone or something that has passed. This is why Levinas used the word trace for the moment when God 'passed by' Moses and showed him – literally: what was after Him or behind Him.[7] From this point of view, the world could be described as a mark of a past event and as the wake left by God's passing. The trace marks the absence in the present of what has passed, the disappearance of its origin: 'The absence of the *other* here-now, of an other transcendental present, of an *other* origin of the world appears as such, presenting itself as an irreducible absence in the presence of the trace' (G, 68). But the trace is, at the same time, an affirmation that something has passed, a vestige which bears the mark of the other: 'the *wholly other* announces itself as such – without any simplicity or identity or resemblance or continuity – in that which is not it' (G, 69). The announcement of the other in the trace it leaves cannot be described as the affirmation of a presence, even of a past presence, for the trace left by someone or something evokes it without presenting an image or a similitude of it and without restoring its presence. A broken branch can signal someone's passing, can evoke something about the person who has passed (his height or strength perhaps), but it leaves in obscurity as much about him as it reveals. This is why Derrida also describes the presentation of the other in the trace as a dissimulation, an occultation, a concealment. Dissimulation, occultation and concealment preserve the otherness of the other. In Derrida's reading, God did not show even Moses his face.[8]

Presentation and occulation recur in the temporal dimension of the trace. To trace is also to trace over something, to 'copy by following and marking its lines on a superimposed sheet through which they are visible'. This aspect of the trace, which Derrida first develops in an early essay on Freud,[9] describes re-presentation as a re-marking of what had been marked out in an other presentation. But re-presentation also contains its own areas of occultation and concealment. For one thing, the re-presentation, the temporal copy is all we have; the origin is always 'repressed': 'Everything begins with reproduction. [It is a case of] always already – that is of depots of a meaning which has never been present, whose signified present is always re-constituted later, *nachträglich* after the event' (ED, 314). For another thing, the becoming space of time, the intervals or delays between re-presentations, give traces a binary character, like the open-closed, present-absent rhythm of a computer: 'Traces only produce the space of their inscription by giving themselves the period of their effacement. From the origin, in the present of their first impression, they are constituted by the double force of repetition and effacement, of readability and unreadability' (ED, 334). Unlike an inscription which has a measure of durability, a trace is a mark that can be effaced.

According to Derrida, traces cover the whole field of being and all of time. The problem is how to return from this multiplicity of signals and pathways to the God who has passed. For, like the Hebrew word used for God in the first sentence of Genesis (*Elohim*), the world as a tracework is not simple or singular; it is plural and complex, a 'plurality of presence'. To seek the One who in the beginning differentiated Himself from the plural God who is the subject of the first sentence of Genesis is to seek a unity capable of generating and encompassing a plurality of differences without sacrificing its unity. And because, as it is written, 'there is no oneness in any form like His', this in turn involves thinking of unity in new ways.

Derrida's solution to this problem is to think of difference as the trace of God's passing and to conceive of it this time not only as a separating principle and as a linking principle, but as an 'opening' which 'grants a possible letting appear' and a possible letting disappear.[10] Difference is the opening which lets both the plural phenomena of the world and their originating unity appear and dis-appear.

Difference as the opening of divisions allows all things to appear. It is the opening between the waters and the waters which made it possible for the heaven and the earth to become present, and the opening between their re-presentations which constitutes their being in time. Difference is the opening of the division between supplement and origin, presence and absence, the sensible and the intelligible, speech and act, subject and object, and between everything else that is distinct. It is the cistern out of which all things are hewn and the source of all oppositions. Difference as the opening which lets all things appear is the One, the unique generator of the plurality of all that is. Irreducible, differentiating, disseminating, difference is 'the principle of life' (G, 284). But difference is also 'the principle of death' (G, 284) and the place where all divisions disappear. For in the opening, in the spacing, in that which is between differentiateds, there are no articulations, no intervals, no determinations and no differences. The opening, the spacing is a pure unity without alterity. In difference is indifference, and indifference, indeterminacy is nothing; it is non-being and death. For Reb Derrida, as for Jewish tradition, the world was created out of nothing: 'There was nothing before "In the beginning"' (G, 357). And the world and everything in it can at any moment return to the nothing whence it came. For as Derrida has been careful to establish, difference is temporal as well as spatial. In accordance with Jewish tradition, Derrida's divine principle is not only the creator, but also the sustainer: 'in His goodness, He renews the creation every day, continually'.[11]

Presentations have to be re-presented; the oppositions have to recur every day, continually. Wherever and whenever there is no difference, there is indifference, non-being, death. Difference as the ever renewing source of life and death is 'both the first and the last'.

Difference is the 'hint at a glimmer of what is beyond closure', the opening to the wholly other outside the oppositions which constitute everything within our orbit. It is 'the opening to the first exteriority in general, the enigmatic relation of the living to its other, and of an inside to an outside' (G, 103). If everything in being is paired and opposed, the difference, the opening, the black hole whence opposites emerge and into which they return is outside the play of oppositions in the world; it is other than they. And if all our knowledge is contained in oppositions, then difference, the opening in which all things become the same, is also that which is outside our knowledge. But difference is, at the same time, always within closure and within knowledge. For difference also occurs and recurs within and between everything in nature, culture and time to separate all things, beings, words, ideas and moments from each other and to make them what they 'are'. Both outside our ken and within it, difference is at once manifest and hidden, at once the supreme mystery forever hidden from us by a veil and the law of the world. And these are not the only contradictions it embraces. Difference is not only both outside and inside, both transcendent and immanent, both hidden and manifest, both absent as being and present in being, both the productive principle of life and the erasing principle of death; difference is also always the same and always different, always unique and always multiple. For if the work of creation is renewed day by day, continually, if difference is an origin and a vanishing point which occurs in every part of every system and is re-presented throughout time; then we have to do with the multiple recurrence of multiple origins and multiple vanishing points which are always the same without ever being identical with one another. As Derrida says: 'The expression "in the beginning" and all the indices one might use to describe it, do not refer to any date, to any event, to any chronology. One can vary the facts without varying the structural invariable' (G, 357). For Derrida, the structural invariable is the space, the interval, the black or blank hole which is always *between* any two signs, and this structural invariable is singular without being single. [12] Not the least part of its singularity is the fact that, by its own principle of in-difference, it can only be one and multiple, outside and inside, transcendent and immanent, absent and present and all the other normally mutually exclusive things it is, by being none of these, by having no identity or at least nothing that we could recognise as an identity or determination.

This 'wholly other' which is also 'always the same' requires a name. The names of God, especially those which may not be pronounced, have traditionally been thought to unite multiple aspects of His nature and manifestations, but Derrida rejects these because they are proper names. The act of giving a proper name, he argues, is an act of violence against what is proper and specific to that which is being named. By classifying it and inscribing it in a system of differences, the proper name 'obliterates' what is unique to that which is being named, and thus repeats what Derrida describes as the 'violence' of the arche-writing: 'To think the unique *in* the system, to inscribe it in [a system] such is the violence of the arche-writing: arche-violence, loss of the proper, loss of absolute proximity, loss of presence to self, loss, in fact, of what has never been. . .' (G, 164). To give the difference which 'alone has made, does make and will make all things' and which has never been a being or a subject a proper name is to rob it of its uniqueness and to inscribe it in the system of differences within closure. Derrida's name will therefore not be a proper name, and it will not be within the system of differences.

A name is only valuable, as far as Derrida is concerned, if it functions as 'a sign marking the necessity for a *supplementary* symbolic content' (ED, 424). A word like *mana*, he explains, can signify a host of different and contradictory things (a force and an action, a quality and a state, something abstract or concrete, omnipresent or localized) and it can function as different parts of speech (substantive, verb or adjective) because it is none of these; it is only a 'zero symbolic value'; it means nothing in itself and therefore marks 'a lack which must be supplied' (ED, 425). A name is only useful, if it lacks any original signified, any original content or meaning of its own, so that this original lack must be supplied by adding contents and multiplying meanings which will substitute themselves for the original signified in a vain attempt to make the name's non-existent original meaning present. A name is a useful sign in other words only if its structure is that of the world as a system of supplements for a 'meaning that is always out of play'.

The best way to find a name which has no meaning (and which

is thus also immediately outside the system of differences) is to make one up. Therefore, although Derrida is otherwise content to 'slide' into extant names and to re-mark them with ex-centric meanings of his own, in this case, he invents one. The name he invents – *différance* is interesting not so much for its supplementary meanings, which are those of difference as described above, as for its structure.

First of all, like the world as arche-writing, the name itself is created by nothing but a slight graphic difference – the difference between writing difference with an a or an e. And yet this difference produces a new word, a new sign. The inaudible nature of the difference between the a and the e in French marks the crucial but imperceptible lack which has to be supplied. The graphic effect of the difference, which is to produce a sign – *différance* – which is different from difference, marks the generative aspect of difference: 'That which is written *différance* is the ludic movement which 'produces' by what is not simply an activity, these differences, these effects of difference . . . *Différance* is the non-full, non-simple 'origin', the structured, differing, and deferring origin of differences' (M, 12). The a in the word *différance* thus marks both the need for and the possibility of supplementation. The a in *différance*, 'silent, secret and discrete as the grave', itself (at least in handwriting) shaped like a small blank hole, also marks the point where all possible supplements and effects of difference within *différance* fade into in-difference and disappear into the nothingness of the grave.

By giving the name *différance* a Latin etymology, Derrida succeeds in placing it at the intersection of space and time – at the point where space becomes time and time becomes space – and thus in providing it with a host of spatial and temporal supplements. Temporally, this name which originally has absolutely no meaning can now be supposed to stand for a deferring, a delay, a reserve and a re-presentation – the reserve of the signified, the deferring of its presence, the delay between re-presentations, and the detour via the sign and the supplement which constitutes the life of all things in the world. Spatially, this name which originally has absolutely no meaning, can now be supposed to stand for 'not being identical, being other, being discernible', for the interval, distance and spacing which is necessary for things to be discernibly other, and even for the conflictual, polemical element in otherness. Such supplements are additions of meaning to a name which originally has no meaning or whose original meaning is 'out of play'. But as Derrida points out, there are also supplements which function as 'non synonymous substitutes' for the meaning which is lacking – such as the arche-writing, the arche-trace, spacing, the supplement and the pharmakon (M, 13).

These supplements and substitutes for *différance* re-produce the structure of the world in two further ways. First of all, Derrida's supplements and substitutes need no more cohere than does the world. As the world can be a 'bundle' (*faisceau*) of signs, some of which connect and some of which do not, while remaining one world and bearing traces of the passing, so the supplements for *différance* can sometimes cohere and sometimes be disparate, sometimes repeat each other, and sometimes oppose each other, while belonging to the same name and remaining traces of the 'wholly other' which is always the same. Space, interval, division, articulation, deferring, delay, reserve, the origin of differences, the different origins, the effects of difference, the death of difference in-difference, the opening which is prior to the emergence of distinct objects or fields of knowledge, that which comprehends, exceeds and unifies all differences and all differentiateds – this bundle of supplementary signs is assembled in a word, *différance*. *Différance* unifies them only in so far as it does not 'really' exist, in so far as it has no determinate meaning of its own; and in so far as it does exist, it exists only in Derridean texts as a unique recurrent, and always somewhat mysterious point of unity for these supplements, which itself has come to 'usurp the place of the King'.

Secondly, Derrida's supplements and substitutes for *différance* resemble the world by heaping plenitude on plenitude without any necessary or foreseeable end. As the phenomena of the world multiply and change while always remaining ultimately the same, so the supplements and substitutes for difference can multiply and change, while yet remaining ultimately the same: hymen can be added and *marge–marque–marche*, and the cave, and the well, and the pyramid, and the pharmacy *ad infinitum* or until in-difference and death. As in the arche-writing of the world, where there are things, waters, images, an infinite reference of one to the other, but no longer any origin, so in Derrida's writings, there can be infinite referentiality among *différance*, hymen, well, pyramid, *entre* and *antre*, envaginations, blanks, columns of zeros and so on – without anything more than a trace either of these words' 'original' meanings as words or of the origin of their Derridean meaning in something other than themselves (whether this other be conceived as an other text, as the unplumbed depths of an other word, or as a divine mystery). Derrida's signs are as readable or as unreadable as the heaven and the earth.

Yet for all its supplements and substitutions, *différance* also conceals and reveals a lack which some might consider more fundamental than that which it so elliptically indicates. As 'Reb Derrida' would no doubt be the first to admit, *différance* is God and is not God. *Différance* may stand in the place of the God indicated by the first four of the thirteen principles of the Jewish faith:[13] 'Author and ruler of everything that has been created', [*différance*] 'alone has made, does make and will make all created things'; 'there is no manner of unity like unto [it]; 'not a body . . . free from all the accidents of matter, and having no form whatsoever, [*différance*] is also 'the first and the last'. But *différance* is not, at the same time, the God 'to whom alone it is right to pray', who 'knows every deed of men and all their thoughts', and who 'rewards those that keep his commandments and punishes those that transgress them'. Like Spinoza's God, *différance* can be approached by the intellect and by study, but not by prayer or experience. *Différance* is exclusively – in Chouraqui's translation of *bereshit*, 'in the beginning', as quoted by Derrida – 'in the head'. *Différance* is not the God encountered; it is not the God who spoke to Moses 'inwardness to inwardness', the God that Maimonedes, Levinas and Buber translated into the language of philosophy;[14] and it is not the righteous God of the rabbis, who fixed the bounds of the sea, as he fixed the bounds of good and evil.

This difference between Derrida and Levinas or Buber, and between Derrida and the rabbis is not incidental; it is not merely a matter of temperament or preference. For it enables Derrida to graft one aspect of Jewish tradition onto the post-Nietzschean view of the world as an absurd and arbitrary game of interpretations and re-interpretations. If the 'living God' has never been encountered, if *différance* lacks and has always lacked a presence, a face-to-face, and a voice, then there has never been any divine explanation or guidance; above all, there has never been any divine judgement of anything or anyone. Dividing everything else from everything else, *différance* has failed to divide the holy from the profane, the sacred from the sinful, and the permitted from the prohibited. Uniting everything else in its quasi-mystical *coincidentia opposito-rium*, it has failed to unite anything to its meaning or to its ground. At once magical and mechanical, *différance* can only suspend all meanings, including 'received' divine meanings, returning the divinity to its almost impenetrable mystery and the world to absurdity, arbitrariness and play. In the infinite self-referentiality of a world 'born by suspending its relation to any origin' (G, 55), whose meaning is 'always out of play', signs, words and ideas circulate without any fixed point of orientation, without anything to anchor them in place to stop them turning and turning about. 'Language turns like the earth' (G, 310), in a void, about its own polar oppositions; and the merest flick of the wrist suffices to make the North displace the South or the South the North, for life to occupy the place of death and death of life, for the absent to become the present and the present what is 'really' absent. If anyone on this globe succeeds in clearing a window through these merely linguistic or semiotic revolutions, what is there to see but the bottomless void, the abyss, the darkness on the face of the deep? At the same time, anyone installing himself in the black hole of difference and looking down at us from a position 'outside' the oppositions which constitute our knowledge and our world, would see much the same spectacle of absurdity. What sense do our oppositions between things and language, or between nature and culture make when these 'entities' are constituted by difference, and when each of them is itself nothing but a system of differences? What sense does our opposition between space and time make when the same opening makes space time and time space? What is the point of opposing origin and structure or structure and history when difference is an origin that occurs through out the system and a structure which is re-presented throughout history – when we have to do with the multiple recurrence of multiple origins? From the point of view of *différance* what are all our categories and oppositions but the supreme vanity of vanities? And what do they all boil down to but some arbitrary divisions of *différance*?

If, as Derrida says, *différance* is the result of 'beginning, strategically, from the place and time where "we" are' (M, 7), then *différance* cannot only be described in terms of some of the more abstruse aspects of the Jewish God; it must also be described as a testimony to the God that post-Nietzschean philosophy and modern linguistics inscribe as dead, and as a deconstruction both of the possibility of any I–Thou relationship to God and of the traditional rabbinical understanding of God as a just and merciful judge who is accessible to human prayer.

Ultimately, *différance* must also be described as a de-construction even of those aspects of Jewish tradition which Derrida seems to be using. As we have seen in our reading of Derrida's early writings as a supplement for – an addition to and substitution for – the first phrase of Genesis, *différance* is the product of 'the regulated transformation of one language by another, of one text by another' (Pos., 31). And as such *différance* 'issues' from the bible in two opposite senses. On the one hand, there are what Derrida calls 'the most visible traits of filiation which show that it descends from the bible'; but on the other hand, *différance* also 'escapes it without any possibility of return, no longer reflects its image' (Diss., 63). One way of describing the way *différance* escapes Genesis is to say that it has been transformed from a moment of theology and metaphysics into a cosmology and graphology. Another way of describing the transformation is to say that Derrida has converted God and Genesis into a limited number of 'structural invariables' by excluding all referents and all signifieds, whether absolute, historical or 'real'. Real and historical referents drop away when Derrida points out, in the continuation of a passage already quoted which is worth quoting again, that Genesis is a fiction: 'The expression 'in the beginning' and all the indices one might use to describe it, do not refer to any date, to any event, to any chronology. One can vary the facts without varying the structural invariable. . . Recourse to factual illustration even to the remote events of the origin, is purely fictitious' (G, 357). The problem here is not whether or not it is still shocking to describe Genesis as fictitious. The problem is the status of the complex Derrida calls *différance* if Genesis is viewed as fictitious – or indeed if Plato, or Hegel or Heidegger, whom Derrida could also be shown to 'transform',[15] are viewed as fictitious. If *différance* is merely a transformation of an already fictitious text; a displacement of a double of an already dubious or incomplete 'reality'; a supplement for what is already a supplement; a transformation of something that never was and that itself reflects no simple or single 'reality' – then in so far as *différance* is visibly filiated to the bible (or to any other 'text'), it is nothing but 'an allusion, but an allusion to nothing', 'a speculum without reality', 'a difference without reference, or rather a reference without referent' (Diss., 234). To build on a fictitious text, even if it be the bible, is not to build on a firm foundation; it is to build on the abyss. Moreover, if the 'original' God of Creation has always held himself in reserve; if this original God, the *Ein Sof*, is always and has always been unfathomable and outside our knowledge, while the God of the bible is merely a re-presentation caught, not only in a fictional text, but also in a system of graphic and semiotic differences which transform him into the subject he is not (either in Derrida or in orthodox Jewish tradition), then God disappears as an absolute referent. There is nothing to which to refer.

By his 'regulated transformation', Derrida effaces all traces of the origin of *différance*: 'He burns his text and effaces the traces of his steps' (M, 163). All that remains of the 'visible filiation' to the bible are the 'structural invariables' Derrida collects under the name *différance*, deprived of all meaning and all reference beyond themselves. This, too, preserves some sort of visible filiation to the bible. For structural invariables inscribed in the world without any meaning beyond themselves are precisely what, basing themselves on the bible, the rabbis have called law or *Ḥok*. The *Ḥok*, the law, is by definition something inscribed or engraved in the world:

> The verb *ḥakkok*, etymologically, signifies the act of engraving, of making incisions in a hard surface such as stone or metal . . . Used in religious law, the term signifies that the *ḥok* is characterized by perpetual validity and is 'graven in the rock for ever'. . . The Decalogue was engraved in two tablets of stone . . . Nature's laws are also *ḥukkim*, unalterable and universal . . . The Bible uses the work *ḥok* in regard to nature, as in Proverbs 8:29: 'When he gave the sea his decree (*ḥukko*) that the waters should not transgress his commandment'.[16]

Moreover, the rabbis traditionally teach that a *ḥok* is a law whose purpose and meaning are not clear to us, which can therefore only be conformed to with simple unquestioning obedience. Where there is no divine lawgiver, this law remains as the law of 'a machine defined by its pure functioning and not by its final utility, its meaning, its yield or its work' (M, 126). The structural invariables of *différance* are the law of the world as machine.

DECONSTRUCTION: GAME, RULE, REPETITION, WRITING

We have already said all that we *wanted to say* . . . Since we have already said it all, people will have to be patient if we go on a little longer. If we extend ourselves by dint of the game. Thus if we *write* a little: Plato already said in the *Phaedrus* that writing can only repeat (itself), that it 'always signifies the same thing', and that it is a 'game' (Diss., 73).

One of the lessons Derrida has taught us is that the most effective way of coming to grips with a text is not necessarily to meet it head on; and that sometimes a more 'oblique' approach, which focuses on apparently incidental, peripheral or extraneous details, reveals more about the workings of a text or about its inner contradictions. As in the passage quoted above, game, repetition and writing are often connected in Derrida's texts, but how they connect only becomes apparent if we begin from somewhere else.

In a passage immediately preceding the one quoted above, Derrida describes both writing and the game in terms of authority, prescription and necessity: 'He will have understood nothing of the game who feels himself *authorised* to add on more, that is to add just anything . . . The supplement of reading or writing *must* be *rigorously prescribed*, but by the *necessity* of a game; this sign *must* be granted the system of all its *powers*' (my italics) (Diss., 72). Elsewhere, again linking writing and the game, Derrida emphasises that the writing is not arbitrary, the game no mere game of chance:

> The adventurous excess of a writing which is no longer guided by any knowledge is not given over to improvisation. The accident or the throw of the dice which 'opens' the text do not contradict the *rigorous necessity* of its *formal ordering*. The game here is a unity of chance and *rule* . . . (Diss., 62).

Describing the repetition he calls 'double reading', 'double writing' and 'double science', Derrida speaks of 'the *rule* according to which each concept *necessarily* receives two similar marks – a repetition without identity – one inside, the other outside the deconstructed system' (Diss., 10). Examples could be multiplied: there is a '*law* that constrains' writing, a '*law* of dissemination' and a '*law* of supplementarity'; the game is often described as '*regulated*'; it has its '*protocol*' and its '*necessary phases*'; and one has only to count the number of times Derrida uses the word *must* (*On doit, Il faut*) in *Positions* or in the *Hors Livre* of *La Dissémination* when describing the necessary textual operations.

The rules are indeed necessary for the writing, the repetition and the game. It is only because it is bound to follow the rules of the game that writing finds itself in the position of only being able to repeat (itself?) and of always signifying the same thing. The rules of the game consist of repeating or re-producing the same 'structural invariables' each time one reads or writes about a text. In other words, they consist of repeatedly re-presenting all the facets of *différance*. This extends writing by making it possible and necessary to keep repeating. Repetitions need not be identical – indeed their pleasure and their wit lie in their apparent difference – but should they fail to reproduce the same structural invariables, should they fail to re-present *différance*, then they would be 'adding just anything' and transgressing the rules of the game. If, as Jonathan Culler has pointed out, deconstruction 'encourages critics to identify and produce certain types of structures',[17] it is because it prescribes the structures which they are to identify and produce. If deconstruction 'brings out inexorable regularities',[18] it is because it also adds them in. So if many readers have complained that 'deconstruction makes everything sound the same',[19] it is because they are accurate readers — it is supposed to.

The rule to be applied and re-applied in the reading and writing of texts is fourfold. Although these four folds have already been explored indirectly in the previous section, it is worth focussing on them here, first to reconsider them in the context of critical reading and writing, and secondly to identify the ways Derrida 'doubles' or 'squares' the rules by using them once in describing his reading of any given text and once in the form he gives his own writing.

The fourfold rule can conveniently be designated by Derrida's figure X. To read this figure, one has to focus on the blanks. The blanks in the sign form four Vs (or folds) placed back to back so that they intersect with one another. As we will see, the four Vs of the fourfold rule – DiVision, Articulation, the PiVot and the Veil of Displacement — are closely intertwined. Derrida usually attempts to get them all into each of his major texts.

1. DiVision

There are two types of division.

The first type of division is always a division of the waters from the waters: in other words, it is always a division of something that we would normally assume constitutes a single entity or that we consider as having an identity of its own. Division is therefore applied to entities which are thought to have a being, a presence, an identity, an essence, a truth, an inherent coherence, a fundamental form or a property of their own, as well as to the concepts of being, presence, identity, essence, truth, form and property themselves. Division differentiates such entities from themselves: it shows that what we thought was one and the same is in fact at least two and different, and that what we thought was identical with itself is in fact divided against itself.

The 'text', whether literary or philosophical, has long been assumed to constitute a single, identifiable entity. The corollary has been that the critic or commentator's task has been understood as that of harmonising any inconstistencies and of explaining any incoherences or obscurities he may find in the text in such a way as to bring out each text's basic unity, fundamental coherence, inherent form or essential point. Division deconstructs this notion of the text as a single, coherent and identifiable entity by seeking out each text's inconsistencies, incoherences and obscurities and by developing them into full scale contradictions. These contradictions are not harmonised in any way. They are held apart, spaced out, in the reading (*mise en écart* or *chiasmus* being the technical terms for this) so that each text is presented as saying first one thing and then its opposite. The text can then be described as playing 'two scenes'. This reduces the text to indeterminacy, since if the text is 'saying' both one thing and its opposite, it is in fact saying nothing. A text which argues against itself is assuming no determinate position. As Derrida points out in *Otobiographies*, to be double is also to be neutral (Ot., 64).

Examples of this technique can be taken from 'La Pharmacie de Platon' and from 'Ouisia et Gramme'. Since Derrida's arguments are lengthy and complex, they can only be sketched out very rapidly here to show their basic structure. In 'La Pharmacie de Platon', Derrida explains why Socrates argues that writing is an evil: for him, knowledge is a living repetition in the mind of man of the Truth, the Idea or the essential Form of things, which can be defended and elucidated by the knower; writing, on the other hand, is merely a dead and mechanical repetition, one which can only repeat the same words and which can, to boot, be used as a crutch for memory and as a substitute for true knowledge. Derrida goes on to show that Socrates also frequently uses the metaphor of writing to describe how the living knowledge he approves is inscribed or engraved in men's memory. There is therefore, Derrida argues, both a good writing and a bad writing, a living writing and a dead writing, a true writing and writing which is only a semblance of the truth. Writing in the text is therefore both good and bad, both living and dead, both true and a sham. Writing 'in itself', if it still has an in-itself, is therefore neither good nor bad, neither truth nor lie; it is either or neither, both or none of these. In 'Ouisia et Gramme', Derrida uses the same technique, explaining first that Aristotle assumed the existence of the present and the continuity of time and then reproducing and developing those arguments in his text which suggest that time is composed of multiple divisible parts and that the present does not as such exist. What is time if it is either a continuum or not a continuum or neither of these? What is the present if it neither exists nor does not exist, or if it both exists and does not exist? And what is an argument that assumes the existence of a present which it also shows does not exist?[20]

The second type of division is always a division of two things or two terms which we would normally assume go together and which seem to us to make sense only in conjunction with one another: as the Creator was separated from his creation, so origins are separated from what has originated, causes are separated from their effects, reality from its representations, the premise of an argument from its consequences and so on. Such familiar couples are uncoupled by cutting away the first term (*coupure, tranche*) and by showing that the second term (what has originated, effects, representations, the consequences of a premise) proliferates without any basis, repeating and re-producing itself completely independently of the first term. This operation is often described as a *mise en abîme* since successive re-presentations (or arguments or effects or whatever) are shown to be built, in effect, on nothing. This operation is also known as a supplementary structure, since each successive re-presentation differs somewhat from the one before, so that it is in fact adding itself to and substituting itself for the fundamental lack.

Derrida uses this type of division to separate the 'text' from any basis or origin it may be thought to have in truth, in reality, in history or in its author and to show that, for all their differences, texts repeat nothing but each other and themselves. For instance, in 'Ouissia et Gramme', Derrida shows how Bergson's text, Hegel's text and Heidegger's text all repeat, with some supplementation, the *problématique* of Aristotle's text, which is itself premised on the existence of a present which it also shows does not exist. In 'La Double Séance', successive imitations or representations are shown to imitate or re-present each other while lacking any original 'imitated': Mallarmé's *Mimique* re-presents a story he has read in a book, which recounts or re-presents a mimetic drama he has seen, which re-presents a crime which never took place. In 'Declarations of Independence' (Ot.), Derrida separates the American Declaration of Independence from any author or author-ity beyond itself by showing that Jefferson (who wrote it but did not sign it) wrote it as the representative of the representatives of the United States of America in congress; and that they in turn first corrected it and then signed it as representatives of a people (and a United States) which did not exist as such before the Declaration was signed. This chain of representation makes it impossible to locate the author or author-ity of the Declaration in any one person or group; and it leaves the Declaration both as the originator and as the guarantor of its own author-ity. The same structure recurs more mystically and apocalyptically in *La Carte Postale* and in *D'un Ton apocalyptique adopté naguère en philosophie*, when Derrida describes the scriptor of a text as an envoy or as an angel, in the sense of the Hebrew word for angel, *malach*, which means messenger. As an envoy or messenger, the scriptor merely receives and transmits that which has been dictated to him by an other who has received it from an other and so on. This chain of envoys again makes it impossible to locate the author of that which is being transmitted, just as it makes it impossible to decide on the destination of what is transmitted, for each envoy is also a receiver, and once inscribed on a square of paper, the transmission is open and accessible to anyone. Each envoy is thus a point of transition for an anonymous transmission to an anonymous destination; and the transmision or missive itself becomes something which is merely transmitted, merely sent. Considered as something inscribed on sheets of paper, it becomes a post(ed) card or a flying letter (*La Lettre volée*).[21]

The abyssal or supplementary structure can also be reversed. In other words, instead of reading a text or a series of texts as supplements for a missing origin, for a missing author, for a missing truth of for a missing reality, it is possible to present a text as holding its meaning or truth in reserve and as postponing or deferring its own meaning by talking about other texts. For instance, Derrida shows that one of Heidegger's notes to the first volume of *Sein and Zeit* is full of suggestions which are hinted at by his references to Aristotle, Bergson and Hegel but deferred to a second volume of *Sein und Zeit*, which may never have been written.

It should also be noted that this second, abyssal, type of division intersects very well with the first, chiasmic, type of division, and Derrida often uses them in conjunction. The origin, cause, premise or basis in reality can be cut away or thrust into the abyss very neatly by showing that, instead of being one identifiable entity, it is either nothing (determinate) or itself already an opposition based on nothing.

Both types of division are repeated in various ways in the forms Derrida gives his own writings.

For instance, the abyssal or supplementary structure recurs in *Marges de la Philosophie* when Derrida presents his own text, 'Ouisia et Gramme' (itself a slightly varied repetition of an earlier published version of the same text) as supplementing a note of Heidegger's – in which Heidegger comments on the way Hegel and Bergson draw on Aristotle's notion of the present – by describing the ways in which Bergson, Hegel, Kant and Heidegger all repeat Aristotle's uncertain notion of time. Here Derrida presents his own 'critical' text, 'Ouisia et Gramme', as part of the same series of variegated repetitions which it describes: as Bergson, Hegel, Kant and Heidegger's texts re-present Aristotle's text, sometimes one way and sometimes another, sometimes acknowledging the debt and sometimes not, so Derrida's text re-presents Aristotle's text and re-presents Bergson, Kant, Hegel and Heidegger's texts re-presenting Aristotle's text. (Derrida's own text also re-presents itself in so far as it contains a commentary on its own reading and a theoretical re-presentation of its own method). If at the same time Aristotle's text is so divided against itself that it undermines its own truth and its own basis in 'reality' and time, then all re-presentations of Artistotle's text – including Derrida's – must lack a basis in truth and reality, unless truth and reality consist in saying, with Derrida, that truth and reality are not present anywhere in this column of representations, and that what is in fact being represented in all these re-presentations of re-presentations is nothing.

The reverse version of this abyssal structure – where the meaning of one text is held in reserve and both hinted at and deferred by talking about other texts – is also apparent in Derrida's writings. As in 'Le puits and la pyramide', Derrida often reminds his readers that he is proceeding 'above all by detours'. What, if anything, Derrida's text, 'Le puits and la pyramide' 'wants to say' about wells or pyramids or signs or anything else can only be arrived at, if at all, by negotiating a series of detours: these consist first (and again) of the representations in Derrida's text of Hegel's texts, of Hegel's representation of Aristotle's text and of Saussure's place in the series; secondly, of 'anticipations' (*pierres d'attente*) of ideas which Derrida does not develop and footnotes in which he overdevelops ideas already developed in the text; and thirdly of the representations in Derrida's text of the methods it is applying to the reading of other texts.

The first type of division – that which separates a text from itself by introducing a chasm or distance between its two opposite meanings – is graphically illustrated in *La Dissémination* when Derrida inserts the essays entitled 'La Double Séance' (which are, among other things, on Mallarmé) between two parts of a single quotation from Mallarmé. The Mallarmé quotation begins at the end of Transe Partition (1) on p. 197 and concludes after the entire text of 'La Double Séance' at the beginning of Transe Partition (2) on p. 318. This marks the fact that literary and philosophical texts are divided from themselves and shown to have two separate and incompatible meanings only by the intervention of the critical text. It is the critical text which 'holds the book open' and prevents its two halves from closing back upon themselves to form a single self-consistent whole. Or to put it another way, it is the critical act of describing the rupture within the literary or philosophical text which produces that rupture. As Derrida says: 'to describe the composition of the mirrors, screens and walls in [Phillipe Sollers'] *Numbers*, the general structure of the machine, is already to be quoting or to be conforming to the prescription of another 'book', which thereby comes to be reinscribed in *Numbers*, preventing them [*Numbers*] from closing back into their own proper sequence' (Diss., 352). This opens the possibility of autobiography or autography: the critical text can inscribe its own 'speculative' or structural story in the literary or philosophical text, and its reading of the content of the literary or philosophical text can then be reapplied to or folded back on itself (see 'Spéculer – Sur Freud').

The first type of division – that which separates a text from itself – is also graphically illustrated in *La Dissémination* when Derrida inserts the page of quotations from Hegel, Sade and Mallarmé entitled Transe Partition (1) into the text of his essay: 'La

Pharmacie de Platon'. 'La Pharmacie de Platon' runs from page 71 to page 196; it is interrupted on p. 197 by the quotations of Transe Partition (1); and it concludes on page 198. This marks the fact that division is not a one-way operation. As the critical text divides the literary or philosophical text from itself, so quotations from literary or philosophical texts inserted in the body of the critical text divide the critical text from itself. The critical text prevents the literary or philosophical text from constituting a single coherent entity by inscribing in it 'the prescriptions of another book'. But quotations from the literary or philosophical text – and indeed the need for the critical text to say what it 'wants to say' by the detour of the literary or philosophical text – also prevents the critical text from closing back on itself as a single identifiable entity. They prevent the critical text from being that 'other book' it keeps trying to inscribe in the literary or philosophical text it is describing.

Whether by chance or by design, or by what Derrida calls 'a union of chance and rule', Transe Partition (1) is inserted in 'La Pharmacie de Platon' in such a way as to separate or partition this argument:

– One ought to distinguish between two repetitions.
– But they repeat each other still, they substitute themselves for each other.

from this argument:

– No they don't; they don't replace, they add.
– Exactly.

Is it always possible to distinguish between repetitions in Derrida's critical texts? Is it always possible to determine where Derrida's text is faithfully re-producing and representing a literary or philosophical text and where it is speaking by the 'detour' of the literary and philosophical text and inscribing in it 'the prescriptions of another book'? Is it always possible to distinguish between Derrida 'reading' Mallarmé or Hegel or Sollers or Plato and Derrida re-writing them and substituting his text and his auto-graph for theirs? Is it always possible to tell where a quotation in Derrida's text represents the text from which it is taken and where it either fuels Derrida's speculations or interrupts them? The transe-partition both partitions Derrida's text and is partitioned by another of Derrida's texts. The partition also falls where there is in fact, in Derridean terms, no partition: for the supplement is a repetition which both substitutes itself for something else and adds to it. Similarly, the representation of the literary or philosophical text and Derrida's critical text supplement each other, each supplying what the other lacks. They are so inserted into one another that it becomes 'undecidable' where one begins and the other ends and 'who is speaking' at any given time. Division in all its forms – as a rupture of self-identity, as a supplementary structure built on the abyss, or as the repetition of these in a writing – always falls back into the indeterminacy and 'undecidability' of *différance*.

2. Articulation

Articulation always joins what we would not normally think of as conjoined. It operates primarily through the word. De Saussure pointed out that 'a word can always evoke everything that can be associated with it in one way or another . . . A particular word is like the centre of a constellation; it is the point of convergence of an indefinite number of co-ordinated terms'.[22] And one of the Talmudic principles of interpretation consists of 'inferring from the similarity of words or phrases occurring in two passages, that what is expressed in the one applies also to the other'. Derrida merges the two. He treats the word both as the trace of all its possible meanings in different passages, texts or contexts, and as the trace of all its differential relations to other words. These relations can be purely phonic (like *marge–marque–marche* or *crise de vers–crise de nerfs–brise d'hivers–brise de verre*); they can be based on a common root (De Saussure's classic example is *faire–défaire–refaire–contrefaire*, Derrida's is *pharmakon–pharmakos–pharmakoi–pharma*); or they can be what Saussure calls mental associations 'formed outside discourse' (like the sign, the pyramid and the well). Where, as Saussure points out, 'the mind naturally discards associations that becloud the intelligibility of discourse', Derrida exploits the fact that contradictory or incongruous meanings (or texts) can be conjoined by virtue of the fact that they all 'hinge' on the same word. By treating the word as the trace of all its possible meanings, contexts, associations and differential relations, and by trying to show that as many of these as possible 'apply' or produce what Derrida calls 'an effect of sense' in any given text or context, Derrida turns the word into 'the centre of a constellation, the point of convergence of an indefinite number of coordinated terms'. He makes the word a 'middle point' (*Mittelpunkt*), 'at once a central point on which all opposite beams converge' and 'a *milieu*, in the sense of an element, the medium in which different meanings and associations can be linked' (M, 92).

If division ruptured 'the text' as a single entity by attacking it from within, articulation attacks the notion of the text as a single, self-enclosed entity by dissolving its boundaries, by de-limiting it. By following the traces of a word both 'in' the text and 'outside' it, and by re-marking the word as it appears 'in' a text with its various meanings, differential relations, associations, and contexts 'outside' that text, articulation joins the 'inside' of a text to its 'outside'. It joins the word or meaning which is 'present' in the text to words, meanings and associations which are 'absent' in the text but implied by the word's chain of associations or differential relations. Of course, the precondition for this operation is to erase such concepts as authorial intention, linguistic intentionality and the difference between conscious and unconscious intentions. Cleverly used, a word in one literary or philosophical text can lead not only to any number of other literary or philosophical texts, but almost anywhere, in a system of 'infinite reference of one to another'. As Derrida explains: 'Any sign can be quoted, placed in quotation marks; in this way, it can break with any context that is given and engender an infinity of new contexts in a way which can never be saturated' (M, 381).

Here, for instance, very briefly, is what happens to the word *pharmakon* in 'La pharmacie de Platon'. *Pharmakon* is developed in terms of its different meanings (charm, philtre, drug, remedy, poison) and in terms of the contradictory implications of these meanings (life and death, sickness and health, beneficent or maleficent effects). It is also developed in terms of its associations with other words formed from the same root, like *pharmakos* (scapegoat, magician, sorcerer, poisoner) or *pharmakeus* (pharmacy) and in terms of the implications of these meanings (the banishment of the scapegoat, the mixture of remedies and poisons in the pharmacy). Once picked out of the *Phaedrus*, the word *pharmakon* with all its meanings and associations is followed into other texts (other Platonic texts, texts on the ritual practices and mythological beliefs of the ancient Greeks and Egyptians, texts on the etymology of Greek words etc.) like a rolling stone which does gather moss wherever it goes. Whatever is associated syntagmatically with the word *pharmakon* (or *pharmakos–pharmakeus*) in any text in which it is found, sticks to it. If Plato once uses the word *pharmakon* (or *pharmakos–pharmakeus*) in connection with writing, or speech, or memory or knowledge or mimesis or law or Socrates, then that in connection with which Plato mentions the word *pharmakon* becomes its new context. The word *pharmakon* acquires new 'meanings' and implications in each of the contexts in which it is thus placed. And conversely, the contexts become aspects of the *pharmakon*: writing, speech, memory, mimesis and the law become life-giving remedies and deathly poisons and Socrates becomes a magician, a sorcerer, the administrator of the remedy and the poison and the scapegoat to be banished. Thus different subjects, different contexts and different characters from different texts, with all their beneficient and maleficent effects, find themselves conjoined by the virtue – or the vice – of the word *pharmakon*. As the point of articulation of all these diverse and contradictory elements, the *word pharmakon* is a pharmacy: the place where the different remedies and poisons are mixed (up).

By following in the traces of a word from one text into other texts and contexts which are 'outside' it, therefore, articulation dissolves the boundaries of 'the text' and 'grafts' all texts on each other (*la greffe*). In the process, as may have become apparent, articulation also decentres the text; the 'text'with its own 'proper' meaning or meanings is no longer either its own centre or at the centre of the critical discourse. Articulation uses a word 'quoted' from one context in one text to draw that text into a constellation of diverse texts, diverse contexts and contradictory meanings, which are all centred on a word. As the point where different topics, different texts and largely incompatible meanings converge, the word now occupies centre stage. It also holds the centre because it remains *between* these different texts, contexts and meanings in all the Derridean senses of between: 'The word "between", whether as confusion or as the interval *between*, carries all the force of the operation' (Diss., 250). To remain between all contexts and contradictions without allowing any one of these to suck it in or take it over, to remain the *Mittelpunkt* on which different meanings and contexts converge and the medium in which they can be linked, the word has to be 'a zero-symbolic value'. It has to lack a determinate meaning of its own; and it has to mark a lack which can be supplied, indifferently, by any member of contexts or meanings. It has, in other words, to consist of 'only its contexts without any absolute anchoring centre' (M, 381). The word thus marks a blank, an interval empty of meaning and a space in which all meanings become in-different. It is always constructed like *Différance* (see previous section).

Derrida insists that the choice of word is not important, that any word can fulfil this function providing it is placed 'in between':

> What counts here is not the lexical richness, the semantic infinity of a word or concept, its profundity or its density, the sedimentation in it of two contradictory significances (continuity and discontinuity, inner and outer, identity and difference etc.). What counts is the formal or syntactical practice which composes and decomposes it . . . The effect is primarily produced by the syntax which sets out the 'between' in such a way that the suspension depends only on the place and not on the content of words' (Diss., 249).

One might point out that Derrida's own practice indicates that some words occupy the place of the between and repeat *différance* more successfully than others: for instance, the *pharmakon*, the *pyramid* and the *hymen* seem to work better than *marge–marque–marche*, *fort–da* in 'Speculer – sur Freud' or the vocabulary of whiteness and blankness in 'La Dissémination'. One might also point out that Latin or Greek words, which are so unfamiliar as to conjure up no image in the mind and which can undergo several transformations in the process of free translation, have the advantage over more common and garden words. But it is perhaps more important to note that articulation intersects neatly with division in so far as it makes it possible to graft a series of textual re-presentations on each other; and that, like division, articulation is produced by the critical text which describes it. It is the 'formal or syntactical practice' of the critical text which joins what we would not normally think of as conjoined and holds incongruous and largely incompatible elements in suspension, in in-difference, in the space of an indeterminate and indifferent word.

If it is still possible, in light of this, to speak of a repetition of the reading in the writing, it is possible only by a certain division of Derrida's text from itself. It is possible only by distinguishing the formal and syntactical practice in Derrida's texts from those texts' own representations of their own practice. Here articulation is marked in two ways.

It is marked first by what might be described as a poetics of *différance*, as a mythology of blankness or as a shifting metaphorology of the *entre* (the between). Derrida not only uses words like hymen, envagination, pyramid, supplement or *différance* to perform a textual operation on other texts. He also uses them to explore the hole, the gap, the blank space, the empty passage, the infinite mystery at the apex of the opening, and the way complex articulations form only to fall back into nothingness at the point of their intersection. And he uses them to discover how language can be silenced, or, to borrow his metaphor, how a text can be punched full of holes and sewn together again in such a way as to re-present the secrets of the void. As he says: 'The writing offers philosophemes – and all the texts of our culture – to be read as some sort of symptom of something which *could not* present itself in the history of philosophy, and which is in any case *present* nowhere' (M, 302). Derrida's texts return to the un-ending obscurities of the infinitely other, as mystical texts return to the intricacies of the Godhead.

Articulation is also graphically represented in texts like 'Tympan' where two entirely different texts are printed on the same page, separated by a wide margin which runs down the centre of the page. Here articulation is represented as an invitation to the reader or critic of Derrida's texts. The margin in the centre of the page is, in the first instance, a mark of the lack which has to be supplied – a mark of the lack of any apparent articulation, connection or relation between the two texts on the page. To articulate or graft these two texts upon each other, the reader or critic has to work both inside and outside each of the two texts; and he has to place himself or his text 'between' the two texts on the page. Needless to say, there have already been critics who have placed their texts in this opening. But the critic who wants his supplement to Derrida to re-present Derrida will ensure that the articulations of his text remain in the space 'between' the two texts on Derrida's page – in other words, that they also preserve or re-present the blankness, the in-difference and the indeterminacy of the spacing.[23]

3.   The PiVot

The pivot reverses accustomed hierarchies. It assumes that in every pair of oppositions – like presence/absence, speech/writing, concept/metaphor and so on – one term is customarily dominant. And it reverses the hierarchy by making the minor term the ground or condition of possibility of both terms of the opposition. For instance, having demonstrated that the whole of Western philosophy privileges presence over absence – by using what is present as its point of departure, either excluding absence or treating it as a form or moment of presence – Derrida will argue that absence (in the form of difference or spacing) is the pre-condition for the presence or absence of any thing. Or, having shown that the whole of Western philosophy privileges speech over writing – by identifying speech with the breath and the breath with spirit or consciousness, reducing writing to a less than adequate graphic copy of speech – Derrida will argue that writing as a global system of differences is the pre-condition both for speech and for that form of writing which merely copies it down. Or having explained how the whole of Western philosophy privileges concepts over metaphor and reduces metaphor at best to a useful illustration and at worst to a source of error and confusion, Derrida will show that metaphors in fact underly all philosophical concepts, and that metaphor must therefore be considered the condition both of philosophical concepts and of what philosophy dismisses as mere metaphor. In the pivot, then, the critical text actively intervenes in the text which is being read by reversing its assumptions.

The pivot intersects very neatly with division and articulation. There is a certain pivoting, a certain reversal of hierarchies, in division when, for instance, the duplicity of a text becomes more important than its unity or when effects replace their cause and supplements their origin. There is also a certain pivoting, a certain reversal of hierarchies, in articulation, when a word which would normally be considered marginal is made central, and when the margin, understood as the blank space of indifference, is made the condition of its centrality. Moreover, values are constantly pivoted around 'within' a word, when it can be used in contrary senses.

But the pivot does not merely reverse hierarchies within an opposition. It also steps outside the opposition and dissolves it. It does this by making the term which comes to ground the opposition so extensive and all encompassing that it ceases to mean anything. As Derrida says, a term 'annuls itself by its illimitation' (Diss., 252). If all reasoning, as well as everything that reasoning opposes to itself as mere metaphor, is metaphorical, then everything is metaphorical. And as Derrida points out: 'When everything becomes metaphorical, there is no longer any proper meaning anywhere, and therefore no longer any metaphor' (Diss., 290). If writing is so extended that it is not only all speech and all writing and all the graphic forms which represent language and speech, but also the global system of differences which makes it possible for all things to be, then 'nothing escapes it' (Diss., 252). It becomes 'so extended that nothing of what *is* can be beyond it' (Diss., 252). If everything in nature and culture, if all things and all languages as well as all books, are writing or 'text', if indeed *'il n'y a pas de hors–texte'* – there is nothing outside the text and nothing except text. But this extends writing and text to the point where they no longer mean anything. It extends them to absurdity. Imagine a child pointing to the sun and saying: 'Writing'; pointing to his food and saying: 'Writing'; pointing to his toys and saying: 'Writing'; pointing to his books and saying: 'Writing'; pointing to the television and saying: 'Writing'; pointing to the ants in the garden and saying: 'Writing! Writing!'

The pivot dissolves oppositions not by reconciling them in a third term which constitutes their essential unity, as the Hegelian dialectic would, but by allowing them to intersect in what Derrida calls 'undecidables' –

> that is, sham or simulated unities, 'false' verbal properties, whether nominal or semantic, which can no longer be understood in terms of (binary) philosophical oppositions and which nevertheless inhabit these oppositions, resisting and disorganising them without ever constituting a third term, without ever giving rise to a solution in the manner of the speculative [Hegelian] dialectic (Pos., 58).

Unities are 'shammed or simulated' by extending a term so that it can mean either one thing or another or any one of a number of things, while meaning none of them. Terms like 'writing' or 'text' or 'dissemination' are 'undecidables', sham unities, simulations, because 'in the last analysis, [they] mean nothing and cannot be pulled together in a definition' (Pos., 61). The problem is only compounded by the fact that used in this way, terms like 'writing' or 'text' or 'spacing' or 'dissemination' or 'difference' are also metaphors. They are metaphors which manifestly lack a 'proper meaning' anywhere, metaphors which refer infinitely to each other, repeating and re-presenting each other through Derrida's texts.

When metaphors without any 'proper meaning' take over the whole space of Derrida's texts, they also suspend them over the abyss. They enable Derrida's texts to produce what he calls 'effects of meaning' or 'supplements of meaning' while lacking any 'proper meaning'.

As Derrida points out, however, there is neverthless a 'rest', a remainder, something which is left over, which escapes the general conflagration. In so far as our thinking is based on metaphors, to change the metaphors is productive: it generates and disseminates new insights. When metaphor is also understood apocalyptically, as the means by which mystics seek to transmit the 'unreceivable', it also becomes a way of re-examining the 'visionary' or spiritual or 'unearthly' dimensions of literature. (See Ton and CP.) In so far as readers and writers are, by definition, always bent over writings, to call everything a writing is liberating: it dissolves the boundaries between disciplines and departments, it removes the opposition between the library and the 'real world', and it allows readers and writers to roam where they will, reading and writing about nature and culture, social formations and philosophic texts, aesthetic and mimetic representations and everything else with equal zest and authority – as indeed they used to do before the University manufactured narrowly delimited competences. In so far as critical texts are always supplements to the texts which came before, and in so far as they always insert 'the prescriptions of another book' in any text they are describing, to call all texts a supplement and all criticism an auto(bio)graphy, is liberating too: like Wilde's program for the critic as artist, it frees the critic from any obligation to seek texts' 'real' or 'original' meaning and allows him to add and substitute a writing of his own. This allows the critic to be not only critical but also subversive of the culture in which he works: for supplementarity is self-fulfilling – in the process of infinite substitutions, the 'real' or 'original' meanings of texts do indeed come to be lost. The idea that all texts are metaphorical and that everything is a text is particularly liberating for literary critics: it places what has come to be treated as a 'marginal' discipline at the centre of all academic work and extends the proper concern of literature departments from the consideration of what used to be called 'literature' to a consideration of all texts in general. Few critics remember that Derrida also pointed out that 'literature annuls itself by its illimitation' (Diss., 252).

But this is of the essence. For one of the most valuable things that 'remains' from Derrida's reversals is that where we thought there was knowledge there is only literature; and 'beyond literature' is another way of saying 'nothing' (n. p. 62 Diss.). What remains from a reading of Derrida is the awareness, demonstrated by Derrida on every page, that all our writings – all the texts that we write to represent texts, referring to yet other texts which re-present texts and arguing with their re-presentations of texts – that all these texts are suspended over an abyss of fundamental ignorance about the origin, truth, presence, essence, reality and nature of the things which we are representing; that all our supplements of knowledge are in fact substitutes for knowledge which we fundamentally and 'originally' lack; that all our reading, all our erudition, and all our metaphors lead us only to an awareness of the limits of our knowledge; and that were we as wise as Solomon, as erudite as Derrida or as encyclopaedic as Hegel, were we to 'give [our] heart to seek and search out by wisdom concerning all things that are done under heaven', we would still only know that 'of making many books there is no end' and that 'no man can find out the work that God maketh from the beginning to the end'.[24]

4.   The Veil of Displacement

As Mallarmé said, 'All methods are fictions'. But, as George Orwell might have said, some are more fictional than others. If Derrida produces the fiction of having an 'original' method, it is largely by casting a veil over the origin of his methods in habits of thought which are as widespread as they are familiar both in traditional academic work and in philosophical texts. And if he produces a 'simulation' of strangeness and unfamiliarity, it is by displacing such familiar habits of thought to new objects and new terms.

Considered purely as structures or as textual 'operations', division is nothing but the making of distinctions, the differentiation of things from each other; and articulation is nothing but the making of connections, the relating of things to each other. And this is precisely what critics, teachers and people who write or talk about texts always do. They contrast a text's themes or characters or formal and linguistic features, for the most part without attempting to make them cohere as the vehicle of any single, ultimate authoritative 'reality' or truth. Critics and teachers also relate the characters, ideas, themes or formal linguistic features of one text to those in other texts, or, depending on their approach, to critical methods, semiological structures, unconscious patterns or socio-historical frameworks which are taken from other texts. In this respect, all critics and teachers of literature are always working both 'inside' a text and 'outside it' and the space of their discourse can always be described as 'between' texts. Critics and teachers of literature or philosophy also often construct their courses and their books by showing how a theme, a character-type (like 'the Fool'), a genre, a metaphor, or an argument (of being, of good and evil) recurs, repeating itself with some differences throughout a series of texts from antiquity or the Renaissance or the eighteenth century or the beginning of the twentieth century to the present day. And, of course, if one is in a field where discussion always begins from a text, then the text necessarily becomes 'the origin of the origin' – the starting point for any consideration of what that text 'signifies' or 'represents' and for any consideration of that text's origin in reality, in history, in universal structures of the mind or in the life, experiences or unconscious of its author; and these in turn become 'undecidable' in so far as they always preserve an area of uncertainty and in so far as they are always subject to various interpretations. The structure which pivots opposites and reverses hierarchies is no less familiar: what else are we doing when we dethrone the Romantics, for instance, and make Donne the condition for reading all literature, or when we show how the nineteenth-century cult of nature and the imagination reversed the eighteenth-century cult of reason and culture, and made nature and imagination the ground and condition of all writing?

The same points about the intrinsic familiarity of division, articulation, the supplementary structure and the pivot could be made, but at considerably greater length, by reference to Aristotle (for whom distinction and connection are the beginning of logic), to Plato (who makes literature an inadequate imitation of an imitation of an imitation of a transcendent Idea), to Hegel (whose dialectic shows how oppositions contain traces of each other and pivots them so that one term of the opposition comes to annul the opposition and to replace it) or to Lacanian Freudianism (with its emphasis on an originating lack).

Derrida displaces these familiar habits of thought in two ways. First, as we have seen, he divides, articulates and pivots in a different place from everyone else: he divides what we are accustomed to thinking of as one or as connected, articulates what we are accustomed to thinking of as distinct, and pivots hierarchies that we had not previously noticed, much less questioned. And secondly, he gives these operations new names (*mise en écart, mise en abîme*, simulated unity, reversal of hierarchies, *la greffe*, etc.). It should, however, be pointed out that inventing new terms for people to learn is normal scientific and academic practice, and that it is always accompanied by an effect of sense.

Derrida also separates himself from familiar forms of division, articulation and pivoting by a thin veil of difference. One, probably non-Derridean, way of describing this difference is to say that where everyone else uses division, articulation and pivoting to try to describe or account for what is present in a text or in a series of texts, Derrida uses division, articulation and pivoting to show the absence of what we think is present and the undecidability of everything we think we know. As we saw, division, articulation and the pivot all return to in-difference, to the chasm, the abyss or to an intrinsically indeterminate and meaningless word. Another way to describe Derrida's difference from traditional methods of analysis is to borrow his reference to Saussure's claim that the signifier and signified relate to each other like two sides of the same sheet of paper. In these terms, what separates Derrida from traditional forms of division, articulation and pivoting is 'the invisible thickness, almost nil, of this *sheet* between the signifier and the signified' (Diss., 127). As Derrida always places a sheet of paper (his own) between the words of a text and their 'proper' meaning, and between the text and its reality, truth and authority, so he always places a sheet of paper (his own) between his own method and its significance. He describes the suspension of differentiation as a 'fiction', a 'game', an 'illusion' a 'simulation', which produces nothing but 'effects of meaning' and 'effects of theoretical theses' or 'readability without a signified'. He describes the words or signs on which texts, contexts and contrary meanings converge as 'undecidables', 'sham or simulated unities' or as 'fantasy making a sign'. He insists that methods can work, texts can be written and read and words can function not only in the absence of any reference to anything or anyone, but also in the absence of any signification, of any intention of communicating, and of anything they 'want to say' (M, 376ff). And he associates deconstruction with the Nietzschean superman who 'burns his text and effaces the traces of his steps', and, having prevented any possibility of return to the old manner of thought, stands back and – laughs (M, 163). One can, I think, see why.

This, then, is the fourfold rule of deconstruction: division, articulation, pivoting and displacement, all leading to the famous Derridean × which crosses out all that is – is – and all leading beyond this to nothing but indeterminacy and in-difference. As we have seen, each of the rule's four folds produces an opening to the infinitely Other – to that which 'can neither be thought nor spoken', to that which 'must preserve the negativity of the indefinite to be other' (ED, 168). This constant opening of what is to the other, to that which cannot be appropriated or absorbed or encompassed or enveloped or mastered by language and thought is the purpose of the fourfold rule and its necessity. As Derrida says: 'without the violent eruption of the other and of non-being, of non-being as other, in the unity of being, writing and its game would not have been necessary' (Diss., 189). It is therefore not so much that the rule is necessary for the playing of the game and for the extension and repetition of the writing, as that the writing, the repetition and the game are necessary because of the rule. The rule is 'necessary' to produce openings to the infinitely other, and in the process, to accomplish a certain destruction and to make a certain affirmation.

What Derrida's rule sets out to destroy is nothing less than the ethno-centrism and self-referentiality of the West: the 'mythology of the white man' who takes his own logos for the universal form of reason, who transforms his own consciousness into a universal form of appropriation, who makes everything and everyone the 'same' as himself, and who makes himself the master of all things (and all beings). The fourfold rule demonstrates that the white man's logos cannot master all being; that his consciousness cannot appropriate all that is; that everything is not the same as himself. It shows him that he has these illusions only because he moves in a closed circle of repetitive texts which refer only to each other and re-present only themselves. It shows him that there are always and everywhere in each of his texts and in every one of his writings unfilled gaps, spaces which escape his mastery and which elude appropriation by consciousness or domination by reason, just as there is always something 'outside' the West's logic and tissue of texts which escapes their comprehension.

As Derrida says: 'The irreductibility of the spacing is the irreductibility of the other' (Pos., 130). To open the logos of the white man to the irreducibility of the spacing is, at the same time, to open it to the irreducibility of the other. And this, as Derrida points out, contains traces of a political, social and ethical affirmation, as well as of an intellectual one. Politically, it may be said to represent an opening to those others outside the West who do not share the white man's logic or consciousness, whose thinking and consciousness are inescapably other, and something approaching a recognition of their right to their otherness. Socially, it may be said to represent an opening to the stranger within, to those who inhabit the texture of Western societies without being of it, and something approaching a recognition of the right of these others to maintain their otherness even within these societies. Ethically, openness to the irreducibility of the other means respect and freedom: Derrida argues in *L'Écriture et la Différence* that where there is mastery, appropriation or assimilation, there is neither respect nor freedom;[25] that respect between men is possible only when they know each other to be other and treat others as distinct and separate from themselves; and that freedom requires separation or separateness, a certain reserve of God and man, of meaning and author-ity, which allows different men, different meanings and different truths the latitude to 'play' indifferently. When Derrida's texts make it uncertain 'who is speaking', when they hold their author-ity and their meaning in reserve, when they try to function without anything they 'want to say', when they produce 'effects of meaning' and 'effects of theoretical theses' which largely self-destruct, they are also presenting this ethical space where different authors, different meanings and different authorities have the latitude to play. If Derrida's texts constantly return to the indeterminacy, the in-definiteness, the in-finity of the space and the *entre*, if they constantly speak of that which is not present and has no determinate being, it is also because, in Derrida's view, only the indeterminate and the in-finite escape 'mastery'. 'Only presence can be mastered' (M, 76).

Paradoxically, then, the fourfold rule must be mastered and repeated 'without any presumption of mastery' (Pos., 126). The fourfold rule is 'necessary' to repeatedly write texts in which nothing is mastered and in which, as Derrida says, 'nothing happens' – in which nothing is mastered *because* nothing happens. Nothing 'happens' to what is present when it is divided from itself on a page of writing and shown not to be – one has only to look up from the page, as Hume did, or to walk across the room. Nothing 'happens' when a book is propped open by a sheet of paper, when it is articulated on other texts by a word 'quoted' out of context and placed in other contexts, nothing happens when a book is cut off from any single meaning, from its author or from its origin in history and reality by the words on a sheet of paper – or at least nothing happens to the book which it has not survived before. 'Nothing happens' to the West or to the white man because a text has represented a space in which differences can play. It is because 'nothing happens' that Derrida describes the game as both serious and unserious, both 'sacred and vicious' and as neither serious nor unserious, neither sacred nor vicious. The rules trigger a game which involves the serious business of constant reading, constant re-search, the constant re-presentation of other texts, the constant reproduction of the rules and the constant repetition of one's writing. But how serious can this writing and this business be if it is based on nothing, if it masters nothing, if it has nothing it 'wants to say' and if it makes 'nothing happen' – if it is, in other words, ultimately a matter of indifference? How serious – and indeed how free – can writing be when it is 'necessarily' ruled by the rules; when it necessarily divides, articulates and pivots in one place or another; when mastery of the rules of writing and repetition is also the submission of writing and repetition to the mastery of the rules?

The 'science' of deconstruction is a 'double science'. It is a double of science – just as, as we have seen, the rules of deconstruction are a double of the rules of constructive 'scientific' discourse in the humanities. As the constructive rules of 'scientific discourse' in the humanities have reproduced themselves in constant re-search, in the constant re-presentation of texts and in the constant repetition of a writing, so the deconstructive rules of the 'other' science can reproduce themselves in constant re-search, in the constant re-presentation of texts and in the constant repetition of a writing. But, as always, there is a difference between constructive science and its de-constructive double. For de-constructive science is a parody of science. It marks the distance between scientific academic discourse as signifiers and what is signified in scientific academic discourse by these signifiers. Deconstructive science allows all the signifiers of scientific academic discourse to proliferate: the rules, the jargon, the close readings, the rigorous argumentation, the erudition, the impersonality, the texts and the writing are all there;

and so are, not only the criticism or the subversion of the status quo, but also the liberalism and academic lack of partisanship which allows incompatible meanings and incompatible values free play in the space of the text and the classroom and reserves judgement on ultimate truths or realities. But deconstructive science says, again and again it says, that by this proliferation of signifiers, nothing has been said. One sense of the double science, then, is that science is non-sense.[26]

As it has in fact become. Derrida's 'double science' not only parodies traditional forms of scientific discourse in the humanities; it also models itself, in significant ways, on scientific discourse in the sciences, which could indeed also be described as a parody of the older science. As one post-modern scientist put it, science has now 'made the known unknown'.[27] Determinism, cause and effect, predictability, stable systems, continuity, conventional logic and intelligibility and teleologies no longer have any place in scientific discourse. Science now explores instabilities in systems, discontinuities, situations in which all directions are equally probable or in which 'incomplete information' is indemic and the behaviour of 'things' whose existence is a fiction. Microphysics produces 'undecidables' – multiple statements about 'the molecule' or its 'parts' which are incompatible in absolute terms and completely paradoxical in pragmatic terms, so that it is no longer possible to put them together as 'properties' proper to one and the 'same' thing. The practice in the sciences of working and publishing in teams puts the whole concept of the 'author' of ideas and of scientific texts in question, which matters very little in the sciences since scientific texts are expected to generate their own authority. But the unintelligibility in conventional or commonsensical terms of the materials they are working on often reduces them to metaphors (the 'charm' of particles, for instance) or to 'putting together a story' to explain their findings.

The 'double science', already a parodic double of conventional scientific discourse in the humanities and a re-presentation in the language of the humanities of scientific discourse in the sciences, also has an other sense which takes it 'outside' or 'beyond' the closed system of scientific academic production altogether. For the 'double science' is also the science which, with the utmost seriousness and dedication, makes 'nothing *happen*'. Nothing becomes a happening in Derrida's texts. Wherever we try to touch ground – in the stable meanings of a text, in the author's conscious or unconscious intentionality, in the structures of language and thought, in the presence, truth, essence or historicity of ideas or words – indeterminacy, undecidability and uncertainty await us. And there is nothing but text, nothing outside texts, nothing except texts – all searching and re-searching; all presenting and re-presenting the same questions; all supplementing the same lacks and sharing the same failures to find stable and certain answers; all marking and re-marking in their different ways the manifold openings to what is outside our ken. After Derrida, it is impossible to look at a page, a writing or an argument without noticing the spaces, the silences and the gaps and without asking where the divisions have been produced. What science in this other sense teaches us is humility: the sense to know how much we do not know and how much of what we know is just an artificial construct; the sense to know that we are always obeying laws who 'ultimate' meanings we do not understand; the sense to remember that there are limits to our knowledge, and a beyond to those limits which, no matter how far we extend our knowledge, our writing and our game, will always remain in-finitely other and incapable of assimilation by us.

Inside closure; outside closure; between. Not unlike Derrida. An Algerian in French society, a Frenchman in American society, a Jew in gentile society: both one and the other; neither one nor the other; between, undecidable. As Derrida never tires of repeating, his science is always inside closure and outside closure: inside texts and outside them; inside the oppositions which constitute our thinking and outside them; inside the Western metaphysic and outside it; inside France and outside it; inside the academy and outside it. Consequently, Derrida's science is also double because it can always be read in two ways. Inside closure, it can be read as a subversion of the accepted meanings of classical texts and of the conventional rules of academic work, as a new rule for the production of critical texts, or as a reversal of the departmental priorities and hierarchies in the academic world. Outside closure, it can be read as a question about what we are 'really' doing and 'really' saying when we teach texts and write about them; as a questioning of our assumptions which brings to light the limits of certainty and decidability; and as a call to beyond-closure where the infinitely Other was, is and will be, eternally veiled from us by infinite reserve, presiding over the All and the Nothing, Life and Death, and forever leaving the traces of his passing in the differences, indifferences and re-presentations of *Différance*.

Come beyond being, this comes from beyond being and calls to beyond being. . . Come is apocalyptic . . . an apocalypse without any vision, any truth or any revelation, some *missives*, addresses without a message or a destination . . . without any eschatology but the intonation of 'Come'. . . But what are you doing, you will say, what is your purpose in coming to tell us, here and now, let's go, come, the apocalypse, it's finished, I say it, that's what happens.

Conclusion:
Recontextualisations

*'Recognise him or not?' our hero wondered in indescribable anguish,
'or pretend that I am not myself, but somebody strikingly like me?
. . . I'm alright. I'm quite alright. It's not I, it's not I, and that's
the fact of the matter.'*

Dostoyevski, *The Double*

Much 'theory' has been extracted from the texts of Lacan, Barthes,
Foucault and Derrida, and diverse attempts have been made to
translate it directly into ideas and methods which can be readily
adopted and applied by those of us who do not read, write or
teach in France. As a result the representations we have been given
of their texts have not always been faithful repetitions, even
allowing for what Lukács called 'normative misunderstandings;'
and signification, connection and context have been lost. They
were lost when, as in the case of the Yale critics, translation
also involved a considerable amount of transformation. American
doctrines of 'revisionary misreading' and of the 'creativity' of
criticism, together with French views of the intrinsic fictionality and
supplementarity of academic writing, freed those who introduced
French ideas into the Anglo-Saxon world to do their own, often
quite diverse, things. It is one of the tenets of 'theory' that
representations of texts need not be 'true' (to them),[1] and there is
no specific exemption for the French. Signification, connection and
context were lost again when, in desperation, some of us sought
to abstract from the confusion of texts a few clear and distinct ideas
or methods – like the political power of the intellectual, the
institutionalisation of academic writing, intertextuality, the
decentred subject, the death of the author, demythologising,
exclusion or aporia. Protesting the insulation of 'theory' from the
practice of teaching English, we began to ask how such ideas and
methods could be applied to teaching, to revising the curriculum

and to our perception of ourselves and of our roles in the university. A great deal of extremely useful and interesting work has emerged in the process of trying to answer such questions, and Lacanian, Foucaldian and Derridean structures and assumptions are finding their way into the academy.[2] But the debate and the reappropriations have for the most part proceeded without taking into account the fact that 'theory' was 'originally' part of the practice of teaching and writing in a French University in very specific and very French cultural and historical circumstances. This 'origin', together with the sense that 'theory' originally made in very various French contexts, have been lost sight of. 'Theory', and many of our current difficulties with it, have been arrived at by extracting 'theory' from texts and texts from the contexts which make them intelligible and in which they answer, in their own terms, many of the questions which they are seen to raise. 'Recontextualisation' – to borrow a term which joins and separates Geoffrey Hartman and William Cain – is needed not only to restore to Lacan, Barthes, Foucault and Derrida's writings their signification, connection and context and to make their answers to our questions more apparent. It is needed also to enable us to begin to ask ourselves where the problems, concerns and solutions of French academic intellectuals have simply been different, and where they match or impinge on our own.

Structurally, Lacan, Barthes, Foucault and Derrida all marked their uncomfortable position as dissenting intellectuals, who were obliged to go on writing, teaching and working within a culture, a university and a society they condemned, in a similar way: as we saw, they all devised methodologies and styles of writing which placed them both inside and outside the pale, and which allowed them to tread a precarious path between conformity and non-conformity, sense and non-sense, clarity and dissimulation. Lacan placed his dialectic at the point where the inside of language and society – the law of the Other, the symbolic order, the socialised ego – and their outside – the 'ex-centric' subject, the unconscious subject in his *aphanisis* – show themselves to be both hopelessly alienated from one another and irrevocably bound to one another. Barthes inscribed his texts as a paradox of participation and exclusion, of re-creation and subversion, repeating the standard topoi of institutionalised political, ideological and critical languages in bourgeois society, but also displacing and combining them in such a way as to construct an 'atopical', a 'ne-utral' space outside them. Foucault placed his 'history of the present' methodologically on the dividing line between the towns and the spaces of exclusion: he traced the changing boundaries between the normal and the abnormal, between reason and folly, truth and error, law and punishment, and reconstructed the ways in which we came to be divided from ourselves in the very process of being made to conform; while Derrida placed both his 'double science' and his spaces of *différance* both inside and outside the logos, the writings and the rules of Western discourse.

Structurally, Lacan, Barthes, Foucault and Derrida also marked the real impossibility of escaping the doubleness of their position as insiders who defined themselves outside the system – or perhaps as outsiders who found themselves inside the system – in a France where revolution had become unforseeable, in a similar way: as we saw, they all constructed a purely theoretical space of non-being. The differences among them – and their own debates about whether non-being should be conceived in Lacanian terms as a lack which conceals the reality and truth of being; in Derridean terms as the indifference of spaces without vision or truth or revelation; in Barthian terms as an absence of place and suspension of meaning; or in Foucaldian terms as an exclusion and a silencing – should not blind us to the fact that for each of them this purely theoretical space of non-being marked the place from which it was still honest and honourable to speak. For all of them, to borrow Derrida's words, non-being was 'a void, but with a vacancy which calls, and which calls, like all enigmas, for a discourse' (CP, 322). Sometimes explanatory, sometimes self-justifying, the discourses called for were inventions from the void of purely theoretical and non-referential – and therefore also fictional – alternatives to the alternatives they found present before them in their disciplines, in their universities, in their culture and in their society.

In recontextualizing Lacan, Barthes, Foucault and Derrida's work, account must be taken of the diverse and sometimes incompatible positions they were thus assuming with regard to French 'realities'. Their relations to the intellectual, institutional, cultural, political and social contexts in which they worked cannot therefore be described merely in terms of 'reflection' – though they certainly reflected much that was going on around them – or merely in terms of subversion – though they certainly sought to subvert much of what they found – or merely in terms of innovation – though they were also clearly great innovators and originators. It is as important to see where they also conformed to bourgeois, institutional or left-wing values, and where they simply sought practical solutions to local problems. It makes little practical difference here however, whether the con-texts to which their texts are returned are regarded as socio-historically 'real', as consisting merely of other equally 'fictional' texts on which their texts have been articulated, or as some sort of mixture of the two. But it does seem to me that the blanket view of the fictionality of all texts promoted by Lacan, Barthes, Foucault and Derrida needs to be re-examined. Historians have known, at least since Bayle in the seventeenth century, that both the testimony of the texts on which historians are bound to draw and the writings of historians themselves are likely to be fictions; and from the eighteenth century at least, novelists have also explored and exploited the fact that fictions are also 'histories'.[3] The real question to be addressed is why post-modern French intellectuals have resorted to a notion of the fictionality of texts which can only be described as seemingly naïve and undifferentiated when compared to that of earlier centuries, and why they have clung so firmly to the idea that 'words create reality'.

It is important too not to be entirely taken in by French fictions. As we will see, there is a great deal in French writing and thinking which is recognizable by Americans, if not always by Englishmen, but the relation of French writing and thinking to American realities and values is a great deal less direct and more ironical than it appears.

The rapid changes introduced in France after the Second World War with the help of the Marshall Plan, which converted what had been a predominantly rural, and agricultural society into a modern, industrialised, 'americanised' 'technological civilisation' in the course of about twenty years, was viewed with intense disfavour by most of the French left. From the late forties, they subjected the new 'programmed society' to a virulent critique. This is the first context in which Lacan, Barthes, Foucault and Derrida's work must be seen. At the same time, it should be noted that French left-wing critics of modernity tended to universalise their insights – this is evident even from the titles of their books: *Daily life in the Modern World*, *The Technological Society*, *The Post-Industrial Society*, *Capitalism and Schizophrenia*. Few remembered what Raymond Aron tried to point out to them: that 'industrialised societies are by no means alike; they differ in their economic systems, social relations, political forms and scales of values'.[4] French left-wing critics of modernity also ignored what Michel Crozier tried to tell them: that in America, the bureaucratic and technological organisation of society had not been accompanied by centralism and *dirigisme*; and that centralised power and planning, authoritarian control of the economy, the media and every aspect of the educational system, hierarchisation and lack of feed-back from the margins to the centre were peculiar to French social and political structures, and had been so at least since Napoleon.[5] As far as French left-wing critics of modernity were concerned, therefore, 'technological civilization' was virtually indistinguishable from state planning and control: 'Technique causes the state to become totalitarian, to absorb the citizen's life completely'.[6] This is why they tend to argue that there is no difference between 'totalitarianisms' in Russia, America and France, and it is why the Hegelian master–slave dialectic as expounded by Kojève became fundamental to the thinking of the whole French left. The identification of technological civilisation with centralised planning and control explains why left-wing critiques of modernity (including those of Lacan, Barthes, Foucault and Derrida) tend to be accompanied by stringent attacks on centralism, hierarchical structures of authority and domination, standardisation, systematisation and programmed conformities, just as it explains their rejection of all theoretical totalisations, whether modelled on Hegel and Marx or on structuralism and semiotics. It also explains why the projected solutions of the French left to the problems of modernity tend to involve revolt, subversion, de-centralisation, pluralism, pluralities, the possibility of being different and *auto-gestion* (self-management and self-determination). By one of the delightful ironies of history, therefore, critics of 'americanisation' ended up by preaching a de-centralisation, a pluralism, a freedom to be different and to make one's differences felt, which are familiar to every American.

What should not be forgotten in the pleasure of discovering shared values is that for the French, de-centralisation, pluralism and the ability to make one's difference felt in the power structure, were concrete realities only for the brief span of the French student uprising of 1968. This is why 1968 marked French thinking so profoundly. Before 1968, and again after 1968, decentralisation, pluralism, difference, the freedom not to conform and *auto-gestion* appear in left-wing writings as purely theoretical and non-referential – and therefore also fictional and unreal – alternatives to the status quo. As we saw, Barthes and Foucault both characterised as fictional their purely textual representations of plural and decentred structures in which individuals or groups are free to be different and to make their differences felt: Foucault spoke of 'fictioning reality' and Barthes of 'utopia', 'atopia' and the novelistic representation of the 'marvel-ously real'. One reason why Barthes, Foucault and Derrida described their texts as fictional, then, was that they were using discontinuous, differential, plural and decentred structures which had no equivalent in French 'reality'.

Lacan, Barthes, Foucault, and Derrida's perceptions of society, of the functioning of the symbolic order and of the subject's place within them are also indebted to the work of early left-wing critics of modern society, like Henri Lefebvre and Jacques Ellul, in other ways. Jacques Ellul's book, *The Technological Society* (1954) could almost be described as a blueprint for much of Foucault's work, but the views expressed in it, which are not entirely unique to him, also had their impact on the others. Ellul portrayed the technological society as a society in which techniques to rationalise means and to maximise functional efficiency acquire a certain autonomy, both vis-à-vis the experts who administer them and the individuals in society. He described it also as a society in which technique begins to take over every aspect of public and private life, 'resulting in the complete conditioning of human behaviour – in the man-machine'. Ellul explains how technique subordinates workers 'body and soul' to 'a human discipline [which] must correspond to technical necessities' in order to maximise perform-ance; how state, juridical and policing techniques of administration and information-gathering provide 'discrete surveillance of every citizen' and ensure that 'everyone can be supervised'; and how 'human techniques' in pedagogy, medicine, psychiatry and psy-choanalysis promote adaptation, conformity, submission and 'psy-chological collectivisation'. Ellul was not alone in describing the technological society as a society 'essentially independent of human beings' in which 'the individual's acts or ideas do not exert any influence on social, political and economic mechanisms'.[7] Fougayrollas, for instance observed that 'modern man has the feeling that, rather than speaking the world, he is spoken and made by technique; he also feels that he is spoken and made by the political apparatus more than he speaks and makes it. We are evolving towards technocratic social forms and towards bureau-cratic political forms which have in common de-individualisation and the anonymity of power'.[8]

Ellul and Henri Lefebvre saw technological societies as societies which hold together and function by discourse. But without any culture to give technique meaning, without common reference points in common sense, in history, in ethics, or in anything else, and without anything in technique itself which can determine to what end it ought to be used, they saw that 'only discourse persists as the foundation of social relations. Without any criterion, any truth or authenticity, even without any objectivity'.[9] In the new technologically-directed consumer society, they argued, one consumes the representations surrounding the object one is consuming; one consumes signs and images; one consumes yesterday's 'contestation' and fragments of yesterday's culture as today's cultural commodities; one devours the fashion of the moment before it becomes obsolete; one consumes passively a verbal and mythical universe which 'reconstructs reality in the minds of its citizens' by emptying signifiers of their meaning and by fashioning 'images of things, events and people which may not reflect reality, but which are truer than reality'; and the act of consumption is as much a fictive and imaginary act as a real one. Between 1948 and 1968, Henri Lefebvre preached *la fête* – revolution as *carnaval*, game, creativity, prodigality, and the bursting of constraints; after 1968, he concluded that creativity had become obsolete, that even the ludic had become degraded, and that all that was left was 'the irreductibility of [unsatisfied] desire'.

Lacan, Barthes, Foucault and Derrida did not simply take over such views; they interacted with them. As we saw, Lacan presented the subject as a being who is conditioned both in his ego and in his unconscious by the symbolic order and who, at all levels, is spoken more than he speaks. As we saw too, his model for man was not the old humanist and Freudian subject with his tri-partite soul, who was capable of using his reason and his will or his ego and his language to master his passions and his problems; nor was it the Hegelian-Marxist subject who creates his world and recognises himself in it; Lacan's model for man was the computer. But Lacan did not accept that psychoanalysis had to promote adaptation, conformity, submission and 'psychological collectivisation' and be a technique to maximalise the functional efficiency of individuals in society. As we saw, he made psychoanalysis champion what he described as 'a fundamentally lost cause'; he made it champion the 'real' subjectivity which was lost in conforming to the law of the other. Foucault and Derrida's subsequent criticisms of the Lacanian unconscious as the hidden location of man's reality and truth and Gilles Deleuze and Felix Guattari's attacks on 'the poor technicians of desire . . . who would subjugate the multiplicity of desire to the two-fold law of structure and lack'[10] should not make us overlook the recurrence of the pattern. In Barthes, in Foucault and even in Derrida, the subject continues to repeat the institutional languages, the cultural fragments, the *epistemes*, the norms, the rules, the writings, the re-presentations and the myths of a symbolic order which remains essentially independent of human beings and which creates reality as we know it. The subject continues to be spoken more than he speaks. The mechanistic image of man recurs in Foucault's cybernetic image of men as power points in a field of forces and in Derrida's image of man as a transmitter for an anonymously transmitted message. And there is a recurrence too of the refusal to accept that the human sciences must be techniques for promoting adaptation, conformity and submission. In their different ways, as we have seen, Barthes, Foucault and Derrida all de-mythified and de-naturalised the illusory verbal universe in which we live, consuming signs and images and fragments of yesterday's culture. Like Lacan too, who used images and myths to say 'I am not', they all tested the limits of myth, image and illusion in their discourses by taking them to the brink of a silence they called 'suspension of meaning', 'undecidability' or 'the non-being of exclusion'.

It would be a mistake, therefore, to conclude too rapidly that in their work either the subject or the author is 'dead'. Their strategy was more complex than this.

On the one hand, they subverted the lingering ideological supremacy of the conscious humanist subject, who either was at one with himself or could become so. Lacan and Derrida did this by showing that the subject was always divided and alienated from himself, always other than himself; Foucault by explaining how the subject had come to be divided and alienated from himself by the human sciences and the community's disciplinary and excluding practices; and Barthes by presenting the subject as his own self-contradictory double. They all subverted the old individualistic creative subject by presenting the subject as a clone who was doomed to repeat and to re-present the myths, the *epistemes*, the norms, the rules, the laws and the writings of the symbolic order. And they dethroned 'man' from his old primacy, de-centred him from his old centrality, by describing his real obsolescence in a signifying and technological order which functioned anonymously and independently of human beings, which always preceded every man or woman, and determined a priori the positions and roles each could assume.

But, on the other hand, they also subverted the determinisms of the new man-machine and sought alternative modes of action and expression for the subject in the new de-personalised, de-individualised mass society. As we saw, Foucault began to conceive of the space of language, culture and society as an open, mobile and dynamic 'field' of interrelations in which power is everywhere and comes from everywhere and in which subjects are power points at which multiple local and specific power-relations intersect. In each of these multiple power relations, the subject is both determined and determining; in each of them he is therefore free either to submit to the constraints and controls exercised against him, or to resist and become a starting point for an opposite strategy. Here the subject remains decentred, both psychologically and socially, without being either a clone or an automaton. As we saw too, Barthes began to represent the space of language, culture and society as a pluralistic space in which no language or meaning or ideology or subject need be either dominant or subjected. Granting Foucault's point that technological societies serialise people by classifying and grading them, he showed how the series could also be made to represent the vision of a world in which the weight of every term and the difference of every individual is respected, and where each is, at the same time, linked to every other by multiple affinities. Granting that we may be doomed to consume and repeat fragments of yesterday's culture and of yesterday's subjectivities, Barthes showed how the subject could become active, performative and free by juxtaposing and combining a multiplicity of fragments. And recognising that structures are both inevitable and necessary, he sought 'unique and varied' structures which, precisely by virtue of their decentredness, allowed for a plurality of individual differences and activities. Derrida, in turn, subverted the indomitable sameness to which men were reduced by rationality by representing the world as a decentred system of differences and by stressing 'the irreducibility of the other' and the dependence of freedom on difference. Granting that the subject may be nothing but an anonymous relay-station for a missive which is not his own, Derrida showed that he was nevertheless still capable of calling and re-calling the infinitely other. Granting that men might be bound to obey a rule, a law or a programme, Derrida showed that by displacing the rule and by holding the meaning of the law in reserve, it was possible to mock at their authority. And granting that men might be doomed to repeat and re-present the writings and re-presentations that precede them, he showed how re-presentations could also be made markedly different. In their various says then, Barthes, Foucault and Derrida not only acknowledged the obsolescence of the old humanist subject and the conditioning of the new programmed and decentred man-machine of mass society. They also sought to show man-machines that they need not be robots and to provide them with new, decentred areas of freedom and activity, with new ways of being individual and different, and with new possibilities of subjectivity.

Their strategy with regard to the author was equally complex. But here, too, the old humanist author whose meaning or intentions governed the text and its interpretation had to die to enable a new, equally creative, but more multiple and decentred author to live. The old humanist author had to die in two senses. He had to die as a real or imagined, historical, biographical or formal constraint on the reading of his texts – it is not by chance that Lacan, Barthes, Foucault and Derrida resolutely ignore even such indisputable formal features of texts as dialogue or peripateia. For, as we saw, following Lacan, they all spoke 'through' the literary, philosophical or historical texts they discussed or 'inserted' themselves within them by puncturing holes in the fabric of the texts and introducing their own structures and their own concerns. As we saw, they were all quite explicit about what they were doing in this respect and about the methods they were using to do it. They also indicated their own authorial positions: Lacan presented himself as an analysand, Barthes as the subject of his writings in both senses of that word, and Derrida as his own autobiographer; while Foucault simply explained that 'the interpretation is the interpreter'.

The old humanist author had to die not only as a constraint on the reading of his text, but as a model of authorship for Lacan, Barthes, Foucault and Derrida. For one thing, they could not ally themselves to the forces of authority, domination and control by imposing a controlling authorial signified, meaning, ideology or reading on their texts and on their readers. This is one reason why Lacan, Barthes and Derrida all developed techniques to suspend meaning, to separate signifiers from all signification and to withold author-ity. Foucault was clearly a partial exception here, for reasons which, as we saw, were connected to his Maoist theory of revolution, but even he disputed the right of authors to speak for others and to determine how they should act.

The old humanist author had to die as a model for authorship, too, because he was too coherent and unified a figure. He could not contain either the ideal freedom, activity and multiplicity of the new decentred subject or the real complexity and contradictoriness of the positions Lacan, Barthes, Foucault and Derrida were assuming as insiders, outsiders, subverters, innovators, conformists, non-conformists and revolutionaries, both in relation to the old humanist culture and in relation to the new technological society. It was because they were assuming such different and incompatible positions that Barthes, Foucault and Derrida indicated that the author (most particularly themselves) had to be thought of in a new way – as multiply divided, as assuming polyvalent strategic positions in his discourse, or as employing a 'concomitant syntax' to present himself as a living contradiction. And it was to enable the author to represent the ideal of decentred freedom, activity and multiplicity that they all presented themselves as authors of a game. As authors of a game, Lacan, Barthes, Foucault and Derrida figured as Nietzschean supermen, as Lefebvrian revolutionaries and as the hidden God. For the game was *carnaval*, creativity, prodigality, waste, the bursting of constraints, and the mocking laughter of the last man in the face of total destruction. For Barthes, as we saw, it was in addition a way for man to re-appropriate himself and his world. The game was god-like too to a generation who answered Einstein's objection that he could not believe in a God who played dice with the world, by proclaiming this God to be the only God in whom they could believe.

But despite the changes they introduced in the profile of the author by making him the multiple, contradictory, unconstraining and partly hidden generator of a game which imposed no ideology on anyone but contained all its value and all its values in itself, Lacan, Barthes, Foucault and Derrida preserved two important features of the old humanist author. First, he was an *écrivain*, a writer, not an academic. Where academics in all fields at least make a stab at describing 'the thing as in itself it really is', even if that thing is a literary or philosophical text, the writer is a generator of ideas and fictions. As Lacan, Barthes, Foucault and Derrida keep pointing out, to speak through other texts, to insert oneself, one's own structures, ideas or self-analysis into other texts, is to produce a fictional representation of those texts – in Lacan, it is to turn all texts into moments of an ongoing self-analysis, in Foucault, it is to turn history into a novel, in Barthes, it is to turn literary criticism and literary theory into a Writing and, in Derrida, it is to turn philosophy into mimicry and mime. And as Barthes and Derrida underline, to write games which have no referent in reality or in anything else, games which are purely self-referential, is to write fictions – both in the traditional sense of creating an autonomous, self-referential world which defines its own values, its own norms, its own structures, and its own language, to say nothing of its own heroes and villains, and in Jakobson's sense of 'literarity' as a preoccupation by the text with its own structures.

By assuming the mantle of the writer, they were also borrowing something of the writer's traditional status and authority in France. There is nothing comparable to it in the Anglo-American world, except possibly for the respect Victorians accorded their writers during the brief period when they expected them to act as moral prophets. In France, both under the III Republic and after the war, to be a writer was to sit above mere ministers at banquets, to enjoy an undisputable moral authority, to have the right and the duty to pass judgment publicly on the social and political issues of the day and to uphold the sacred principles of liberty, fraternity and equality in the face of all infractions. This Lacan, Barthes, Foucault and Derrida did, even if they re-defined liberty as the right to self-determination and self-management (*auto-gestion*), equality as pluralism and the abolition of dominations and subjections, and fraternity as respect for the right to be different.

They also sometimes sought to reinforce the more traditional view that writers' 'writings are also acts whose import often exceeds ministerial decisions'[11] by borrowing import and importance from the way 'words create reality' in technological societies. As we saw, Barthes argued that 'practice follows speech and is absolutely determined by it' and that as our lives are repetitions of books and of myths, to change the words, the books and the myths is also to change peoples' lives. And Foucault insisted that fictions could in the long run create new realities. It should not disturb us to find them borrowing some of the moral and political authority of the old humanist writer and some of the power of language in modern society, while at the same time seeking to silence all languages and to subvert all author-ity, including their own. For one thing, these are just two of the many contradictions they inhabited. For another, they needed what leverage they could get in a France where the situation of intellectuals and academics was thought to have deteriorated badly.

Henri Bérenger, writing in 1898, was among the first to note this deterioration and to speak of an 'intellectual proletariat'. Explaining that members of the liberal professions were no longer bourgeois of independent means, but largely poor men who looked to their professions to support them, he defined the intellectual proletariat as 'regimented and subjected people, aspirants to the bourgeoisie who finish up by being candidates for starvation'. He blamed the universities for producing too many graduates, so that most graduates could do little more than scrape a miserable living, if indeed they were lucky enough to find work. Made ambitious by their education, deprived of their liberty and equality first by the stringent competitiveness of the French educational system and then by what he called the 'servility' and 'bondage' of work which reduced them to regimented employees, proletarian intellectuals – a class which included doctors, journalists, teachers, lawyers, professors, artists, and small functionaries – were, he said, bound to revolt and to turn to socialism for redress.[12]

As we saw, French left-wing sociological writing took up all these themes after the war. In such books as Kanapa's *Situation de l'Intellectuel*, Serge Mallet's *The New Working Class*, Bon and Burnier's *Les Nouveaux Intellectuels*, Pierre Naville's *Révolution des Intellectuels*, Henri Lefebvre's *Position: Contre les Technocrates*, and Sartre's *Plaidoyer pour les Intellectuels*, to name only the most well-known, the proletarianisation of intellectuals, their regimentation in their places of work and the inevitability of their revolt were all developed, but with some differences. For Bérenger, the intellectual proletariat consisted essentially of that class of intellectuals which had either failed to find work, or which was forced to work either on the fringes of their professions or in low-paying professions like teaching. In the writings of the 1960s, proletarianisation was extended to all intellectuals because it was now clearly linked to their new role of experts and technicians in the new technological society and to the subjection of intellectuals to a new ruling class of technocrats, who exploited their know-how, made the decisions, and sought to turn society into a rationalised and coherent system.[13] Sartre even goes so far as to predict that 'under American influence', intellectuals would lose their old universalising and revolutionary functions completely, and be entirely reduced to specialists, experts, technicians and anonymous members of teams. In this post-war literature, the sociological deterioration of intellectuals (which now includes all Bérenger's categories, plus engineers, computer experts, lab workers and all the specialists of the new science and technology) is described in terms of a new marginalisation and a new centrality of intellectuals in technological civilisation. Foucault was not alone in realising that modern technological societies depend heavily for their progress, prosperity and power on intelligence, knowledge and expertise – Lyotard in fact traces this insight back to a remark of Marx's in the *Grundrisse*[14] – nor was he alone in realising that intellectuals therefore acquired a new centrality and importance in modern societies. At the same time, it was felt that intellectuals had lost their old place in the social and political pecking order with the fall of the old governing liberal élite of the III Republic and with the emergence of the new ruling class of technocrats.

The University was seen as very much part of this process of proletarianisation and of social and political marginalisation of the intellectual. Bérenger had already compared French schools and universities to military barracks, and complained of the effects of Napoleon's 'militarisation' and regimentation on all spheres of intellectual work, and the comparison of schools and universities to barracks and factories recurs quite frequently in post-war left-wing literature. The French university, with a central bureaucracy in Paris dictating what was to be taught in every subject in every department of every university in France and with a feudal internal organisation which made one or two politically appointed professors the *grands patrons* of everyone beneath them, was perceived neither as an ivory tower nor as a bastion of freedom. It was perceived as a coercive, authoritarian and regimented institution which was run on the same lines as other Napoleonic institutions, which permitted very little personal freedom (even for faculty members), and which forced students to cram and conform in order to pass highly competitive examinations which were designed to weed people out all the way up the educational ladder rather than to enable them to acquire paper qualifications. After the war too, the universities, the *grandes écoles* and the institutes of higher learning began to lose their old functions as training grounds for a homogeneous, liberal and humanist, governing élite; what was now increasingly demanded of them was that they produce the expertise required for the modernisation of France. Within the universities, subjects like French and Philosophy, once the mainstay of the education of the old humanist élite, became increasingly marginalised by the new demand for technical expertise; and students in the humanities and in some of the social sciences found themselves superannuated and unable to find work. This was one of the factors which led to the student uprising of 1968.[15]

Moreover, it was no longer as clear to post-war French intellectuals as it had been to Bérenger that intellectuals could turn to socialism for redress. Or rather, it gradually became clearer that if intellectuals as a class or caste were to be able to turn to socialism, it would have to be to a socialism purified of the taint of Stalinism and of the authoritarianism and establishmentarianism of the French Communist Party, and to a socialism which transcended the fracturing and factional disputes of the French left in the post-war years. The only thing that was still undisputably honourable about the link between intellectuals and socialism was the pre-Marxist, home-grown oppositional role which French intellectuals had acquired, with their name of *intellectuel*, during the Dreyfus affair. Jean Vigier of the CNRS defined this role as follows: 'An intellectual is someone who gives society a critical account of itself: permanently contesting it, holding up to it a savage mirror which incites – helps? – to transform it. Historically, it is in this sense that the noun 'intellectual' was born at the time of the Dreyfus affair'.[16]

As we saw, Lacan, Barthes, Foucault and Derrida, all addressed themselves to intellectuals rather than to the proletariat or to the general informed reader; they all assumed the role of the intellectual as it had emerged during the Dreyfus affair; and they all sought to reverse marginalities.

Lacan, Barthes and Foucault, as we saw, sought to give the marginalised intellectual a new identity and a new centrality. Lacan initiated this movement by reminding French intellectuals that they need not employ their know-how merely in the service of the technocrats and by giving analysts a role, and writers and teachers the model of a role, which did not simply involve helping people to conform and adapt to the demands and constraints of the established order. Foucault concretised both this insight and this role. His historical analyses of the ways in which modern intellectuals had been created by specific events (like the birth of the clinic and the asylum, or the policy of collecting information about the population) and of the ways intellectuals continued to be determined by the authoritarian nature of the institutions in which they worked, by the roles of surveillance and control these imposed on them and by the regimes of truth and the forms of exclusion and control to which they were themselves subject, served two functions. On the one hand, such analyses helped intellectuals to become aware of where they were themselves being constrained and where they were specifically engaged in forcing others to conform to the demands of the established order. On the other hand, such analyses showed intellectuals that, far from being marginal to society, they had from the beginning, played central roles in the development of the institutions of modern society, and that they were still key figures in the day-to-day operation of these institutions. Foucault used this fact, together with the increased importance of knowledge in what he called the 'technico-scientific structures' of modern society, to ground his claim that knowledge is power and that intellectuals can work and struggle, each in his own specific area and by mutual exchange and support, to overthrow the political, economic, institutional, cultural and epistemic chains that bind them and to 'constitute a new politics of truth'. Foucault not only brought 'subjugated knowledges' back into view; and he not only brought such excluded and marginalised figures as the madman and the prisoner back into the mainstream of the social and historial order; he did the same for the intellectual.

Barthes' manner of centralising marginalities was, as we saw, quite different. Barthes accepted and affirmed multiple marginalities – the marginality of the intellectual, of the *grand bourgeois* of the past, of the atheist, the homosexual, the amorous subject and of all forms of pleasure in modern ideologies – and he transformed these marginalities into positive creative and intellectual resources. Barthes celebrated the pleasures of reading, writing and cruising on the atopical fringes of society, outside the power-structure, without any need to choose among competing ideologies and without any need to obey institutional demands except by the mere appearance of conformity. In Barthes' writings, marginality became central to the ideally free, plural and active subject whose *jouissance* he engineered.

However, the most important single step taken by Lacan, Barthes, Foucault and Derrida to reverse both the marginality of intellectuals and their own marginality as professors of what had now become marginal subjects was, in appearance, the most innocent and the most politically under-determined. Intertextuality seemed to be grounded in a purely theoretical assessment of the inter-connection and inter-relation of all texts and all languages in language. And after semiotics, structuralism and Marxist analyses of the inter-relation of different aspects of the super-structure with each other and with characteristic features of the infrastructure, who could argue with intertextuality? But unlike semiotics, which assumed that society is a single complex system of signs, unlike structuralism which assumed that the same unconscious structures determine all cultural, ideological and linguistic formations, and unlike Marxist analyses which assumed that being determines consciousness in the social totality, intertextuality simply qualified the intellectual to speak of anything and everything in language. As we saw, it made it possible for Lacan, Barthes, Foucault and Derrida to roam at will among different types of discourse and among different types of text, pulling things together and making what sense of them they would, without conforming to the traditional delimitations and prescriptions of any one discipline or any one text.

In the light of the pretty standard left-wing characterisation of technological societies as societies which rule by dividing intellectuals into narrowly defined areas of specialisation, this was an extremely significant move. For, it was argued, the study of man had been so divided up among different fields of expertise and different areas of research, that no single expert or specialist in any field or sub-field could any longer perceive or understand the real implications and consequences of his theories, his practices or his research.[17] Intertextuality was a means of bringing the human sciences together and of providing a more coherent, complex and critical view not only of man's positions in modern society, but also of the ways in which language, reason and the human sciences themselves contributed to making man into a machine. By extending their disciplines through intertextuality and by gearing their scholarship 'directly to the needs and problems of today', (rather than, let us say, to the way being had determined con-sciousness in the past), Lacan, Barthes, Foucault and Derrida were able to give their marginalised disciplines a new centrality and importance. Psychoanalysis could be seen to address itself not merely to the private and subjective psychological problems of individuals, but to the more generalised problems of conformity and subjectivity in modern society. 'French' could be seen to address itself not merely to the *explication* of ancient classical texts, but to the operation of language, myth and ideology in the media, in society at large and in the human sciences themselves. History, frankly redefined as 'a history of the present', could deal with a whole range of contemporary political, social and intellectual issues and explore the operation of language, power and control both in society's institutions and in the human sciences too. And philosophy could be seen to address itself not merely to the reasonings of ancient philosophers, but to the hubris and the limitations of reason, rationality and language themselves. This extension of their disciplines enabled Lacan, Barthes, Foucault and Derrida to speak to a wider cross-section of intellectuals and to provide a much needed broadening of intellectual horizons. And if Lacan alone succeeded in providing his students with a potentially remunerative form of expertise, the others could at least claim, if they wished to, that through their work, Letters regained their importance for the training and formation of France's intellectual élite.

It would be misleading to describe Lacan, Barthes, Foucault and Derrida as merely gearing their disciplines to the needs and problems of the present. Their *renversement* of accepted values and of traditional modes of analysis in their own disciplines was much more complex and contradictory than this. For, on the one hand, they all gave the study of the past dignity and importance by showing the extent to which the past dominates the present. As the child's first image of himself in the mirror or in the form of a symbolic and cultural order which precedes every individual's entry into it; as a body of myths and texts from the past which are taught in the schools and vulgarised in the media of mass society; as the historical emergence of the components of over-arching modern abstractions like justice or madness or truth; as the logos modern man has inherited from the Greeks or in the form of the writing of the world as a system of differences, the past invariably leaves its indelible mark on the present. Moreover, in their various ways, Lacan, Barthes, Foucault and Derrida all demonstrated the value of texts from the past. Lacan showed that literary texts have provided men with their pre-determined roles and the myths they live out, as well as with the means to speak of these myths and these roles. Barthes characterised literature as the discipline which would have to be saved if all others were destroyed: the history of literature, he argued, is the history of all human knowledge, the history of men's shifting and unsuccessful attempts to capture and understand the real, as well as the history of men's attempts to construct an ideal and utopian space in which man is free to speak 'according to the truth of his desire'. Foucault and Derrida demonstrated the value of the past as a means of changing our perspective on the present. Foucault used the specificity and internal coherence of past periods of history to denaturalise the present by showing that completely different values and ways of doing things made sense in their own very different configurations of truth. And Derrida countered the long history of the logos in Western writings by drawing on an alternative, but no less ancient, body of texts.

But, at the same time, Lacan, Barthes, Foucault and Derrida also subverted the past and loosened its hold on the present. As we saw, Lacan emptied past philosophical systems of their meaning by using their key words to mean something other than they meant within the philosophical system in question; he restructured received ideas by his use of gaps or omissions; and he used all received texts and all received cultural reference systems as vehicles for the same subjective message: 'I, the real subject, am not'. Derrida, as we saw, de-constructed both the logos inherited from the Greeks and the alternative body of ancient Jewish texts on which he drew most heavily. His four-fold rule of division, articulation, pivoting and displacement was designed to reduce all received philosophical and literary texts to undecidability and in-*différance*. And his doctrine of critical writing as a constant process of substitution for and addition to earlier writings ensured that the origin – here the original meaning and context of any text – did indeed come in time to be lost. The 'supervised ruptures, fake conformities and indirect destructions' in Barthes' game-texts were designed to 'explode' received cultural myths, past ideologies, institutionalised theoretical and critical methods and the time-bound meanings of literary texts and to reduce Barthes' own commentary to silence by suspending all meanings. Foucault, as always, stands a little apart, but he, too, used discontinuity, differentiation and dispersion to break down the familiar units, categories, continuities and totalities through which history, society and the symbolic order are traditionally interpreted. He described these methods as 'tools made not for understanding, but for cutting', and his account of the past was often governed more by his desire for *renversement* than by his faithfulness to things as in themselves they might have been.

It is certainly true that the methods Lacan, Barthes, Foucault and Derrida used to deconstruct the past and to suspend its meanings 'provide new ways of explicating classical texts, texts that might have seemed exhausted, "used up" and unable to grant still more readings'.[18] And it is certainly true that this use of the past provided Lacan, Barthes, Foucault and Derrida with a virtually unlimited possibility of speaking, writing and publishing, a fact which none of them overlooked. For once each had determined the method he was going to use to deconstruct the past and to empty it of all or some of its meanings, and once each had decided on what Barthes described as 'the one sentence each of us speaks which can only be interrupted by death', each had only to repeat. Indeed, they all argued in their different ways that it was impossible for speech and writing to do anything but repeat themselves. 'Ludic repetition' ensured that each repetition should be somewhat different to the one before, and therefore witty, novel and interesting. But, as Lacan pointed out, 'everything in repetition which is varied and modulated is only an alienation of its meaning'. And indeed, ultimately, as we saw, Lacan, Barthes and Derrida's ludic repetitions only alienated the same structures and the same (non) meanings, only made them seem 'other', by putting them in different terms and in different contexts. This in-built possibility of repeating their writing and their speech enabled Lacan, Barthes, Foucault and Derrida to conform to institutional demands that they keep on speaking and writing. It kept them within an institution from which they dissented, and it kept them rising in its ranks.

In assessing the value of the methods they used to deconstruct the past and to suspend its meanings, one important fact should not be overlooked. They all belonged to generations which had been thoroughly grounded in the classical texts of literature and philosophy by the disciplines and educational system they sought to subvert, and so did their students and readers in France. It is against this stable background of common reference points and of solidly acquired knowledge of the past that they are witty, novel, interesting and different. Hence their very ambiguous relation to the past: their sense of the value and importance of that which they set out to silence. As Barthes put it, they all needed the literature, philosophy and culture of the past to 'originalise themselves'. Separated from this past, their texts have no body and no being; they are nothing but empty and recurrent structures which cannot be fleshed out. This symbiotic relationship to the past helps to explain their paralysis in the Oedipal phase of development: their obsession with the Father, their Oedipal rivalry, their desire to kill the Father and put themselves in his place. To substitute their recurrent structures for a genuine study of the past in our teaching and writing practice is not only to disturb the fine balance on which the *brio* and the brilliance of their texts depend. It is also to leave future generations without that which we all still share with Lacan, Barthes, Foucault and Derrida – namely whatever knowledge of the past can be gleaned from fallible human scholarship. This would be tantamount to leaving future generations without a past, and therefore without any defence against the empty structures imposed on them in the present. And it would be tantamount to depriving them of a non-Oedipal relation to the past, a relation based on respect, interest and a sense of our difference.

Lacan, Barthes, Foucault and Derrida's destructions of the past could be explained in Lacanian terms as a repetition of languages' 'original murder of the thing' and as a manifestation of the only real freedom Lacan left the subject in modern society – the freedom to annihilate all that is. But it is perhaps more usefully discussed in terms of the French intellectual's traditional role of giving society a critical account of itself and of inciting it to change. For one thing their methods were all designed to do was to take the *parole vide* of cultural reference systems, cultural myths, critical methods, methods of analysis in the human sciences, historical discursive formations and rational forms of argumentation to their limits – to the point where they teetered and where, again to borrow Lacan's phrase, 'the moorings of speech were loosened'. In this context, their areas of non-being – the place of the subject as pure negativity, as pure absence and pure lack; the atopical place of the ne-uter, the neither/nor; the space between the great dualities of Western consciousness; and the spaces of *différance* – represented 'the beyond which is nothing' except the pure possibility of standing outside extant structures and methods and of being able to perceive them critically against their limits. Placing cultural reference systems, cultural myths, critical approaches, methods of analysis in the human sciences, rational forms of argumentation in philosophy and historical discursive formations against their limits in this way enabled Lacan, Barthes, Foucault and Derrida to bring out their limitations, their shortcomings and their faults. It enabled them to denaturalise the ways in which we are accustomed to thinking and speaking, in the academy and outside it, by making our ways of thinking and speaking cease to appear to be the only obvious and natural ways of approaching things. As Foucault made clear, such critical analyses were potentially of revolutionary value. They made it possible to conceive of change and to see what needed to be torn down. By providing a topological and geographical survey of potential battlegrounds – of areas where peoples' lives had been dominated, where peoples' minds had been subjected, and where peoples' language had been ordered, by imposed conformities – they helped to free people from them. And by demonstrating the automatism, the clichés, the divisions and the over-rationality in academic thinking, in culture and in society, they incited people to transform them. How far they really hoped to have a revolutionary impact on society as well as on thought is absolutely clear only in the case of Foucault. But George Lichtheim may well be right in saying that 'no critic of existing institutions ever supposed that his freedom was limited to contemplation'.[19]

Alienation was a central theme in all their work, as we saw. It was also the great obsession of the French left in the post-war years. Existentialist Marxists who gathered around Sartre and Merleau-Ponty at Les Temps Modernes, the Trotskyist founders of Socialisme ou Barbarie, the Arguments group which included Henri Lefebvre and Barthes, and the Situationists, all made alienation a central category of their analyses of modern technological society. Where the 'official Marxism' of the French Communist party stressed Kapital and Anti-Dühring, this revisionary French Marxism turned to the early Marx of the Paris Manuscripts, to Lukács' History and Class Consciousness, and to Karl Korsch and mixed them with liberal doses of Hegel as filtered through the teaching of Alexandre Kojève and Jean Hyppolite.[20] In this alienation-centred revisionary French Marxism, alienation was no longer perceived as a fundamentally economic problem which principally affected the working class. Alienation became characteristic of all classes of people in technological society, including the 'masters', and of all spheres of life – psychological, sexual, cultural, ideological, everyday life in the city, leisure and so on. In the work of the situationists, in Henri Lefebvre and in Guy Debord's unreadable but influential Société du Spectacle, particular emphasis was placed on the 'totalitarian management' which shaped and modelled people's everyday behaviour, on the evils of conformity, and on the way cybernetics and the media intervened in consumer societies to alienate men from their desires and to prevent them from acting on the world.

Moreover, while they all perceived the desirability of overcoming alienation, some doubt was expressed about whether this would be possible, even at the end of history. It was certainly not going to be possible in the foreseeable future. The Hegelian-Marxist dialectic had therefore to be radically revised. The Hegelian-Marxist notion of transcending alienation by re-uniting subject and object and by reconciling man to the world had to be abandoned, and with it the dialectical moment of *Aufhebung*. Being now confronted Nothing without any possibility of *Aufhebung* in Becoming. Subject faced object and self the other, identity confronted difference, and the dialectic became binary. The impossibility of overcoming alienation in reality had two further consequences.[21] First, failing to recognise himself in the world and to transform it by his labour, the subject could now only define his subjectivity (and his humanity) as difference from the world, as otherness from the alien other, as a negation of the given. Kojève had taught that 'freedom can exist only as negation' and that negation is creative, and this became a guiding principle for two generations of French left-wing intellectuals. Despite the high-flown philosophical language, we should note that this negation was a value judgment: disliking what they found in being, they chose non-being; unable to accept what was present, they chose what was not; failing to find fulfilment in society, they chose freedom from it. Secondly, the Hegelian identity of subject and object at the end of history could now only be conceived abstractly as an end of history in which men encountered nothing outside themselves to impede their projects and to prevent the fulfilment of their desires. Kojève characterised this end of history as the reign of frivolity and play, as a time when there was nothing left to be done. The announcement by Kojève, and then by others, that history had already ended, that men were already living in the aftermath of history, was therefore not only a transposition of the identity of subject and object to the sphere of creativity, frivolity and play, a sense that the subject could now only be identical with the object in creativity and play. It also represented a doubt that there was anything left to be done about history. This is how members of the *Arguments* group, like Fougayrollas, Axelos and Henri Lefebvre came to preach fluid and 'open' totalities which allowed for constant new creation, the importance of human creativity and participation, and the ideal of a 'civilization of play'.

In Lacan, as we saw, alienation was essentially a no-exit situation. If the child identified with his image, if he saw himself in his conformist and socialised ego, he lost himself; if he spoke in the language of the symbolic order and obeyed its laws, he alienated himself from reality and from himself. And yet he could not do otherwise, for he needed the image, the ego, the language of the symbolic order and the law of the other to be. Without them, the subject was 'no one' even in his unconscious. But this no one, this nothing, this ex-centric other subject who was not and could not be, was also the negation of the given and the precondition for genuine being. The lost and ex-centric subject represented the freedom to subvert and annihilate all that is and to open a path to an impossible possibility of being. By a strange twist, therefore, and for the first time, alienation became a positive good: if there were nothing left in man that was alienated and other, if man were only what society and the symbolic order made him, if he really recognised himself in the social other, then men would no longer be able to 'speak as men'; they would have become mere members of the herd. In Lacan, otherness from the other was the condition for authenticity, humanity, reality, being and truth.

Barthes went a step further. In his work, alienation was the precondition for pleasure, play and writing, and pleasure, play and writing were means of reuniting subject and object and of overcoming alienation intellectually. Barthes' play-texts were negations of the given which, as he made clear, proceeded from a non-place, from a 'scandalous atopicality'. By cutting themselves adrift from the standard topoi of culture, society, language and personal identity; by playing off against each other the multiple cultural plagiarisms and multiple conformities to the 'canonical languages' of culture and the human sciences; by erasing any magisterial voice pleading a theory or a cause; and by 'exploding' all possible meanings, Barthes' play-texts not only marked the freedom to negate and destroy all that is. They also marked Barthes' alienation and his formal otherness from everyone else. At the same time, this destruction of all conformities and all established meanings freed text, writer and reader from all the obstacles outside themselves which could impede their projects and the fulfilment of their desires. Writing and reading could become a praxis free of all real constraints, in which, as we saw, writers and readers could overcome their alienation from themselves, from each other and from extant cultural forms by constructing what meanings, structures or connections they wished and by being once again able to recognise themselves and each other in and through the text object. Freed of all real conformities, constraints and established meanings, the text could also become a space where Barthes, at least, could use forms like the fragment or the series to create and represent the utopian world which accorded with his desires. But Barthes did not see this as a real *Aufhebung*. Writing might be a 'sacred' space where the ideal unity of subject and object could be realised, but the subject remained bound to 'live to the full the contradictions of his time'. He might be able to reject the either/ors of society, but this only left him a somewhat castrated ne-uter. It left him where Lacan's subject had been left, without any real social place.

Foucault was more optimistic. Foucault wrote from the centre of alienation, from the dividing lines where men were made other to each other and to themselves. He analysed 'the dividing practices' in which 'the subject is either divided inside himself or divided from others' and he showed how these dividing practices were built into the discursive and institutional order of society, determining our subjectivations and alienating us from others and from ourselves. Foucault's histories were to be negations of the given: 'scalpels, molotov cocktails or minefields'. But they were also spaces in which real conformities and conventional 'policing of discourse' could be evaded: in Foucault's histories, the writer was free to cut and connect historical materials and to 'fiction history'; he was free to operate *renversements* which had as yet no being in reality; and he was free to 'fiction' spaces for power and knowledge and spaces for the creation of new regimes of truth. Foucault taught society to recognise itself in that which it had alienated and made other, and he incited men to transform their world and to re-appropriate their power to do so. But he also showed that men could no longer overcome alienation by any Hegelian or Marxist *Aufhebung* and that the model of identity of subject and object would have to be abandoned, both as a model for knowledge and as a model for society. Alienation could not be transcended by trying to unite man with himself or with his world; it could only be superseded by complex and uncentred multiplicities and interactions.

Derrida went further than anyone else in his rejection of *Aufhebung* and of the ideal of identity between subject and object.

For Derrida too, otherness from the other was the non-place from which the given could be deconstructed and in which extant meanings could be collapsed into indeterminacy. But Derrida multiplied otherness and sacralised it. God's otherness from the world became the condition for human freedom; men's otherness from each other, their refusal to make others the same, became the condition not only for freedom in and between societies, but also for respect and tolerance among men. Excluded from rationality in the Western logos where reason traditionally sought to absorb and appropriate everything that was its other, otherness in Derrida became the supreme mystery and the supreme law. But the law of otherness ruled only over writing; and to extend its rule to all things in creation, it had to suppress the reality of every object, and turn all things into writing and text. And then, to mark and re-mark its otherness from every other, it had in its turn to suppress the otherness of all others and to convert all writings into itself.

In the work of Lacan, Barthes, Foucault and Derrida, then, otherness became the mark of individuality, of an individuality free not only to annihilate all that is, but to understand its own complex relationships to the sameness of conformity. In their work, otherness shows both its need of the symbolic order to be and its ability to be despite the symbolic order; it shows the multiple ways in which it is determined and subjected by the given, and tests its own power to determine and subject the given too. In their work, there is a growing realisation that individuals can find the ideal unity of subject and object, the absolute freedom to control and create what is outside them, only in the sphere of literature, writing and play; and that for the rest, individuals must accept each others' otherness and view society as a multitude of others, each of whom is free to assert his otherness in his own way.

The last context in which Lacan, Barthes, Foucault and Derrida need to be seen is that of the French educational system. If English and American universities are, as Caplow and McGee have said 'remarkable for pursuing an intricate program with little agreement about fundamental purposes',[22] the French could not be more different. From the Napoleonic period, the French educational system was organised on the assumption that 'there will be no firm and fixed political state without a teaching body with firm and fixed principles'[23] and on the assumption that the primary function of education is to inculcate these firm and uniform convictions in everyone. French and Philosophy became the pillars of an education designed to produce citizens with firm and uniform convictions. French privileged classical authors like Corneille, Racine, Bossuet, La Bruyère and la Rochefoucauld, often taught either in bowlderized versions or in *morceaux choisis* (selected passages), because they provided models of honour, dignity, nobility, virtue, courage, sacrifice and the ability to prefer reason and duty to passion and self-interest. The teaching of French literature was to result in 'elevation of thought, nobility of style, and thence seriousness of character'.[24] In Philosophy, where Plato and Descartes were given pride of place, students were taught that man is a rational and conscious being, who has imagination, passion and volition and who is capable of choosing the good. The goal of philosophy was to produce serious, rational reasonably cultivated citizens, who could deliberate about human nature, about the human condition and about the good, the beautiful and the true.[25] Philosophy was taught all the way up the educational ladder – in secondary schools, in the universities and *grandes écoles* to students of science, public administration, business and everything else.

Teaching, as might be expected in a system designed to transmit firm and fixed principles and established ways of speaking and writing, was rigid, frontal and authoritarian. It constrained junior and middle-rank faculty as well as students. Here is Derrida's description of his own job at the ENS: '*Répétiteur*, the teacher for the degree, ought to produce nothing, if produce means innovate, transform, adduce something new. He is intended to repeat and to get others to repeat, to reproduce and make others reproduce: forms, norms and a content'.[26] Even middle-rank faculty were bound by the need to prepare their students for the rigorous state examination which conferred the degree. Their job was 'to assist both the professors and the pupils'. From the other side, things looked equally rigid. As one student has put it, perched on his platform behind his desk or lectern, the 'master – the term takes on all its meaning – distributes knowledge and inculcates principles rigorously defined by other adults',[27] which students are expected to accept and reproduce passively and without question. Not only is there great emphasis in the French educational system on learning by heart, but the *dissertation* (an essay or paper) on which success in the highly selective school and university system depends, essentially requires students to give appropriate, or if possible brilliant, expression to received ideas.

At the same time, it should be pointed out that this essentially left-wing and oppositional portrayal of the system completely fails to explain both the long tradition of dissent in French universities, and the creativity and originality, to say nothing of the high level of argument, of French dissent.[28] Before condemning unquestioningly the rigours of the French system, it is worth wondering how it managed to get so many people to think for themselves.

By the late 1960s and early 1970s, the absolutist and humanist model of education began to teeter, especially in left-wing colleges like Vincennes, not merely because the 'firm and fixed' humanist principles which it inculcated were under attack, but also because it was thought that the development of science had undermined the possibility of any 'firm and fixed' rational body of knowledge and truth. Kouchner and Burnier explained, for instance, that 'Given the evolution of science and technology, no master can pretend to incarnate knowledge, the established positions are swept away. Master and pupil are simply situated on different rungs of the ladder of non-knowledge'.[29] Jean Fourastié argued that the university could no longer pursue its traditional goal of teaching 'the most brilliant expression of ideas held in common' because to do so was to hide from students 'the complexity of the real and the difficulty man has in understanding it . . . the immense lacunae in human knowledge and the contradictions in science itself'.[30] And writing at the end of the 1970s, Jean-François Lyotard explained that knowledge in the university had lost all sources of legitimation other than those constantly changing rules for the production of scientific discourses which each type of scientific discourse is constantly giving itself. Post-modern thinkers, he said, know that as a result of developments in physics, science has lost all referent in reality; they see that there is not one true and binding form of scientific discourse but 'an indefinite number of games of language which obey different rules', including machine languages, new non-denotative logics, the language of the genetic code and so on. They therefore conclude that 'legitimation can only come from their linguistic practice and from their communicational interaction'. They conclude that the legitimation of a discourse depends on the formulation of rules (which include defining the symbols to be used, the forms of acceptable argument and the operations permitted) and on the agreement of one's interlocutors to play by these rules. Invention then consists either in combining and rearranging the givens within the framework of the old rules or of 'the invention of new rules and therefore of a change of game'.[31] And Lyotard pointed out (yet again!) that for post-modern thinkers, science understood in these terms constituted a *contestation* of the deterministic, rationalist and totalising system of the technocrats. With such ideas in the air from the late 1960s on, it is hardly surprising that the vogue of semiotics and structuralism should have been so short.

Beginning to teach and to write in the late 1950s and early 1960s, Lacan's theory and practice was in many respects an inverted mirror image of the absolutist humanist model of education. Lacan still had a truth to impart; he still had 'firm and fixed principles'; and he still had all the moral and philosophical abstractions – as we saw, he merely reproduced Truth, Reality, Goodness, Language and Being in inverted form in the subjective realm of negativity. Moreover, as the history of his various psychoanalytic groups showed, Lacan still taught very much in the tradition of a master distributing knowledge which he did not expect to have questioned. Derrida's writings, on the other hand, are very much in the newer tradition. The essays of the late 1960s, especially those collected in *L'Écriture et la Différence*, are still in quest of truth. They question the literary and philosophical texts they discuss and try to decide where the ideas presented can be agreed with and where not. But thereafter, Derrida begins to stress the lacunae in human knowledge, the difficulty man has in understanding the real, the complexity of all things and the coexistence of contradictions in scientific discourse. He also develops rules which legitimate the writing and the game – he defines the symbols to be used, the forms of acceptable language and the operations permitted in deconstruction and in the process, as we saw, he shifts and changes the old rules of 'scientific discourse' in the humanities and starts a new game. Far from pretending to incarnate knowledge, Derrida presents himself as master of non-knowledge and insists that he has no truth to impart and nothing he 'wants to say'. However, judging by what he says in 'Où commence et comment finit un corps enseignant', even as late as 1975, he did not dare do much of this in his teaching, and his students postponed reading his writings until after they had obtained their degrees.

Foucault and the later Barthes, too, are very much in the newer tradition. Foucault's discursive formations behave like transitory scientific languages: they are rules which govern the truth or falsity of statements in a given era; one is only 'in the true' (*dans le vrai*) if one obeys the discursive policy of the moment. But it is always possible to do what he tried to do in *Les Mots et les Choses* and in *Histoire de la Sexualité*, and to change the rules of the discursive game. Barthes innovated by combining and rearranging 'fragments of the language which already exists' and he did all he could to 'deconstruct the dissertation' and to 'loosen' and baffle the power of professorial discourse. Writing by fragments and lecturing by discontinuous digressions around his subject were methods intended to prevent the direct transmission of any 'firm and fixed principles' and to allow his readers and his students to construct their own readings and their own messages. And his seminars, too, were designed to get students to think for themselves and to 'originalise themselves' each in his own way.

At the same time, Lacan, Barthes, Foucault and Derrida remained in the tradition of humanist magisterial teaching in one important respect. In the humanist model of French education, the professor was supposed to demonstrate in his lectures and in his writings the standards of rationality, clarity, organisation and rhetorical excellence which his students were expected to emulate. He was the model to which they were supposed to aspire. Lacan, Barthes Foucault and Derrida all preserved this tradition; they merely changed the model. They were offering models of freedom of thought and freedom of discourse. They all understood freedom here in Sartre's sense of a 'permanent rupture of determinism'. And for all of them, as for Sartre, this permanent rupture of determinism was a fictional product of the imagination, which had no being.[32] They all manifested this imaginative freedom most markedly in their rupture of semiological and structuralist determinisms.

One way they ruptured semiological determinism was by rupturing the unity of signifier and signified. Saussure had defined language as 'a system of signs in which the only essential thing is the union of meanings and sound-images' and he had insisted that these unions are fixed and not free with respect to each linguistic community, so that no individual can modify signs on his own.[33] Lacan, Barthes, Foucault and Derrida set out in their different ways to show that this was not so. Lacan, as we saw, turned words like 'trimethylamin' in Freud's dream of Irma into signifiers without any signified, and he made signifiers like dialectic, being or other signify things that they did not signify to the linguistic community at large. For Barthes, as we saw, 'to imagine is to unfold a sign'. The meanings Barthes attached to each signifier in his named fragments and the configurations he gave them went beyond dictionary definitions and the pacts of any linguistic community; they represented Barthes' own imaginative elaboration and structuration – what he called 'the novelistic quality of the intellect' – and showed, among other things, that the imagination was in no way bound by any predetermined union of sound and concept. Derrida not only showed that it is possible to use words to produce 'readability without a signified' and that signifiers can function perfectly well without any signification or anything they 'want to say'. He also hoist Saussure with his own petard. Saussure had pointed out that 'a word can evoke everything that is associated with it', and Derrida, as we saw, associated so many contradictory or incongruous meanings, contexts and differential relations to signifiers like hymen of *différance* or writing that they ceased to have any decidable meaning at all. Foucault broke down the automatic union of signifier and signified in the linguistic community by showing that signifiers like punishment or discipline or truth were composed of multiple signifieds, each of which had its own different, and often shocking, origin in an earlier period of history.

Another way Barthes, Foucault and Derrida showed their freedom from the determinism of language was by interfering with the paradigmatic oppositions which, according to modern linguistics, ground all meaning. Barthes, as we saw had two ways of doing this. One was to remove the separation between opposites like male/female or literature/criticism, work/play, either by producing texts which were neither one nor the other but somewhere between the two, or by inscribing oppositions within the same body. The other way he used was to coin his own paradigmatic oppositions: as we saw, he coined such paradigmatic oppositions as Literature/Text, *Écrivant/Écrivain*, System/*Systématique*, Doxa/Paradoxa, and such 'drifting' paradigmatic oppositions within the same word as Politics/Politics, History/History and Subject/Subject. This permitted him to generate meanings and to make affirmations which were 'outside' the possibilities already embodied in language's paradigmatic code. Derrida also freed himself from the determinism of paradigmatic oppositions in two ways: one was, as we saw, to join paradigmatic oppositions and to divide and oppose where language as given would see no paradigmatic opposition; the other was to reverse the hierarchy in established paradigmatic oppositions like speech / writing, to make the supposedly inferior term the condition of the possibility of both terms of the opposition, and then to dissolve the entire opposition by making the grounding term so extensive and all-encompassing that it ceases to mean anything at all. Foucault escaped the determinism of such paradigmatic oppositions as normal/abnormal or reason/madness by using history to show that they were not fixed and absolute, but dependent on *epistemes* or discursive formations which changed in the course of history and could be changed again.

Robert Scholes has explained that for semioticians, 'the producers of texts are themselves creatures of culture who have attained a human subjectivity through language. What they produce as literary text is achieved by their acceptance of the constraints of discursive and generic norms'.[34] Barthes, Foucault and Derrida transgressed discursive and generic norms to show that producers of texts and discourses need not be merely creatures of culture. They ruptured the constraints of language and genre to show that human subjects are not merely determined by language and by the conventions of writing; they are also free to create their own languages and to determine their own conventions of writing. This desire to demonstrate their freedom to 'permanently rupture the determinisms' of language and writing is one reason why their texts occupy the boundary between communication and non-communication, and why they are often so hard to understand. It is also a characteristic of their writing which places them in the realm of the literary and the poetic, where conventions of language and genre have always been broken (except perhaps in formulaic oral poetry).

Lacan, Barthes, Foucault and Derrida ruptured the determinism of structuralism by demonstrating their freedom from its most fundamental assumption. Structuralism assumed that everything in culture, in society and in the mind is governed by the same universal and unconscious structures, and it set itself the task of discovering what these are. Lacan, Barthes, Foucault and Derrida countered this by inventing their own structures, and by showing that it is possible for different individuals to invent different structures. Lacan showed that it is possible to change extant structures by introducing 'the notation of an absence'. Barthes invented multiple different systématiques, like the fragment and the series. Foucault devised discursive formations and Derrida produced such structures as the chasm, the structure of supplementarity or *mise-en-abîme* and the indeterminate structure of *différance*. In countering structuralism by showing that it is possible for individuals to invent their own structures, Barthes, Foucault and Derrida were careful not to fall back into the old determinism. Barthes tried to avoid determinism, as we saw, by inventing *systématiques* which were 'at once unique and varied' and which provided for multiple individual differences. Foucault avoided determinism by making it quite clear that the discursive structures he was describing would be different if he had selected different groups of human sciences or different types of material. And he made it clear not only that 'the law which governs what may be said and the system which regulates the appearance of statements' has already been changed several times in the course of history, but also that they can always be changed again. Derrida avoids the old determinism by insisting that his structures are the rules of a game. Derrida's rules are 'necessary' for the playing of his game; but without any referent in reality or in some transcendental absolute, the rules depend for their legitimation first on their ability to produce 'effects of meaning' and secondly, on other people's readiness to accept them as rules for the production of 'effects of meaning'. Should other people not agree to accept them, or should someone else invent different rules that people agreed to accept, there would simply be a change of game.

Foucault and Derrida were thus using the new scientific paradigm of knowledge to counter the determinism of the old scientific paradigm in structuralism. David Bleich – who called this new scientific paradigm a 'subjective paradigm' because it assumes that 'knowledge is made not found'[35] – has shown that it has a very respectable scientific genealogy. He relates it to Einstein's discovery of the variability of space, time and mass according to the frame of reference of the observer; to Heisenberg's uncertainty principle; and to Heisenberg's statement that 'the transparent clarity of mathematics . . . no longer describes the behaviour of the elementary particles, but only our knowledge of this behaviour. . . For the first time in the course of history, modern man on this earth confronts himself alone'.[36] Bleich also relates the subjective paradigm to Husserl's argument that when scientists create the edifice of science in this way, objectivity can only be grounded in communal authority: 'Even what is straightforwardly perceptual is communalized'.[37] Before accepting all this and agreeing that 'scientific discourse' can now only be scientific on a communal and subjective basis and that it is intrinsically fictional, it is worth remembering that philosophers also fell back on the same subjective paradigm the last time scientists discovered that there is more to nature and reality than they had previously realised or understood. One has only to read Locke or Addison's Papers on the Imagination to find similar statements: that knowledge is a matter of ideas in the head, that the appearance of things changes according to one's frame of reference (only then it was the telescope, the microscope and the inability to explain colour which upset everyone); that man looking at the world sees only the fictions produced by his own senses; and that perception can only be grounded communally – only then the communal authority was human nature. Where the eighteenth century perhaps differed from the present was that despite often extreme scepticism about man's ability to know the 'thing as in itself it really is', they defined their problem as that of trying to discover where and how the fictions of the mind intersect with reality – as intersect they must, or science and human life would not be possible at all.

It is worth reconsidering the value of transposing the subjective paradigm of scientific knowledge to the human sciences. It clearly does have some value. For instance, it is valuable as a way of 'rupturing determinisms' and dogmatisms when they exist. It is valuable within 'theory' to teach rabid semiologists and structuralists (if they exist) to temper their ambitions and to historicise their structures. And its importance is clear in an education system which inculcates 'firm and fixed principles' and rules of rational discourse which no one is allowed to question – for it reminds teachers and students that institutional and discursive norms are man-made, that they can be changed, and that instead of copying and repeating them, students and teachers ought to try and learn to 'originalise' themselves.

However, the subjective paradigm may be unhelpful in a university system already 'remarkable for pursuing an intricate program with little agreement about fundamental purposes', where the freedom to 'originalise' oneself already exists if one is willing and able to do so. In already pluralistic universities and societies, the subjective paradigm of knowledge as an indefinite number of fictional communal games which obey different rules, all of which keep changing, is not a call to liberation from totalitarian constraint. It is a description of the status quo and of the problem to be resolved if education is to be about anything at all. In an already decentred and pluralistic university and social system, where there is a perceived lack of 'firm and fixed principles' on which to base a programme of study, the subjective paradigm of non-knowledge and intellectual gamesmanship can appear as a cop-out – as 'the critic's doomed attempt to retreat from a social landscape of fragmentation and alienation'.[38] As we have seen, Lacan, Barthes, Foucault and Derrida did not opt out of French education and French society. Not only was the subjective paradigm itself a strategy to counter some of the perceived abuses of the French educational system, but it was counter-balanced or even contradicted by their adherence to the republican and democratic principles of liberty, equality and fraternity and by their invention of structural paradigms to embody these ideals.

Lacan, Barthes, Foucault and Derrida were all to some extent myth-makers as well as myth breakers. If they subverted the possibility of knowledge and truth by showing that all forms of knowledge and truth are fictional, they also produced new fictions and new myths. Even those who believe that all principles and all forms of knowledge are fictions are not exempt from the responsibility of choosing and deciding which they think it important to transmit, but they can do so with less fear, on the assumption that others will be able to challenge and change the values that they transmit. Lacan, Barthes, Foucault and Derrida appear to have realised what Horkheimer once pointed out: that societies and cultures are remarkable for their ability to function perfectly adequately on the basis of myths, fictions, false principles and erroneous beliefs. What societies, cultures and educational systems cannot do is function without any myths, fictions, principles or beliefs at all.

The multiple and often contradictory positions Lacan, Barthes, Foucault and Derrida were assuming in their writings turned their texts into what they sometimes described as a tissue or weave. In their texts, multiple and often contradictory positions are woven together by what French commentators have called a 'style'. This style is the style of the rag, of the mock-serious put-on, the style of the peculiarly French *canular*. The *canular* depends on a developed 'sense of the fantastic, which is often translated by a marked bent towards farce and mystification'. Officially defined as 'creative mystification, farce which attains the status of myth', the *canular* 'simulates and dissimulates, forbidding the joy which it gives rise to and constraining itself to adopt the solemnity which it derides'.[39] Not the least attractive trait in Lacan, Barthes and Derrida is that they took themselves so much less seriously than other people take them, that they were always turning their pedantry into a fiction and their solemnity into parody, mockery and laughter — and waiting to see just how far they would be allowed to go.

The picture which emerges from recontextualisation of Lacan, Barthes, Foucault and Derrida is a complex and composite one. But the doubleness of their position as dissenting intellectuals working within the institutions and the society from which they dissented runs all the way through, in the counter-balancing of negations by affirmations. Their critique of the old bourgeois and of the new technological society was counterbalanced by their championship of updated versions of the old republican and democratic ideals of liberty, equality and fraternity and by their adherence to modernised versions of the old bourgeois virtues of individuality and originality. Their dissolution of the old humanist subject and their critique of man-machines was accompanied by new models of subjectivity for technological society. Their refusal to act as mental technicians was counter-balanced by their enthusiasm for devising and teaching techniques of their own. Their use of fragmentation, discontinuity and gaps was offset by intertextuality, and their deconstruction of the standards of 'scientific' discourse in their disciplines by the interconnections they establish among the human sciences as a whole. Their suspensions of meaning and destructions of past writings was counter-balanced by their attempts to reverse marginalities and to renew Letters' central role in the formation of France's intellectual élite. Their attacks on totalitarian systematicity and on rational sameness were more than compensated for by the often rigid and repetitive laws of their subjective paradigms. Their rejection of the old Marxist ideal of unity of subject and object was counterbalanced by a new ideal of Otherness, and their rejection of semiology and structuralism by the creation of signs and structures of their own. Their apparent nihilism and non-knowledge were offset not only by the rigours of the French educational system and by the fact that their students were coming to them with a solid knowledge of classical texts and with an excesss of 'firm and fixed principles', but also, paradoxically, by their advocacy of plurality, difference, and decentralization. And their refusal of author-ity was more than countered by their invention of structures to which all 'other' texts were ineluctably subjected.

Perhaps the most important single lesson we have learned from Lacan, Barthes, Foucault and Derrida is that languages, structures and theories in the human sciences can no longer be considered ideologically, educationally, socially or politically 'neutral' and 'innocent' – even when they present themselves as fictional games and seem to suspend all meaning. They have taught us that theoretical languages and structures are always informed by positions taken on ideological, educational, social and political issues, and that university intellectuals therefore have more social, political and ideological power than they used to think. At the same time, as I have tried to suggest, these theoretical languages and structures represent *particular* conformities and *particular* dialogical responses to *particular* social, cultural, institutional and discursive contexts, however abstract or universal their formulations may be. It follows from this that the intellectual's exercise of power and of social political responsibility begins with her or his choice among languages, structures and theories, and with his or her carefully considered judgments about the applicability of theoretical languages and structures and of the positions they imply to 'other' social, institutional and discursive contexts, past and present.

In making such judgments, it seems to me that we need to break free of binary antagonisms which appear to be inspired largely by the contestatory political situation in which French theorists were working: centralisation *versus* decentralisation, *dirigisme versus* plurality, standardization *versus* difference, conformity *versus* freedom, repetition *versus* revolution, authority *versus* dissent. Such binary antagonisms have not only proved unhelpful in resolving social and institutional problems in France; they are also too simplistic. Even plural and decentred societies draw on some residuum of central organisation and direction. It is possible to cultivate *différance* within a repetitive tradition, and marginalities in society's most prestigious centres of learning. There are different kinds of freedom, and different kinds of conformity and constraint. There are traditional freedoms; and there is conformity in dissent. Repetition and conformity clearly have their dangers; but they are also necessary, even on the left, to give people a sense of community, continuity and place. All ideas, forms and values are not necessarily wrong because we have learned them from our predecessors and now that we have grown up, *we* are society's institutions, and we have our fathers' authority, whether we approve of authority or not, and whether we use it for construction, for conservation, or for dissent.

Notes and References

Introduction: The Voice of Someone

1. John Sturrock (ed.), *Structuralism and Since: From Lévi-Strauss to Derrida* (Oxford UP, 1979) p. 3.
2. Henri Lefebvre, *Position: Contre les Technocrates* (Paris: Gonthier, 1967) pp. 88–9. Lefebvre is less well known outside France than he deserves to be. He was a provocative and original thinker and a very important figure in Parisian intellectual life in the 1950s and 1960s. He also did more than anyone else to prepare the ground for the French students' 'revolution' in 1968 and for the rise of the New Left.
3. Ibid., p. 71.
4. Ibid., p. 81.
5. Frédéric Bon and Michèl-Antoine Burnier, *Les Nouveaux Intellectuels* (Paris: Cujas, 1966) p. 64.
6. Edward Said, *The World, The Text and the Critic* (London: Faber & Faber, 1984) p. 147.
7. Barry Cooper, *Michel Foucault: an introduction to the study of his thought* (New York: The Edwin Mellen Press, 1981) p. 1.
8. See, for instance, Allan Bloom's much disputed *The Closing of the American Mind* (New York, Simon & Schuster, 1987).
9. 'The Critic as Artist' is most accessible in the *Norton Anthology of English Literature*, Vol. II, 3rd edn (New York: Norton Press, 1974) pp. 1699–1708.

1 Lacan and the Alienation of Language

The vel of alienation
1. These quotations are from: Stuart Schneiderman, *Jacques Lacan: the death of an intellectual hero* (Cambridge, Mass: Harvard UP, 1983); Anika Lemaire, *Jacques Lacan* (London: Routledge & Kegan Paul, 1977); Catherine Clément, *Vies et Légendes de Jacques Lacan* (Paris: Grasset 1981) p. 63–4; and Sherry Turkle, *Psychoanalytic Politics* (London, 1979) p. 53, 54. Jane Gallop has gone even further, stating that: 'After years

266

of study, I have come to believe Lacan's texts impossible to understand fully, impossible to master – and that is a particularly good illustration of everyone's inevitable "castration" in language'. See Jane Gallop, *Reading Lacan* (New York. Cornell UP, 1985) p. 20.

2. Catherine Clément, *Vies et Légendes*, p. 64.
3. Lacan frequently indicates his differences from Hegel, his supposed mentor. In 'Fonction et champ de la parole et du language' (Ec. I), for instance, he argues *contra* Hegel that the dialectic only authentically touches the subject if it decentres him from his self-consciousness. He denies that the end of history can be absolute knowledge (Sem. II, 91) and rejects any reference to unity or totality either within the individual or within society on the grounds that 'the subject introduces division' (Ec. I, 173–4). When his son-in-law, Jean-Alain Miller, accuses him of shamming and asks 'ought we not to understand – Lacan *against* Hegel?' Lacan agrees, preferring this reading to those who call him the 'son of Hegel' – whereupon another seminar member is heard to mutter: 'Sons kill their fathers' (Sem XI, 195). For some 'fertile parallels' between Lacan and Hegel, as well as some further differences, see Edwin S. Casey and J. Melvin Woody, 'Hegel, Heidegger Lacan: The Dialectic of Desire' and Wilfred ver Eecke, 'Hegel as Lacan's Source for Necessity in Psychoanalytic Theory' in Joseph H. Smith and William Kerrigan (eds), *Interpreting Lacan* (New Haven: Yale UP, 1983). For Lacan's debt to Kojève's reading of Hegel, see Mark Poster, *Existential Marxism in Post-War France: From Sartre to Althusser* (New Jersey: Princeton UP, 1975). For Lacan's relation to the ideas of Freud, Lévi-Strauss, Norman O. Brown, Sartre, Husserl, Heidegger, Merleau-Ponty, Saussure, Derrida, Laing and Jakobson, see Anthony Wilden's very useful essay, 'Lacan and the Discourse of the Other' and his notes to Jacques Lacan, *The Language of the Self: The Function of Language in Psychoanalysis*, translated and with notes and commentary by Anthony Wilden (New York: Delta Books, 1968).
4. For a free exploration and elaboration of the machine paradigm, see Martin Stanton, *Outside the Dream: Lacan and French Styles of Psychoanalysis* (London: Routledge & Kegan Paul, 1983).
5. 'I is a verbal form, the use of which is learned in a certain reference to the other, and this reference is a spoken reference. The I is born in reference to the you' (Sem I, 188). Lacan denies the existence of any Buberian I–Thou relationship and, in opposition to Husserl and Heidegger, denies the presence of empathy. To him, all the 'registers of being' are in language, and there is nothing behind or beyond this.
6. To Lacan, sexuality itself represents the death of the individual – he returns to this almost obsessively. In reproducing oneself sexually, one loses one's individuality, and this loss is a lack which returns to haunt man. This too might be contrasted with Hegel's (much healthier) view of sexual reproduction as an *Aufhebung* of mother and father.
7. Lacan sums up these different aspects of language in his interpretation of Freud's 'Fort-Da' anecdote about his grandson. For him, these two phonemes 'incarnate the mechanisms of alienation' (Sem XI, 216).
8. See also Sem. II, 92, where Lacan says: 'the reality of each man is in

the being of the other. In the last analysis, there is reciprocal alienation . . . and I must insist it is irreducible, insoluble . . . this reciprocal alienation will remain to the end'.

The beyond in this life

9. Speaking of the 'hole' at the heart of man, Lacan points out that it can be called being or nothing – depending on how one envisages it, and that this is essentially a matter of language (Sem I, 297).

10. For the use of this Zero in and outside Lacan, see Anthony Wilden, *System and Structure: Essays in Communication and Exchange* (London: Tavistock, 1972).

11. From Freud, *The Interpretation of Dreams*, translated by James Strachey (London: George Allen & Unwin Ltd, 1967) p. 107. Freud's observation that he has not exhausted the meaning of the dream gives Lacan his opening to read into the image of Irma's gullet and into the term trimethylamin something more and other than Freud reads into it, and he uses it to give the dream a structure which Freud, with his line by line associative analysis, does not attempt to give it. Lacan's transformations of this dream are already an example of the way he speaks 'through' texts (see next section). For Lacan's interpretation of the dream in relation to Erik Erikson's classical reinterpretation, of the same dream, see William J. Richardson, 'Lacan and the Subject of Psychoanalysis' in Smith and Kerrigan (eds), *Interpreting Lacan* (New Haven: Yale UP, 1983).

12. This and the following part of the dream constitute for Lacan a genuine parole because he argues that what characterises parole, wherever it is found, is the ability to make itself heard ludically in all other languages, while being absolutely particular to the subject because it grasps his desire (Ec. I, 175). For Lacan's own ludic expression of his subjectivity, see next section.

Repetition and innovation

13. Modern critics, who have made a great deal of Lacan's definitions of metaphor and metonymy, have generally seen them as principles applicable to literary language and to literary texts *per se*. An exception is Jean-Baptiste Fages, *Comprendre Jacques Lacan* (Paris: Pensée/Privat, 1971). Fages uses Lacanian principles of rhetoric to bring out aspects of Lacan's play with language which are not discussed below. Lacan insists that 'it is a fundamental law of sane criticism to apply to a work the same principles which it itself gives for its construction' (Sem. II, 141). Besides making it surprising that Lacan has not been applied to himself more frequently, this actually raises the question about the validity of applying linguistic or other theories across the board to texts.

14. Lacan also pointed out in *Ornicar?* (Jan. 1977) that 'the unconscious is not Freud's; it is Lacan's'. For a trenchantly witty critique of Lacan's manner of training students in the art of listening to Lacan and for a description of its dangers and shortcomings, see François George, *L'Effet 'Yau de Poêle' de Lacan et des Lacaniens* (Paris: Hachette, 1979).

15. See, for instance, David Lodge's novel, *Small World*.

16. Lacan points out that there is a parallel between 'The Purloined Letter' and *Oedipus Rex*: 'Oedipus's unconscious is that fundamental discourse which means that for a long time, since forever, Oedipus's history has been there, written, that we know it, and that Oedipus is completely unaware of it, even though it is played out in him from the beginning' (Sem. II, 245).

The intellectual and the other

17. *The Language of the Self*, p. 299.

18. Jean Fourastié, *Faillite de l'Université?* (Paris: Gallimard, 1972) p. 13.

19. Lacan points out that since human life consists of assuming roles like that of king or psychoanalyst, and since these roles have nothing to do with any individual's real ability, examinations must be seen as purely initiatory exercises (Sem. II, 304ff).

20. This is what, throughout his writings, Lacan attacks Anna Freud and American ego psychology for doing. For an ethical reading of Lacan, see John Rajchman, 'Lacan and the Ethics of Modernity', *Representations* 15 (Summer 1986) pp. 42–56.

21. See Charles Posner (ed.), *Reflections on the Revolution in France: 1968* (Harmondsworth: Penguin, 1970) p. 19; and Patrick Seale and Maureen McConville, *French Revolution: 1968* (London: Heinemann, 1968) pp. 215–6. Seale points out that: 'A tiny revolutionary avant-garde detonated a large-scale, spontaneous movement of student protest. This mass, generating its own dynamic, could only be loosely manipulated by the revolutionary core' (p. 20). The revolutionary core were students too.

22. *Psychoanalytic Politics*, p. 72.

23. Most accessible in Marshall Blonsky (ed.) *On Signs* (Oxford: Blackwell, 1985) pp. 84–97.

24. Translated by Geoffrey Wall (London: Routledge & Kegan Paul, 1978).

25. Ibid., p. 27.

26. Ibid., p. 58.

27. Ibid., pp. 85–6.

28. Ibid., p. 85.

29. Ibid., p. 154.

30. Ibid., p. 141.

31. Ibid., p. 6.

2 Barthes and the Pleasures of Alienation

1. The combination of consistency and change in Barthes' work was noted quite early on. See, for instance, Guy de Mallac and Margaret Eberbach, *Barthes* (Paris: Eds universitaires, 1971); Louis-Jean Calvet, *Roland Barthes: Un Regard Politique sur le Signe* (Paris: Payot, 1973); Stephen Heath, *Le Vertige du Déplacement* (Paris: Arthème Fayard, 1974) and Philip Thody, *Roland Barthes: A Conservative Estimate* (London: Macmillan, 1977).

The duplicities of critical play

2. That there are three actors is clear from v. 28 where we are told that Jacob was renamed Israel because he had 'power with God and with men' and from v. 24 where we are told that Jacob wrestled 'with a *man*' till break of day. The word angel, with its ambiguous connotations does not occur anywhere in the text. If one wished to be literal-minded, one would also have to point out that God is only mentioned in relation to Jacob. Barthes' article has been translated and anthologised by Stephen Heath in *Image–Text–Music* (London: Fontana, 1977) and I am using his translation.

3. For Barthes' problematical relationship to structuralism, see Sturrock's essay on Barthes in John Sturrock (ed.) *Structuralism and Since* (Oxford UP, 1979); Annette Lavers, *Roland Barthes: Structuralism and After* (London: Methuen, 1982); Jonathan Culler, *Barthes* (London: Fontana, 1983); and Howard Felperin, *Beyond Deconstruction: The Uses and Abuses of Literary Theory* (Oxford: Clarendon P, 1985) esp. pp. 97–103.

4. In *Qu'est ce que la littéature?*, Sarte presents this ideal situation where the reader is potentially a writer as characteristic of the seventeenth century. For Walter Benjamin, it appears at the end of history. This ideal situation of writers and readers has also been attributed to writers and readers of eighteenth-century periodicals in Jon P. Klancher, *The Making of English Reading Audiences 1790–1832* (U of Wisconsin P, 1987). It seems to me that care needs to be taken not to allow this ideal to turn into a new myth of historical studies.

5. This is very much Lukacs' position too. See Eve Tavor, 'Art and Alienation: Lukacs' Late Aesthetic', *Orbis Litterarum* 37 (1982) pp. 109–21.

6. Jacques-Alain Miller, Lacan's son-in-law who studied with Barthes, describes him as 'amoral and democratic' – Colloque de Cerisy, *Prétexte: Roland Barthes* (Paris: Union Generale D'Editions, 1978) p. 205; and Philippe Sollers too calls Barthes' politics 'inflexibly and naturally democratic' – *Tel Quel* No. 47 (Autumn 1971) p. 20.

'The intellectual writer that I am'

7. Robbe-Grillet complained of Barthes' reviews of his novels *Les Gommes* and *Le Voyeur*: 'I had the impression that Barthes had said nothing about me, but on the contrary that he was beginning to talk to himself . . . and that the novelist Barthes was already beginning to develop in his texts.' In *Prétexte: Roland Barthes*, p. 258.

8. For Barthes' relationship to the avant-garde in France, see Charles Russell, *Poets, Prophets and Revolutionaries: The Literary Avant-Garde from Rimbaud through Post-Modernism* (Oxford UP, 1985). For the close relationship between writers and the university in France and for the 'intellectual novel' see Victor Brombert's classic *The Intellectual Hero: Studies in the French Novel 1880–1955* (London: Faber & Faber, 1960).

9. Barthes' notion of seriality should not only be seen in connection with the linguistic concept, but also as an answer to Sartre's notion of seriality in *Critque de la Raison Dialectique*. For Sartre, seriality was the field of alienation in culture (as opposed to the organic group). See

Arthur Hirsch, *The French Left* (Montreal: Black Rose Books, 1982) pp. 75ff.

Mythologies of otherness
10. There are shades of Verlaine and Rimbaud here, both of whom associated homosexuality with crossing the boundary and escaping established limits. See Jerrold Seigel, *Bohemian Paris: Culture, Politics and the Boundaries of Bourgeois Life 1830–1930* (New York: Viking, 1986) pp. 252ff.
11. This notion of contradiction is Maoist. For Mao 'there is nothing that does not contain contradiction', 'both aspects co-exist in an entity' and 'each of the two contradictory aspects, according to given conditions, tend to transform itself each into the other'. Mao Tse-Tung, *On Contradiction* (Peking: Foreign Language Press, 1953) pp. 11, 49. See also Philippe Sollers, 'Sur la Contradiction', *Tel Quel*, No. 45 (Spring 1971) pp. 3–22.
12. For Barthes' relation to Picard and to university criticism, see Annette Lavers, *Roland Barthes: Structuralism and After* (op. cit.) and Jonathan Culler's chapter 'Polemicist' in *Barthes*.

3 Foucault and the Archeology of Alienation

1. Michel Foucault, 'The Subject and Power', Afterword in Hubert L. Dreyfus and Paul Rabinow, *Michel Foucault: Beyond Structuralism and Hermeneutics* (Brighton: The Harvester P, 1982) p. 208.
2. Michel Foucault, 'Histoire des systèmes de pensée', Résumés of courses of lectures given by Foucault in *Annuaire du Collège de France*, 1971–ff, reprinted in A. Kremer-Marietti, *Michel Foucault* (Paris: Seghers, 1974) p. 194.
3. For Foucault's relation to Marxism, Existentialism and Critical Theory, see Mark Poster, *Foucault, Marxism and History: Mode of Production versus Mode of Information* (Cambridge: Polity Press, 1984). For Foucault in relation to Structuralism and Phenomenology, see Dreyfus and Rabinow, *Beyond Structuralism and Hermeneutics* (op. cit.). For his general intellectual context, Barry Cooper, *Michel Foucault: an introduction to the study of his thought* (New York: Edwin Mellen Press, 1981) and Alan Sheridan, *Michel Foucault: The Will to Truth* (London: Tavistock, 1980).
4. See, for instance, Sheridan, *The Will to Truth*, pp. 205, 208, 225; Poster, *Foucault, Marxism and History*, pp. 24, 72–3; Mark Cousins and Athar Hussain, *Michel Foucault* (London: Macmillan, 1984) p. 253; Diane Macdonall, *Theories of Discourse* (Oxford: Blackwell, 1986) pp. 83–4.
5. Poster, *Foucault, Marxism and History*, pp. 65, 97, 104, 138, 149; Cousins and Hussain, *Michel Foucault*, pp. 6, 76; Annie Guedez, *Foucault* (Paris Eds Universitaires, 1972) pp. 103, 106.
6. Guedez, p. 102.
7. Friedrich Nietzsche, *The Gay Science*, translated and with commentary by Walter Kaufmann (New York: Vintage, 1974) p. 218.

8. Gilles Deleuze, *Un Nouvel Archiviste* (Paris: Fata Morgana, 1972) p. 41. It is generally assumed that there is a break in Foucault's work between AS and SP, and though the continuities are sometimes acknowledged, they are rarely explored.

Instruments for a history of the present
9. For a critique of this approach to history, see J. G. Merquior, *Foucault* (London: Fontana, 1985).
10. Foucault, 'The Subject and power', in Dreyfus and Rabinow, p. 216.
11. Friedrich Nietzsche, *The Genealogy of Morals*, translated by Francis Golffing (New York: Doubleday, 1956) p. 151.
12. Ibid., pp. 256, 249.
13. Ibid., p. 283.
14. See Foucault's essays: 'A Preface to Transgression' (1963) (LCP); 'Nietzsche, Genealogy and History' (1971) (LCP); 'Two Lectures' (1977) (PK); and 'Truth and Power' (1977) (PK).
15. *'Une désinvolture studieuse'* is usually rendered 'a kind of studied casualness', but the word *désinvolture* also contains the idea of cocking the snook and being able to carry it off elegantly. This connotation is important in Foucault.
16. Walter Kaufman, *The Gay Science*, n. 6, p. 79 and Kaufman, *Nietzsche: Philosopher, Psychologist, Antichrist* (Princeton UP, 1974). In other respects, however, my reading of Nietzsche is closer to that of Allan Megill in *Prophets of Extremity: Nietzsche, Heidegger, Foucault, Derrida* (Berkeley: U of California P, 1985).
17. 'Foucault répond à Sartre', *La Quinzaine Littéraire* (1 March 1969) p. 21. See also, Barry Cooper, *Michel Foucault*, p. 3.
18. *The Genealology of Morals*, p. 212.
19. Ibid., p. 210.
20. Ibid., p. 160.
21. Ibid., p. 209. See also *Résumé* in Kremer-Marietti, pp. 198–9.
22. *Résumé* in Kremer-Marietti, pp. 206ff and 201ff.
23. 'Marx, Nietzsche, Freud' in *Cahiers de Rougeaumont*.
24. *The Genealogy of Morals*, pp. 156, 210.
25. See Pamela Major-Poetzl, *Michel Foucault's Archeology of Western Culture* (Brighton: The Harvester P, 1983); Dominique Lecourt, *Marxism and Epistemology: Bachelard, Canguilhem, Foucault* (London: New Left Books, 1975); and for the influence of the Annales school of history, see Troian Stoaianovich, *French Historical Method: The Annales Paradigm* (Ithaca: Cornell UP, 1976).
26. Bellour, 'Deuxième Entretiens avec Michel Foucault: sur les façons d'écrire l'histoire', *Les Lettres Françaises* 1187 (15–21 June 1967) p. 9.
27. Jean Louis Ezine (interviewer), 'Sur la Sellette: Michel Foucault' quoted in Major-Poetzl, p. 43.
28. Bellour, 'Deuxième Entretiens', p. 19.
29. 'Nietzsche, Marx and Freud', in *Cahiers de Rougeaumont*, pp. 191–2.

Alienation, social exclusion and mental integration
30. For an interesting perspective on the link between Lacan and Foucault,

see Althusser's essay 'Freud and Lacan', especially the concluding questions, in *Lenin and Philosophy and other essays*, tr. Ben Brewster (London: New Left Books, 1971) p. 200. Althusser was Foucault's teacher at the ENS and also the person who encouraged Lacan to teach there. This article was written in defence of Lacanian Psychoanalysis in 1964 and 'corrected' in 1969, well after the publication of HF in 1961. It shows the natural continuity in Althusser's Marxist perspective between Lacanian psychoanalysis with its emphasis on what Althusser calls 'the law of culture . . . the dialectic of human order, of the human norm . . . in the form of the order of the signifier itself' and the sort of socio-historical questions about the basis of the psychoanalytical order itself which Foucault went on to ask.

31. Gilles Deleuze, *Nietzsche et la Philosophie* (Paris: Presses Universitaires de France, 1967) p. 3.
32. Ibid., pp. 83, 45.
33. Ibid., p. 4.
34. Ibid., p. 97.
35. Ibid., p. 88.
36. Ibid., p. 97.
37. Ibid., p. 89.
38. Ibid., p. 168.
39. Ibid., p. 126.
40. 'The Subject and Power' in Dreyfus and Rabinow, p. 209.
41. Alain Schnapp and Pierre Vidal-Naquet, *The French Student Uprising, November 1967–June 1968: An Analytical Record* (Boston: Beacon P, 1971) Document 232. It should be pointed out, however, that many of the students' ideas derived directly or indirectly from the earlier writings of Henri Lefebvre and the 'Situationists'.
42. Ibid., Document 165.
43. Ibid., Document 185.
44. Ibid., Document 183, 164, 167a.
45. Ibid., Document 172, 165.
46. Ibid., Document 184, 168.
47. For instance: 'As the events of May showed convincingly, [the communication of knowledge] functions as a double repression: in terms of those it excludes from the process and in terms of the model and standard (the bars) it imposes on those receiving this knowledge'. 'Knowledge implies a certain political conformity in its presentation'. 'It is of the utmost importance that [in May] thousands of people exercised a power which did not assume the form of a hierarchical organization' (LCP, 219, 232 – originally from an interview in *Actuel* in Nov. 1971). 'Intellectuals are themselves agents of the struggle of power'. 'This is a struggle against power, a struggle aimed at revealing and undermining power where it is most invisible and most insidious'. 'In the fight against power, all those on whom power is exercised to their detriment, all those who find it intolerable can begin the struggle on their own terrain for their own interests, and with methods only they can determine' (LCP, pp. 207, 208, 216, an interview with Gilles Deleuze of March 1972).

48. Schnapp and Vidal-Naquet, pp. 593–5.
49. 'Michel Foucault: On Attica, an interview', *Telos* 19 (1974) pp. 160, 159, 161. The interview was originally given in 1972. The name *Groupe d'Information sur les Prisons* and Foucault's position on non-intervention from outside link him and the group to a spontaneist section of the New Left called *Information Correspondence Ouvrière* (ICO) which had split off from the *Socialisme ou Barbarie group*. ICO believed that 'the emancipation of workers must come from the workers themselves' without 'outside' or Party interference, that workers' major problems were due to the fundamental divisions between directors and operatives; that the battle must be fought against hierarchies, authority and the exploitative system; and that militant intellectuals could contribute to the struggle only by helping to disseminate 'information' about what was going on. For the ICO, see Richard Gombin, *The Origins of Modern Leftism* (Harmondsworth: Penguin, 1971).
50. Foucault explains the relation of SP to the methodology of HF thus: 'To understand better who is punished and why one punishes, I asked the question: how does one punish? In doing this, I was not doing anything but follow the path I borrowed for madness; rather than ask in a given period what is considered madness and what is considered non-madness, what is mental illness and what normal behaviour, I asked how the division between them was operated. This seems to me to provide, I don't say all possible illumination, but quite a fruitful form of intelligibility'. In Michelle Perrot (ed.), *L'Impossible Prison: Recherches sur le système pénitentiaire au 19ème siècle* (Paris: Seuil, 1980) p. 42.
51. Ibid., pp. 42–3.

The divided subject and the death of man
52. 'Power and Sex: an Interview with Michel Foucault', *Telos* 32 (1977) p. 160.
53. In Dreyfus and Rabinow, p. 208.
54. Ibid.

The specific, positive intellectual
55. 'The Political Function of the Intellectual', translated by C. Gordon, in *Radical Philsophy* 17 (1977) p. 12.
56. Ibid.
57. Ibid., p. 13.
58. Ibid.
59. Ibid.
60. Ibid.
61. Ibid., p. 12.
62. Ibid., p. 14.
63. 'Interview with J. K. Simon', *Partisan Review*, Vol. 38 (1971) pp. 193–4.
64. Ibid., p. 194.
65. Ibid., pp. 195–6.
66. Ibid., pp. 194, 196.

67. 'On the Archeology of the Sciences', *Theoretical Practice* 3 & 4 (Nov. 1971) pp. 114, 122.
68. 'The Political Function of the Intellectual', p. 12.
69. Anthony Giddens, *The Constitution of Society: Outline of a Theory of Structuration* (Cambridge: Polity P, 1984) pp. 17, 136, 145ff.
70. *L'Impossible Prison*, p. 35.
71. Ibid., p. 41.
72. Ibid., p. 52.
73. 'The Political Function of the Intellectual', p. 14.
74. 'Interview with J. K. Simon', p. 201

4 Derrida and the Wholly Other

1. For other readings of Derrida's relation to Judaism, see Geoffrey Hartman, *Saving the Text: Literature/Derrida/Philosophy* (Baltimore: Johns Hopkins UP, 1981); Harold Bloom, *Kabbalah and Criticism* (New York: Continuum, 1975); Allan Megill, *Prophets of Extremity: Nietzsche, Heidegger, Foucault, Derrida* (Berkeley: U of California P, 1985); Jean-Francois Lyotard, 'Jewish Oedipus', *Genre* 10 (1977), 395–411; Susan Handelman, 'Jacques Derrida and the Heretic Hermeneutic' in Mark Krupnick (ed.), *Displacement and After* (Bloomington: Indiana UP, 1983).
2. Before Levinas and Derrida, this necessity was perceived by a whole series of Jewish thinkers, of whom Buber and Maimonedes are probably the most familiar. Christian thinkers found themselves in the same situation. For Derrida's assessment of the relation between theology, mysticism and philosophy, see his *D'un Ton Apocalyptique adopté naguère en philosophie* (1983).
3. Leo Baeck, *Man and God in Judaism* (London: Valentine, Mitchell and Co, 1958) pp. 19–20. See also Derrida's discussion of *gala* (revelation) and the 'unreceivable' in *Ton*.
4. Jabès has said the following: 'The true Jew is a rebel. He often exiles himself from the Jews. For instance, the prophets upset people by questioning traditional Jewish thought. A Jew cannot be a Jew if he does not question. All Jewish thought is based on endless commentary and discussion that is often contradictory. If a new question is asked which contradicts Jewish thought, it is still Jewish.' Interview with Jabès in Melinda Camber Porter, *Through Parisian Eyes: Reflections on Contemporary French Arts and Culture* (Oxford UP, 1986) p. 145. This is not in fact altogether true to historical fact (one has only to think of Spinoza), but it does describe one way for Jabès – and Derrida – to have their cake and eat it.

Reconstructing the text
5. There is a distinction to be made between Derrida's earlier writings which are concerned with what is known as *Ma'aseh Bereshit*, with questions of creation and cosmogony, and later writings which draw on the tradition of *Ma'aseh Merkavah* or questions of the mystery – that

which Derrida sometimes calls the apocalypse. But in Derrida's work, the same structures recur (see the next section) and the later work is more easily accessible through the earlier.

6. Verbs in the Hebrew bible are usually in the future tense.

7. Exodus 33: 22–3. *Achorei* also means behind as in 'back parts'. With slightly different vowelling, the word can also mean delay or lateness.

8. Levinas argued that a face-to-face encounter is possible. Derrida's article on Levinas, 'Violence et metaphysique' in ED is largely devoted to showing that it is not.

9. The practice of speaking obscurely by *mashal*, by example or parable, is an ancient practice in Jewish exegesis just as it is a constant characteristic of esoteric writing to speak 'through' another text. In his early writings, Derrida hints that this is what he is doing (see, for example, ED, 337–8); later this becomes a theory of criticism and a theory of autobiography (see next section).

10. These are Heidegger's words. See Mark C. Taylor (ed.) *Deconstruction in Context* (U of Chicago P, 1986) p. 250. Derrida's opening and letting appear to differ from Heidegger's, as Derrida himself repeatedly points out, because Heidegger is thinking in the context of the metaphysics of presence, while Derrida is not.

11. Taken from the daily service in the Jewish Prayer Book.

12. As Derrida points out, in Hebrew the word 'between' (*ben*) can take the plural (*benot*): 'We have said the "between(s)" and this plural is in some sort "primary"' (Diss., note p. 251–2).

13. These were formulated by Maimonedes and are reproduced in the Jewish Prayer Book.

14. The Hebrew words for face-to-face, *panim-el-panim*, can also be read *pnim-el-pnim*, which means inwardness to inwardness. This is certainly the way Buber and Levinas read it.

15. For Derrida's relation to other philosophers, see Mark C. Taylor's excellent introduction to *Deconstruction in Context* (U of Chicago P, 1986) as well as the texts anthologised in it; Vincent Descombes, *Modern French Philosophy*, tr. L. Scott-Fox and J. M. Harding (Cambridge UP, 1980); Henry Staten, *Wittgenstein and Derrida* (Lincoln: U of Nebraska P, 1984); Gayatri Spivak's 'Translator's Preface' to *Of Grammatology* (Baltimore: Johns Hopkins UP, 1974); Richard Rorty, 'Philosophy as a kind of writing', *NLH* 10 (1978) pp. 141–60; Frederic Jameson, *The Prison-House of Language* (Princeton UP, 1972); Frank Lentricchia, *After the New Criticism* (London: Athlone, 1980).

16. Abraham R. Besdin, *Reflections of the Rav: adapted from the lectures of Rabbi Joseph B. Soloveitchik* (Jerusalem: Dept of Tora Education and Culture in WZO, 1979) pp. 101—2.

Deconstruction: Game, Rule, Repetition, Writing

17. Jonathan Culler, *On Deconstruction: The Theory of Criticism after Structuralism* (London: Routledge & Kegan Paul, 1983) p. 213.

18. Ibid., p. 223.

19. Ibid., p. 220.

20. Paul de Man's book, *Blindness and Insight* (London: Methuen, 1983),

for instance, is based on this kind of division, although he tends to privilege the text's implicit counter-argument rather than to return opposites to indifference.

21. For an analysis of Derrida's analysis of *La Lettre Volée* ('The purloined letter') in relation to Lacan's treatment of the 'same' story, see Barbara Johnson: 'The Frame of Reference: Poe, Lacan, Derrida' in *Yale French Studies* 5536 (1977) pp. 457–505.

22. Ferdinand de Saussure, *Course in General Linguistics*, tr. Wade Baskin (New York: McGraw-Hill, 1966) p. 126.

23. The principle is the same in *Glas*, but here Derrida also partly articulates the texts on the page on each other.

24. *Ecclesiastes* I:13; XII:12; III:11.

25. Like Levinas, Derrida sees 'the tautology of ipseity as an egoism'. See Levinas, 'La Trace de l'Autre', *Schrift fuer Filosofie* 9 (1963).

26. For a provocative analysis of the similarities between conventional criticism and deconstruction, see Rodolphe Gaschè, 'Deconstruction as Criticism', *Glyph* 6 (1979) pp. 177–215.

27. Ph. Breton, quoted in Jean-Francois Lyotard, *La Condition Postmoderne: Rapport sur le Savoir* (Paris: Minuit, 1979) n. 207, p. 97, from which many of these perspectives on postmodern science are taken.

Conclusion: Recontextualisations

1. See Jonathan Culler's analysis of the Yale critics in *The Pursuit of Signs* (London: Routledge & Kegan Paul, 1981); Richard Rorty, *Consequences of Pragmatism* (Brighton: Harvester P, 1982) esp. ch. 8; Frank Lentricchia, *After the New Criticism* (London: Athlone, 1980) esp. 'History or the Abyss'.

2. See especially, Robert Scholes, *Textual Power: Literary Theory and the Teaching of English* (New Haven: Yale UP, 1985); Gerald Graff and Reginald Gibbons (eds) *Criticism in the University* (Northwestern UP 1985); William E. Cain, *The Crisis in Criticism: Theory, Literature and Reform in English Studies* (Baltimore: Johns Hopkins UP, 1984); W.J.T. Mitchell (ed.), *Against Theory: Literary Studies and the New Pragmatism* (U of Chicago P, 1985); Frederick Crews, *Skeptical Engagements* (Oxford UP, 1986).

3. See Eve Tavor, *Scepticism, Society and the 18th Century Novel* (Macmillan & St. Martin's Press, 1987).

4. Raymond Aron, *The Industrial Society: Three Essays on Ideology and Development* (London: Weidenfeld & Nicolson, 1967) p. 62.

5. Michel Crozier, *The Bureaucratic Phenomenon* (U of Chicago P, 1964).

6. Jacques Ellul, *The Technological Society*, tr. John Wilkinson (London: Jonathan Cape, 1965) p. 284. Originally published in France as *La Technique ou l'Enjeu du Siècle* in 1954.

7. Ibid., pp. 395, 409, 306, xxvi.

8. In Louis Soubise, *Le Marxisme après Marx (1956–65): Quatres marxistes dissidents français* (Paris: Montaigne, 1967) p. 46.

9. Henri Lefebvre, *La Vie Quotidienne dans le monde moderne* (Paris:

Gallimard, 1968) p. 221. What follows is a montage of Lefebvre and Ellul.

10. Gilles Deleuze and Felix Guattari, *Anti-Oedipus: Capitalism and Schizophrenia* (New York: Viking, 1977) pp. xii–xiii. Originally published in France in 1972.

11. Maurice Schumann, *Le Vrai Malaise des Intellectuels de Gauche* (Paris: Plon, 1957) p. v.

12. Henri Bérenger, *Les Prolétaires Intellectuels en France* (Paris: Eds de la Revue, undated) and in Bon and Burnier, *Les Nouveaux Intellectuels* (Paris: Cujas, 1966); Antoine Prost, *Histoire de l'Enseignement en France, 1800–1967* (Paris: Armand Colin, 1968) pp. 77ff, 145ff, 362ff; Louis Bodin and Jean Touchard, 'Les Intellectuels dans la société française contemporaine', *Revue Française de Science Politique*, Vol. 9, No. 4 (1959) pp. 835–59.

13. It is interesting to note that even anti-left-wing analyses of the situation of intellectuals had to adopt this frame of reference. See for instance Raymond Aron, *The Opium of the Intellectuals*, tr. Terence Kilmartin (Connecticut: Greenwood, 1977). The original French version appeared in 1955. For one possible American source of French analyses of intellectuals in technological societies, see Florian Znaniecki, *The Social Role of the Man of Knowledge* (New York: Columbia UP, 1940).

14. Jean-Francois Lyotard, *La Condition Postmoderne: Rapport sur le Savoir* (Paris: Minuit, 1979) note p. 14.

15. For discussions of the situation in the university, see Pierre Naville, *La Formation Professionnelle et l'École* (Paris: PUF, 1948); Jean Chardonnet, *L'Université en Question* (Paris: France-Empire, 1968); Antoine Prost, *Histoire de l'Enseignement en France 1800–1967* (Paris: Armand Colin, 1968); P. H. Chombart de Lauwe, *Pour L'Université* (Paris: Payot, 1968); Alain Touraine, *The May Movement: Revolt and Reform* (New York: Random House, 1971); and Marc Zamansky, *Mort ou Resurrection de l'Université* (Paris: Plon, 1969).

16. Jean Vigier's introduction to Bon and Burnier, *Les Nouveaux Intellectuels* pp. 19–20.

17. This idea was already present in the 1950s.

18. William Cain in Graff and Gibbons, (eds) *Criticism in the University*, p. 90.

19. George Lichtheim, *Marxism in Modern France* (New York: Columbia UP, 1966) p. 2.

20. See especially Mark Poster, *Existential Marxism in Post-War France: From Sartre to Althusser* (Princeton UP, 1975); Richard Gombin, *The Origins of Modern Leftism* (Harmondsworth: Penguin, 1971); H. Stuart Hughes *The Obstructed Path: French Social Thought in the Years of Desperation 1930–1960* (New York: Harper & Row, 1968); Michelle Perrot and Annie Kriegel, *Le Socialisme Français et le Pouvoir* (Paris: EDI, 1966); David Caute, *Communism and the French Intellectuals 1914–1960* (London: Deutsch, 1964); and Louis Soubise, *Le Marxisme après Marx* (Paris: Montaigne, 1967).

21. I am indebted to much of what follows about Kojève to Vincent Descombes, *Modern French Philosophy* (Cambridge UP, 1980).

22. Theodore Caplow and Reece J. Mcgee, *The Academic Market Place* (New York: Basic Books, 1958) p. 4.
23. Fourcroy to Napoleon in 1806, extracted in Prost, *Histoire de l'Enseignement en France*, p. 41.
24. Ibid., p. 53.
25. For an analysis of the ideological content of the traditional philosophy programme, see François Châtelet, *La Philosophie des Professeurs* (Paris: Grasset, 1970) and for a critique, see Dominique Grisoni (ed.) *Politiques de la Philosophie Châtelet, Derrida, Foucault, Lyotard, Serves* (Paris: Grasset, 1976).
26. In 'Où commence et comment finit un corps enseignant' in Grisoni, p. 68.
27. Émile Copferman, *Problèmes de la Jeunesse* (Paris: Maspéro, 1967) p. 37.
28. For some explanations of French University Dissent, see Léon Emery, 'L'Université française et l'Idéologie politique' in *Le Contrat Social*, Vol. II, No. 1 (Jan 1958) pp. 1-8 and Edgar Morin, 'Intellectuels: critique du mythe and mythe de la critique', *Arguments*, 4 No. 20 (1960) pp. 35–40. Also Kenneth Douglas 'The French Intellectuals: Situation and Outlook' in Edward Meade Earle, *Modern France* (Princeton UP, 1951).
29. Bernard Kouchner and Michel-Antoine Burnier, *La France Sauvage* (Paris: Publications Premières, 1970) p. 91.
30. Jean Fourastié, *Faillite de l'Université?* (Paris: Gallimard, 1972) pp. 107, 115.
31. Lyotard, *La Condition Postmoderne*, pp. 66–7, 68, 71–2.
32. For Sartre's 'Les Imaginaires', see Lentricchia, *After the New Criticism*.
33. Saussure, *Course in General Linguistics*, pp. 15 and 71.
34. Robert Scholes, *Semiotics and Interpretation* (New Haven: Yale UP, 1982) p. 14.
35. David Bleich, *Subjective Criticism* (Baltimore: Johns Hopkins UP, 1978) p. 18.
36. Ibid., p. 17.
37. Ibid., p. 22.
38. Lentricchia, *After the New Criticism*, p. 186.
39. For the *canular*, see Alain Peyrefitte, *Rue d'Ulm: Chroniques de la Vie normalienne* (Paris: Flammarion, 1977, 3rd edn) esp. pp. 24, 358, 439.

Bibliography

ALTHUSSER, Louis, *Lenin and Philosophy and other essays*, (London: New Left Books, 1971).

ARON, Raymond, *The Opium of the Intellectuals*, (Connecticut: Greenwood Press, 1977).

——, *The Industrial Society: Three Essays on Ideology and Development* (London: Weidenfeld & Nicolson, 1967).

BAECK, Leo, *Man and God in Judaism* (London: Valentine, Mitchell & Co., 1958).

BARTHES, Roland, *Michelet* (Paris: Seuil, 1975).

——, *Mythologies* (Paris: Seuil, 1957).

——, *Le Degré Zéro de l'Écriture, suivi de Nouveaux Essais Critiques* (Paris: Seuil, 1973).

——, *Sur Racine* (Paris: Seuil, 1963).

——, *Éssais Critiques* (Paris: Seuil, 1964).

——, *Critique et Vérité* (Paris: Seuil, 1966).

——, *L'Empire des Signes* (Paris: Flammarion, 1970).

——, *S/Z* (Paris: Seuil, 1970).

——, *Le Plaisir du Texte* (Paris: Seuil, 1973).

——, *Sade, Fourier, Loyola* (Paris: Seuil, 1971).

——, *Sollers Écrivain* (Paris: Seuil, 1979).

——, *Roland Barthes par Roland Barthes* (Paris: Seuil, 1980).

——, *Fragments d'un discours amoureux* (Paris: Seuil, 1977).

——, *Le Grain de la Voix: Entretiens 1962–80* (Paris: Seuil, 1981).

——, *Éssais Critiques IV: Le bruissement de la langue* (Paris: Seuil, 1984).

——, 'Réponses', *Tel Quel* 47 (Autumn 1971) pp. 89–107.

——, *Image–Text–Music*, essays selected and translated by Stephen Heath (London: Fontana, 1977).

——, *A Barthes Reader*, ed. and intro. by Susan Sontag (London: Jonathan Cape, 1982).

——, Roland Barthes edition, *Tel Quel* 47 (Autumn 1971).

BARZUN, Jacques, *The House of Intellect* (London: Secker & Warburg, 1959).

BELOFF, Max, 'Intellectual classes and ruling classes in France', *Occident* 10, No. 1 (1954) pp. 54–60.

BELSEY, Catherine, *Critical Practice* (London: Methuen, 1980).

BÉRENGER, Henri, *Les Prolétaires intellectuels en France* (Paris: Eds de la Revue, no date).

BESDIN, Abraham R., *Reflections of the Rav: adapted from the lectures of Rabbi Joseph B. Soloveitchik* (Jerusalem: Dept of Tora Education and Culture of WZO, 1979).

BLEICH, David, *Subjective Criticism* (Baltimore: Johns Hopkins UP, 1978).

BLOOM, Allan, *The Closing of the American Mind* (New York: Simon & Schuster, 1987).

BLOOM, Harold, *Kabbalah and Criticism* (New York: Continuum, 1975).

——, *A Map of Misreading* (Oxford UP, 1975).

BLOOM, Harold; DE MAN, Paul; DERRIDA, Jacques; HARTMAN, Geoffrey; MILLER J. Hillis, *Deconstruction and Criticism* (London: Routledge & Kegan Paul, 1979).

BODIN, Louis and TOUCHARD, Jean, 'Les intellectuels dans la société française contemporaine', *Revue Française de Science Politique* 9. No. 4 (1959) pp. 835–59.

BON, Frederic and BURNIER, Michel-Antoine, *Les Nouveaux Intellectuels* (Paris: Cujas, 1966).

BROMBERT, Victor, *The Intellectual Hero: Studies in the French Novel 1880–1955* (London: Faber & Faber, 1960).

CAIN, William E., *The Crisis in Criticism: Theory, Literature and Reform in English Studies* (Baltimore: Johns Hopkins UP, 1984).

CAMBER PORTER, Melinda, *Through Parisian Eyes: Reflections on Contemporary French Arts and Culture* (Oxford UP, 1986).

CAPLOW, Theodore and MCGEE, Reece J., *The Academic Market Place* (New York: Basic Books, 1958).

CAUTE, David, *Communism and the French Intellectuals 1914–1960* (London: Deutsch, 1964).

COLLOQUE DE CERISY, *Prétexte: Roland Barthes* (Paris: Union Générale d'Editions, 1978).

CHARDONNET, Jean, *L'Université en question* (Paris: France-Empire, 1968).

CHÂTELET, François, *La Philosophie des Professeurs* (Paris: Grasset, 1970).

CHOMBART DE LAUWE, P. H., *Pour l'Université* (Paris: Payot, 1968).

CLEMENT, Catherine, *Vies et Légendes de Jacques Lacan* (Paris: Grasset, 1981).

COOPER, Barry, *Michel Foucault: an introduction to the study of his thought* (New York: Edwin Mellen Press, 1981).

COPFERMAN, Émile, *Problèmes de la Jeunesse* (Paris: Maspéro, 1967).

COUSINS, Mark and HUSSEIN, Athar, *Michel Foucault* (London: Macmillan, 1984).

CREWS, Frederick, *Skeptical Engagements* (Oxford UP, 1986).

CROZIER, Michel, *The Bureaucratic Phenomenon* (U of Chicago P, 1964).

CULLER, Jonathan, *The Pursuit of Signs* (London: Routledge & Kegan Paul, 1981).

——, *On Deconstruction: The Theory of Criticism after Structuralism* (London: Routledge & Kegan Paul, 1983).

——, *Barthes* (London: Fontana, 1983).

DE HUSZAR, George B. (ed.), *The Intellectuals: A Controversial Portrait* (Illinois: The Free Press of Glencoe, 1960).

DELEUZE, Gilles, *Nietzsche et la Philosophie* (Paris: PUF, 1967).
——, *Un Nouveau Archiviste* (Paris: Fata Morgana, 1972).
—— and GUATTARI, Felix, *Anti-Oedipus: Capitalism and Schizophrenia* (New York: Viking, 1977).
DE MAN, Paul, *Blindness and Insight: Essays in the Rhetoric of Contemporary Criticism* (London: Methuen, 1983).
DERRIDA, Jacques, *La Voix et le Phenomène* (Paris: PUF, 1983).
——, *L'Écriture et la Différence* (Paris; Seuil, 1967).
——, *De la Grammatologie* (Paris: Minuit, 1967).
——, *La Dissémination* (Paris: Seuil, 1972).
——, *Marges de la Philosophie* (Paris; Minuit, 1972).
——, *Positions* (Paris; Minuit, 1972).
——, *La Carte Postale de Socrate à Freud et au-delà* (Paris: Flammarion, 1980).
——, *Glas I & II* (Paris: Gonthier, 1981).
——, *D'un Ton apocaliptique adopté naguère en philosophie* (Paris: Galilee, 1983).
——, *Otobiographies: L'enseignement de Nietzsche et la politique du nom propre* (Paris: Galilee, 1984).
——, *Parages* (Paris: Galilee, 1986).
——, *Shibboleth* (Paris: Galilee, 1986).
DESCOMBES, Vincent, *Modern French Philosophy* (Cambridge UP, 1980).
DREYFUS, Hubert L. and Rabinow, Paul, *Michel Foucault: Beyond Structuralism and Hermeneutics* (Brighton: The Harvester P, 1982).
EARLE, Edward Mead (ed.), *Modern France: Problems of the III and IV Republics* (Princeton UP, 1951).
ELLUL, Jacques, *The Technological Society* (London: Jonathan Cape, 1965).
ELSTER, Jon, *Sour Grapes: Studies in the subversion of rationality* (Cambridge UP, 1985).
EMERY, Léon, 'L'université française et l'idéologie politique', *Le Contrat Social*, Vol. II, No. 1 (Jan. 1958) pp. 1–8.
FAGES, Jean-Baptiste, *Comprendre Jacques Lacan* (Paris: Pensée/Privat, 1971).
FELPERIN, Howard, *Beyond Deconstruction: The Uses and Abuses of Literary Theory* (Oxford: Clarendon P., 1985).
FOUCAULT, Michel, *La Naissance de la Clinique* (Paris: PUF, 1983).
——, *Histoire de la Folie à l'âge classique* (Paris: Gallimard, 1972).
——, *Les Mots et les Choses* (Paris: Gallimard, 1966).
——, *L'Archéologie du Savoir* (Paris: Gallimard, 1969).
——, *L'Ordre du Discours* (Paris: Gallimard, 1971).
——, *Surveiller et Punir* (Paris: Gallimard, 1975).
——, *Histoire de la Sexualité* (Paris: Gallimard, 1976).
——, 'Deuxième Entretiens avec Michel Foucault: sur les façons d'écrire l'Histoire' avec Bellour, *Les Lettres Françaises* 1187 (June 1967) p. 9.
——, 'On the Archeology of the Sciences', *Theoretical Practice* 3 & 4 (Nov. 1971) pp. 108–127.
——, 'Monstrosities in Criticism', *Diacritics*, Vol I (Fall 1971) pp. 57–60.
——, 'John K. Simon: A Conversation with Michel Foucault', *Partisan Review*, Vol. 38 (1971) pp. 199–201.
——, 'Michel Foucault on Attica: an Interview', *Telos* 19 (1974) pp. 154–161.

——, 'Power and Sex: an Interview with Michel Foucault', *Telos* 32 (1977) pp. 152–161.

——, 'The Political Function of the Intellectual', *Radical Philosophy* 17 (1977) pp. 12–15.

——, 'Politics and the Study of Discourse', *Ideology and Consciousness* No. 3 (1978) pp. 7–26.

——, 'Governmentality', *Ideology and Consciousness* No. 6 (1979) pp. 5–21.

——, *Power, Truth, Strategy*, ed. Morris, Meaghan and Patton, Paul (Sydney: Feral Publications, 1979).

——, *Language, Counter-Memory, Practice: Selected Essays and Interviews* ed. Bouchard, Donald F. (Oxford: Blackwell, 1977).

——, *Power/Knowledge: Selected Interviews and other Writings 1972–1977* ed. Gordon, Colin (Brighton: The Harvester Press, 1980).

FOURASTIÉ, Jean, *Faillité de l'Université?* (Paris: Gallimard, 1972).

GALLOP, Jane, *Reading Lacan* (Ithaca: Cornell UP, 1985).

GASCHÉ, Rodolphe, 'Deconstruction as Criticism', *Glyph* 6 (1979) pp. 177–215.

GIDDENS, Anthony, *The Constitution of Society: Outline of a Theory of Structuration* (Cambridge: Polity P, 1984).

——, *The Class Structure of Advanced Societies* (London: Hutchinson, 1973).

——, *The Nation-State and Violence* (Cambridge: Polity P, 1985).

GEORGE, François, *L'Effet 'Yau de Poêle'* (Paris: Hachette, 1979).

GLUCKSMANN, André, *Stratégie et Révolution en France 1968* (Paris: Christian Bourgois, 1968).

GOMBIN, Richard, *The Origins of Modern Leftism* (Harmondsworth: Penguin, 1975).

GRAFF, Gerald and GIBBONS, Reginald (eds), *Criticism in the University* (Illinois: Northwestern UP, 1985).

GRISONI, Dominique (ed.), *Politiques de la Philosophie: Châtelet, Derrida, Foucault, Lyotard, Serves* (Paris: Grasset, 1976).

GUEDEZ, Annie, *Foucault* (Paris: PUF, 1972).

HARTMAN, Geoffrey, *Saving the Text: Literature/Derrida/Philosophy* (Baltimore: Johns Hopkins UP, 1981).

——, *Criticism in the Wilderness: The Study of Literature Today* (New Haven: Yale UP, 1980).

HEATH, Stephen, *Vertige du Déplacement* (Paris: Arthème Fayard, 1974).

HIRSCH, Arthur, *The French Left: A History and Overview* (Montreal: Black Rose Books, 1982).

HOFSTADTER, Richard, *Anti-Intellectualism in American Life* (London: Jonathan Cape 1964).

HOY, David Couzens, *Foucault: A Critical Reader* (Oxford: Blackwell, 1986).

HUGHES, H. Stuart, *The Obstructed Path: French Social Thought in the Years of Desperation 1930–1960* (New York: Harper & Row, 1968).

JAMESON, Frederic, *The Prison-House of Language* (Princeton UP, 1972).

JOHNSON, Barbara, 'The Frame of Reference: Poe, Lacan, Derrida', *Yale French Studies* 55/6 (1977) pp. 457–505.

JOHNSON, Terence J., *Professions and Power* (London: Macmillan, 1981).

KANAPA, Jean, *Situation de l'Intellectuel* (Paris: Eds Sociales, 1957).

KOFMAN, Sarah, *Lectures de Derrida* (Paris: Galilee, 1984).

KOUCHNER, Bernard and BURNIER, Michel-Antoine, *La France Sauvage* (Paris: Eds Publications Premières, 1970).

KREMER-MARIETTI, Angèle, *Michel Foucault* (Paris: Seghers, 1974).

KRUPNICK, Mark (ed.), *Displacement and After* (Bloomington: Indiana UP, 1983).

LACAN, Jacques, *Écrits I* (Paris: Seuil, 1966).

——, *Écrits II* (Paris: Seuil, 1971).

——, *Le Séminaire: Livre I, Les écrits techniques de Freud* (Paris: Seuil, 1975).

——, *Le Séminaire: Livre II, Le moi dans la théorie de Freud et dans la technique de la psychanalyse* (Paris: Seuil, 1978).

——, *Le Séminaire: Livre III, Les psychoses* (Paris: Seuil, 1981).

——, *Le Séminaire: Livre XI, Les quatres concepts fondamentaux de la psychanalyse* (Paris: Seuil, 1973).

——, *Le Séminaire: Livre XX, Encore* (Paris: Seuil, 1975).

——, *Télévision* (Paris: Seuil, 1974).

——, *De la psychose paranoiaque dans ses rapports avec la personnalité* (Paris: Seuil, 1980).

LAVERS, Annette, *Roland Barthes: Structuralism and After* (London: Methuen, 1982).

LECLAIRE, S. (ed.), *Psychanalyse et Politique* (Paris: Seuil, 1974).

LECOURT, Dominique, *Marxism and Epistemology: Bachelard, Canguilhem, Foucault* (London: New Left Books, 1975).

LEFEBVRE, Henri, *Position: Contre les Technocrates* (Paris: Gonthier, 1967).

——, *La Vie Quotidienne dans le Monde Moderne* (Paris: Gallimard, 1968).

LEMAIRE, Anika, *Jacques Lacan* (London: Routledge & Kegan Paul, 1977).

LENTRICCHIA, Frank, *After the New Criticism* (London: Athlone P, 1980).

LEVINAS, Emmanuel, 'La Trace de l'Autre', *Schrift vor Filosophie* 9 (1963).

LICHTHEIM, George, *Marxism in Modern France* (New York: Columbia UP, 1966).

LYOTARD, Jean-François, *La Condition Postmoderne: Rapport sur le Savoir* (Paris: Minuit, 1979).

——, 'Jewish Oedipus', *Genre* 10 (1977) pp. 395–411.

MACDONELL, Diane, *Theories of Discourse* (Oxford: Blackwell, 1986).

MACHEREY, Pierre, *A Theory of Literary Production* (London: Routledge & Kegan Paul, 1978).

MAJOR-POETZL, Pamela, *Michel Foucault's Archeology of Western Culture* (Brighton: The Harvester P, 1983).

MALLACH, Guy de and EBERBACH, Margaret, *Barthes* (Paris: Eds Universitaires, 1971).

MALLET, Serge, *La Nouvelle Classe Ouvrière* (Paris: Seuil, 1963).

MAO Tse-Tung, *On Contradiction* (Peking: Foreign Language P, 1953).

MEGILL Allan, *Prophets of Extremity: Nietzsche, Heidegger, Foucault, Derrida* (Berkeley: U of California P, 1985).

MILLER, Jean-Alain, *L'Excommunication*, special edition of *Ornicar?*, Supplement au No. 8 (1978).

MERQUIOR, J. G., *Foucault* (London: Fontana, 1985).

MORIN, Edgar, 'Intellectuels: critique du mythe et mythe de la critique', *Arguments* 4, No. 20 (1960) pp. 35–40.

MITCHELL, W.J.T. (ed.), *Against Theory: Literary Studies and the New Pragmatism* (U of Chicago P, 1985).

NAVILLE, Pierre, *La Révolution et les Intellectuels* (Paris: Gallimard, 1975).

——, *La formation Professionnelle et l'Ecole* (Paris: PUF, 1948).

NORRIS, Christopher, *Theory and Practice* (London: Methuen, 1982).

PERROT, Michelle (ed.), *L'Impossible Prison: Recherches sur le Système penitentiaire au 19ème Siècle* (Paris: Seuil, 1980).

—— and KRIEGEL, Annie, *Le Socialisme français et le Pouvoir* (Paris: EDI, 1966).

PEYREFITTE, Alain, *Rue d'Ulm: Chroniques de la vie normalienne* (Paris: Flammarion, 1977).

POSNER, Charles (ed.), *Reflections on the Revolution in France: 1968* (Harmondsworth: Penguin, 1970).

POSTER, Mark, *Existential Marxism in Post-War France: From Sartre to Althusser* (New Jersey: Princeton UP, 1975).

——, *Foucault, Marxism and History: Mode of Production versus Mode of Information* (Cambridge: Polity P, 1984).

PROST, Antoine, *Histoire de l'Enseignement en France 1800–1967* (Paris: Armand Colin, 1968).

RACEVSKIS, Karlis, *Michel Foucault and the Subversion of Intellect* (Ithaca: Cornell UP, 1983).

RAJCHMAN, John, 'Lacan and the Ethics of Modernity', *Representations* 15 (Summer 1986) pp. 42–56.

RORTY, Richard, *Consequences of Pragmatism* (Brighton: The Harvester P, 1982).

——, 'Philosophy as a kind of writing: an essay on Derrida', *NLH* 10 (1978) pp. 141–60.

ROTH, Michael S., 'Foucault's "History of the Present"', *History and Theory* 20 (1981).

RUSSELL, Charles, *Poets, Prophets, Revolutionaries: The Literary Avant-Garde from Rimbaud through Postmodernism* (Oxford UP, 1985).

SAID, Edward W., *Beginnings: Intention and Method* (Baltimore: Johns Hopkins UP, 1975).

——, *The World, the Text and the Critic* (London: Faber & Faber, 1984).

SARTRE, Jean-Paul, *Plaidoyer pour les Intellectuels* (Paris: Gallimard, 1972).

SAUSSURE, Ferdinand de, *Course in General Linguistics* (New York: McGraw Hill, 1959).

SCHNAPP, Alain and VIDAL-NAQUET, Pierre, *The French Student Uprising, November 1967–June 1968: An Analytical Record* (Boston: Beacon P, 1971).

SCHNEIDERMAN, Stuart, *Jacques Lacan: the death of an intellectual hero* (Cambridge, Mass: Harvard UP, 1983).

SCHOLES, Robert, *Semiotics and Interpretation* (New Haven: Yale UP, 1982).

——, *Textual Power: Literary Theory and the Teaching of English* (New Haven: Yale UP, 1985).

SCHUMANN, Maurice, *Le vrai malaise des intellectuels de gauche* (Paris: Plon, 1957).

SEALE, Patrick and MCCONVILLE, Maureen, *French Revolution: 1968* (London: Heinemann, 1968).

SEIGEL, Jerrold, *Bohemian Paris: Culture, Politics and the Boundaries of Bourgeois Life 1830–1930* (New York: Viking, 1986).

SHERIDAN, Alan, *Michel Foucault: The Will to Truth* (London: Tavistock, 1980).

SMART, Barry, *Foucault, Marxism and Critique* (London: Routledge & Kegan Paul, 1983).

SMITH, Joseph H and KERRIGAN, William, *Interpreting Lacan* (New Haven: Yale UP, 1983).

SOLLERS, Philippe, 'Sur la Contradiction', *Tel Quel* 45 (Spring 1971) pp. 3–22.

SOUBISE, Louis, *Le Marxisme après Marx (1956–1965): Quatre marxistes dissidents français* (Paris: Montaigne, 1967).

STANTON, Martin, *Outside the Dream: Lacan and French Styles of Psychoanalysis* (London: Routledge & Kegan Paul, 1983).

STATEN, Henry, *Wittgenstein and Derrida* (Lincoln: U of Nebraska P, 1984).

STOIANOVICH, Traian, *French Historical Method: The Annales Paradigm* (Ithaca: Cornell UP, 1976).

STURROCK, John (ed.), *Structuralism and Since: From Lévi-Strauss to Derrida* (Oxford UP, 1979).

TAYLOR, Mark C. (ed.), *Deconstruction in Context: Literature and Philosophy* (U of Chicago P, 1986).

TAVOR, Eve, *Scepticism, Society and the 18th Century Novel* (London and New York: Macmillan and St Martin's P, 1987).

——, 'Art and Alienation: Lukacs' Late Aesthetic', *Orbis Litterarum* 37, (1982) pp. 109–21.

THIBAUDET, Albert, *La République des Professeurs* (Paris: Grasset, 1927).

——, 'Pour l'histoire du Parti intellectuel', *Nouvelle Revue Française* 20 (1932) pp. 265–72.

THODY, Philip, *Roland Barthes: A Conservative Estimate* (London: Macmillan, 1977).

TOURAINE, Alain, *The May Movement: Revolt and Reform* (New York: Random House, 1971).

——, *The Post-Industrial Society: Classes, Conflicts and Culture in the Programmed Society* (London: Wildwood House, 1971).

TURKLE, Sherry, *Psychoanalytic Politics* (London, 1979).

VEYNE, Paul, *Comment on écrit l'histoire, suivi de Foucault revolutionne l'histoire* (Paris: Deuil, 1978).

WILDEN, Anthony, *System and Structure: Essays in Communication and Exchange* (London: Tavistock, 1972).

——, 'Lacan and the Discourse of the Other' in *The Language of the Self: The Function of Language in Psychoanalysis* by Jacques Lacan, tr. and with notes by Anthony Wilden (New York: Delta, 1968).

ZAMANSKY, Marc, *Mort ou Resurrection de l'Université* (Paris: Plon, 1969).

ZNANIECKI, Florian, *The Social Role of the Man of Knowledge* (New York: Columbia UP, 1940).

Index

demasking
(centre)
reversing

Intl
regime
hegemony
immanent